GILBERT MURRAY A LIFE

Francis West

CROOM HELM
London & Canberra

ST. MARTIN'S PRESS
New York

 1984 Francis West
Croom Helm Ltd, Provident House, Burrell Row,
Beckenham, Kent BR3 1AT

Croom Helm Australia Pty Ltd,
28 Kembla Street, Fyshwick,
ACT 2609, Australia

British Library Cataloguing in Publication Data

West, Francis
   Gilbert Murray.
   1. Murray, Gilbert
   I. Title
   880.09   PA85.M/
   ISBN 0-7099-2792-4

Printed in Great Britain
First published in the United States of America in 1984
ISBN 0-312-32720-X
Library of Congress Card Catalog Number: 83-40591

Printed and bound in Great Britain

CONTENTS

PREFACE

In most memoirs and collections of letters, autobiographies and biographies of the first half of the twentieth century, the chances are that the name of Gilbert Murray will appear in the index. What is surprising is the extent of the different fields covered by these books. In classical scholarship, Murray appears in the recollections of Maurice Bowra, Eric Dodds, Herbert Fisher and Sandy Lindsey. In Poetry and literature, he is to be found with Andrew Bradley, Rupert Brooke, John Buchan, A. E. Housman, Andrew Lang, Rose Macaulay, John Masefield and T. S. Eliot. In the theatre, he keeps company with Lewis Casson, Harley Granville-Barker, George Bernard Shaw and Sybil Thorndike. In the world of ideas, he figures in the lives of Bertrand Russell and Arnold Toynbee, Oliver Wendell Holmes, Harold Laski, the Coles and the Hammonds. In politics and public life, in Britain and on the international scene of the League of Nations and the United Nations, he is the associate of Asquith, Lord Robert Cecil, Eric Drummond, Anthony Eden, Viscount Grey of Fallodon, Edouard Herriot, Julian Huxley, Salvador de Madariaga and Philip Noel-Baker. In family life, he is to be found in the aristocratic Whig circle of Rosalind, the radical Countess of Carlisle. In Shaw's play *Major Barbara* he is caricatured on the stage as Professor Adolphus Cusins. In person he regularly appeared on the BBC Brains Trust and as a frequent speaker on the Third Programme. By proxy he has appeared in many a school production of Greek tragedy performed in English translation. He has been woven into contemporary life, not simply because one of his family's houses, Castle Howard, was the location for the television production of *Brideshead Revisited*, but because some of his family were models for Evelyn Waugh's fictional characters. Indeed, on the great issues of life and death, it was tempting to subtitle this biography *Brideshead Before It Was Revisited*.

Gilbert Murray's life touched many others. The names mentioned earlier look like a roll-call of many of the great and famous in this century. That they were influenced by Murray is part of his significance in understanding the not-too-distant past. That the causes for which he stood were lost ones or ones which have become unfashionable — the two are not the same thing — does not detract from his importance. His own contemporaries thought that he was important, even when they attacked him and what he stood for. He was, after all, awarded the rare Order of Merit and his ashes lie in Westminster Abbey. It is not, however, simply that many of his contemporaries believed that he was 'A Great Man' which makes his life interesting. What is of interest is that the questions he faced and tried to resolve — what scholarship is all about; how you translate one language and culture for another; what must be done to prevent war in order to preserve civilisation; how religion and ethics meet human needs — are still questions our own contemporaries try to answer. Gilbert Murray's answers may seem, as at the end of his life they seemed to him, Victorian. He did not scorn the title 'the last of the Victorians', notwithstanding Lytton Strachey. And it is always helpful to know that we are not re-inventing the wheel.

ACKNOWLEDGEMENTS

The first of my many debts to be acknowledged with great gratitude must be to the late Arnold Toynbee, who, as Gilbert Murray's Literary Executor, initiated this book and who, with his wife Veronica, provided invaluable help; and then to Alexander Murray, now Literary Executor, and to other members of the family: Stephen, Gilbert Murray's youngest son, Lawrence and Philip Toynbee his grandsons, and Margery Murray, wife of Patrick, Gilbert's nephew. To these should be added Louise Orr who, as Arnold Toynbee's secretary, did everything she could to facilitate the work.

My next debt of gratitude is to all those who so willingly talked about Gilbert Murray and/or provided other material for the book. The list is long, and it is invidious to mention some rather than all names. To those who are not mentioned by name I apologise but hope that they will accept my thanks. To the following I owe particular debts: Constance Babington-Smith, Sir Maurice Bowra, Dame Kathleen Courtney, Dr E. Dingwall, Professor Eric Dodds, Professor Frank Eyck, Mrs Mary Fletcher, Lady Fulton, Professor

V. H. Galbraith, Sir Roy Harrod, Mrs Rosalind Heyward, Professor Sir Keith Hancock, Professor Alec Hope, Professor Hugh Lloyd-Jones, Sir John Masterman, Mr John McCallum-Scott, Lord Noel-Baker, Professor Lucy Mair, Mr Salvador de Madariaga, Sir Denys Page, Baroness Stocks, Dame Sybil Thorndike, Professor Dale Trendall, Sir Kenneth Wheare, Mr Douglas Woodruff.

My remaining debts are to institutions which gave me assistance without which the research and the writing could never have been completed. The Australian National University gave me two years of unpaid leave to begin collecting the material, while the British Academy, by electing me to the 'Thank Offering to Britain' Fellowship, the Ford Foundation, by a Travel and Study Award, and the Rockefeller Foundation, by a special grant, made the leave possible. The Gilbert Murray Trust helped towards the preparation of the manuscript. Christ Church, Oxford, offered me hospitality and lodging while much of the research was being done, and the Master and Fellows of Churchill College, Cambridge, by electing me as a Fellow Commoner, enabled me to put the finishing touches to the book. My debt to the Bodleian Library and to Mr Porter of its staff is obvious.

Finally, I must record what I owe to those who helped actually to produce a manuscript and to check its contents: Wendy Brazil, Rosemary Boston, Anthony Esau, Sue Leach and Robyn Walker.

In acknowledging all of these debts, I think that I should also record an apology. This book should really have been completed some four years ago. I can only plead that involvement in setting up two new universities had a large claim on my time and energy; and the Gilbert Murray Trust, at least, thought Gilbert Murray himself would have approved of such a claim. I very much regret, in particular, that neither Arnold Toynbee nor Eric Dodds lived to see its completion, but I draw some consolation from the fact that both were able to read and approve the first four chapters in draft, and that Arnold Toynbee was able to say that this was Gilbert Murray as he knew him.

1 AN AUSTRALIAN CHILDHOOD

'The memories of a small child are like a broken mirror: bright spots and blanks and occasional misarrangements.' When Gilbert Murray came in old age to write of his boyhood, he began his unfinished autobiography with that sentence. He recognised that in all human testimony memory plays tricks; that although he intended to tell the truth, he might often recollect inexactly; and that what at over 90 he believed to be his own direct memories might really be things that he had been told by other members of his family or had read for himself in the family papers he had collected early in his long life. In any case, the Murray family enjoyed stories about themselves and their ancestors. Gilbert Murray was no exception. When, as an accomplished raconteur, he entertained his guests with anecdote after anecdote, the stories grew more polished as the years went by and sometimes they were improved for purposes of artistry. His nephew's wife, Margery, recalled that his wife, Lady Mary Murray, would remonstrate: 'Gilbert, you know that's not true.' And he would reply, with his charming smile, 'I may have improved it in my mind.' And those stories of his childhood, whether or not they were direct memories, were recollected and related as he grew older, not merely to entertain family and guests but also to explain to himself as well as to others how a little boy from the Australian bush had come to be the man he was: a 'great' man, holder of the rare Order of Merit, destined for burial in Westminster Abbey.

One family story described the remoter ancestry of the Murrays. They were, it was related, descended from the 22nd King of Connaught. Gilbert himself was apt to ask: 'If the 22nd, why not the 21st? There must have been some funny business there.' Funny, indeed. The story recounted that the Murrays' remote ancestor was the first Milesian king of all Ireland. In this tale, six brothers, one of them a druid, invaded Ireland, fought with the race of magicians who then ruled it, drove them into the hills where they became the fairies of today, and conquered the land. 'Queer old stuff, is it not?' asked Hubert, Gilbert's elder brother, who collected such genealogy. But Hubert, as he told Gilbert's daughter, Rosalind, had collected this story from an old Irish bookseller in Brisbane 40

1

years after he and his brother were grown men, so the story is plainly not a childhood memory of Gilbert. What was actually known in the family while Gilbert was growing up was contained in one entry in the family bible, made by a Patrick Murray on 15 September 1758. Patrick recorded that his grandfather Denis had held extensive lands in Antrim and Derry, and had then settled with his mother in Limerick after his father and most of his male relations were killed fighting for King James at the Boyne. In 1758 Denis was a fine active old man of 72 from whom Patrick recorded that he had this story directly, concluding that 'therefore it may be depended on as correct'. Beyond that bible entry there is simply Hubert Murray's speculation in the 1930s that his ancestors had gone over to Scotland when the Campbells and the rest of the Gaels went and then had returned to settle in Antrim where Patrick's story puts them in the Seventeenth century. What is common to the Murray family's stories is a tradition that their ancestry was distinguished, that it was a fighting ancestry opposed to any oppression and usually 'agin the government'. Nevertheless, this Irish tradition, in the Murray children's reading, became mixed up with a Scottish cavalier image. Gilbert in his autobiography recalled that, when he fell down during a family walk, his immediate reaction was to quote one of Aytoun's lays which he knew by heart and which formed a kind of normal speech for him:

Not a Scottish foot went backward,
When the royal lion fell.

Gilbert Murray's direct memories of childhood were dominated by his father, Terence Aubrey Murray, although he was only seven years old when his father died in 1873. Gilbert was born, although not under that name — his birth was registered as George. Forster Wise Murray — on 2 January 1866. Known in the family as 'Georgie', he was baptised three years later in the Catholic College of St John at Sydney University in the names George Gilbert Aimé. Gilbert clearly recalled his father's dominating physical presence. Terence Aubrey was a massively-built man of over six feet. Often clad in white ducks, his appearance was stern and majestic, but he was always ready to answer the boys' call 'Kicket, puppa'. When he tried to insist that his family call him 'Sir', his attempt was a failure. He was a father for whom his children's affection outweighed their reverence. His voice, with its soft Irish burr, stuck in

Gilbert's memory. So did the tales Terence Aubrey told of his own father, another Terence. Grandfather Terence Murray — the 'best man of the lot of us' in Hubert's later judgement — was a nephew of the Patrick Murray who had made the family bible entry in 1758. Patrick had a brother called Thomas. Thomas married Bridget O'Brien by whom he had Terence, Gilbert's grandfather, amongst whose adolescent memories was the summons to his father's side after the latter's leg had been shattered in the Irish rebellion of 1798. Young Terence was asked to hold a candle while the surgeon amputated, and his hand shook. His father then held the light himself, remarking 'Terry, Terry my boy, you will never make a soldier'. But the boy did make a soldier. Although his later army commission forbade him, as a Catholic, to bear arms he was nevertheless a paymaster in the Brigade of Guards as a result, or so Gilbert's brother, Hubert, later believed, of the influence of Mrs Fitzherbert with George IV. Terence served with Wellington in the Peninsula, and was believed by the Murray family to have been present at Waterloo — their material evidence was the 'Waterloo' sword which hung above the fireplace — although there is no clear proof that he was actually at the battle. In 1817 Terence Murray transferred to the 48th Regiment of Foot, sailing with it on guard duty to the Australian penal colony in New South Wales. After seven years of this colonial service, followed by a brief period of service in India from which he retired sick to London, Terence sold his commission as captain and retired on half-pay to New South Wales where his service had entitled him to a free grant of land. When he came back to Sydney in 1827 Murray brought with him his daughter Anna Maria and his son Terence Aubrey, the younger children by his wife Ellen Fitzgerald, kin to the 'Great Liberator', who had died while he was serving in the Peninsular War. An older son, James, was left to complete his medical course in Scotland. The Murrays then became Australian landed gentry.

Captain Terence Murray finally received his grant of land in the southern tablelands, the high sheep country across the mountains from the east coast of the Australian continent between the northern end of Lake George and the town of Goulburn. His son, Terence Aubrey, although only aged 17, received an adjoining grant in his own name. The boy worked hard in the lonely, often uncomfortable, Australian bush to establish and run the Murray properties with the help of the assigned convict labour to which his father was entitled. This hard work was duly recognised by his father who, at his death in 1837, left the whole of these estates to Terence Aubrey, land which amounted to 20,000 acres acquired by grant and extended by later purchases. On one of the stations, Winderadeen, which still exists near the little town of Collector, the young Murray built himself a house fit for a gentleman. Fit, too, to entertain the governor of the colony of New South Wales, and equipped with a good library, brought with him from Dublin, where he had been privately and classically educated under Dr William White. Terence Aubrey became a prominent figure in the district; his education and Catholicism, while it marked him off from his neighbours, nevertheless made him a local leader. Known locally as 'the Duke', he developed a lordly and distinctive swagger and ruled over something like a feudal community on his other great station, Yarralumla (now Government House, Canberra), numbering over 100 at the census of 1841.

Murray's landed position in the Canberra/Lake George area put him among the social elite of New South Wales. When representative government was granted to the colony in 1843, he went into Parliament. He had already been made a commissioner for the peace in 1831, playing his part in handling the lawlessness of bushrangers and escaped convicts in his district. This role, with its risk of danger and possibilities of desperate adventure, made good tales to tell his children. In 1843 he was elected to the Lower House of Parliament unopposed. In the same year he married into another prominent New South Wales family. His wife was Mary (Minnie) Gibbes, daughter of the Collector of Customs in the colony, a man who was said by the Murrays to be either the child of George IV and Mrs Fitzherbert or the illegitimate son of George IV's brother, the Grand Old Duke of York. (If the first were true, then Terence Aubrey's son by that marriage was, claimed Hubert Murray later, the rightful King of England.) Minnie bore Terence Aubrey three children, Leila, Evelyn and Aubrey, but she died in giving birth to the last in 1857. This personal loss was a heavy blow to her husband who had neglected both his government duties as Minister for Lands and his political duties in order to be with her during her long illness. It was also a more material loss for, believing that his wife would survive him, Murray had arranged that, while retaining Winderadeen in order to qualify himself for election, his other properties were transferred to his wife; on her death they passed under her Will into the trusteeship of her father and brother with whom Terence Aubrey quarrelled. Murray was not only left a widower with three children, but also a man in reduced circumstances. He had already faced the possibility of ruin in the 1840s when there was a general depression in the colony while he had outstanding debts incurred by the purchase of Yarralumla, but when the threat passed he had continued to live as generously as before, with as little care for financial detail. His wife's death caused him to lose control of much of his property and it confirmed his already evident inclination to turn away from pastoral life to politics and to the city, an inclination strengthened still further by his second marriage.

As a widower with three children, Terence Aubrey was at first looked after by his sister but, because a more permanent arrangement was necessary, a housekeeper or governess was sought. Agnes Anne Edwards, a cousin of William Schwenck Gilbert (of Gilbert and Sullivan), had come out to the colony as governess to the children of the Chief Justice of New South Wales, Sir Alfred Stephen. Agnes was then a lively woman in her mid-twenties, a gay and vivacious linguist, an accomplished musician, who dressed with considerable chic and possessed what was often described as 'a regal bearing'. She was a woman of character, taste and ambition. When Sir Alfred Stephen's salary was unexpectedly reduced by the New South Wales Parliament when he proposed to take leave in England, much to the regret of his large family — and to Agnes's own regret for she greatly admired the judge — the Stephens were obliged to give up their governess. But they thought of the widowed Murray whose sister promptly engaged Agnes. At their first meeting Agnes thought Terence a fine figure of a man and, when presently he proposed marriage, she accepted. They were married at Murray's surviving property, Winderadeen, in August 1860, first in a Catholic ceremony, then in an Anglican one. Agnes Murray enjoyed the country. She loved riding and, as a family story related, she could cope with the dangers. When bush-rangers approached Winderadeen, she collected the available men, barricaded the house and then went out alone to parley, refusing to give the outlaws arms and then holding out until help arrived. But her real home, with her husband's political career, was in Sydney, in the social and political life of which she made the Murray household a centre. There, on 29 December 1861, she gave birth to John Hubert Plunkett Murray and, on 2 January 1866, to George, later Gilbert. Between the two births the urban character of the Murray household had become complete. In 1865, when there was a great drought and extensive sheep-disease, Terence Aubrey Murray, still blaming his ruin upon debts incurred by the purchase of Yarralumla, finally lost his land and most of his money. He was sold up at Goulburn. Friends rallied round to save him from actual bankruptcy, paying off debts to the amount of £25,000 so that he might still continue in politics. For, after having become Speaker of the Lower House of Assembly, he was then President of the Upper House, the Legislative Council of New South Wales. After 1865 the Murrays were in fact dependent upon the salary of this post.

Of the prosperous, landed position of his father and grandfather, and of the crash of the family fortunes, Gilbert Murray had no first-hand knowledge. Although his mother was carrying him, he was not born until five months after the Goulburn sale. His own direct memory was of a succession of smaller and smaller houses in Sydney but not of the depression and the melancholy that failure had bred in his father which did not show itself in crossness with the children. Whatever consciousness the boy had of declining family fortunes came from the later memories and the stories of his parents, of his halfsisters and halfbrother, and of his own brother, Hubert, because even reduced to his parliamentary salary Terence Aubrey Murray was not poor. There were always servants in the house. And there was social position, formally recognised in 1869 when his father was knighted. His losses notwithstanding, Sir Terence maintained his position as a gentleman by ancestry and birth. But not exactly a gentleman in the English pattern. As an Irishman and a Catholic his was not a common figure in the Establishment of the colony. He had little in common with what he and his children called the Ascendancy. His Catholicism, although in the circumstances of New South Wales liberal to the point of eccentricity, set him apart from his social and political equals. Moreover, his political views were themselves eclectic. When first elected to Parliament in 1843 he had declared that he knew no such distinction as Whig and Tory; he believed, he said, in liberal and equal laws for all parties and sects. Sir Terence, in short, was a good party man in neither politics nor religion. He did not stand reliably with the colonial landed interest in politics. He was not even present at his sons' Catholic baptisms, and his Will specifically left their spiritual fortunes to his Anglican wife. Terence Aubrey Murray was a man of generous, emotional impulses, often full of indignation against injustice and oppression, rather than a man of reason and intellectual consistency or dogma. His career in politics, although he became Speaker of the House and then President of the Legislative Council, was only moderately successful. He held various ministerial offices but was never a serious candidate for the Premiership. Pity, as Gilbert Murray later used to say, is a rebel passion.

Terence Murray's children were not exactly brought up to be eccentric but they were, in Gilbert's later recollection, brought up to suspect Authority, to take a stand for the unpopular cause and the downtrodden. They were also brought up in an educated household. Terence Aubrey had had to sell the greater part of his library before Gilbert's birth, but had saved some of his books. His tastes had been wide. He had preserved the classical texts from his schooldays in Dublin, when he had won a prize for his Greek iambics, and he had added to his library a considerable collection of theology, modern history and political thought, modern poetry and modern science. Aristotle and Gibbon were there. So were Burke, Mill and Darwin. One of Gilbert Murray's direct memories was being asked by his father at the age of five to read some Josephus to a guest. Another was the regular appearance of such periodicals as *Notes and Queries* and the *Revue des deux mondes*, known to Gilbert as 'The Duck's Mounds' and to his brother as 'The Duke's Mondays'. Above all, Gilbert made the acquaintance through their published work of John Stuart Mill, Shelley, Keats and Tennyson. He grew up in a household in which these were well-known names, as were the principles and views of Mill, and the rhythms and imagery of these poets.

In this lively, liberal household, Agnes Murray played a large part. In the face of her husband's financial losses and in support of his political career, she maintained a close and affectionate family circle which obscured from Gilbert the depression lurking behind Sir Terence's demeanour and which he confided to his diary. 'Georgie' — Gilbert — was her darling baby for whom she made great plans: she wished him to be Prime Minister of England. Lady Murray, like many another British woman of her time in New South Wales, regarded the colony as a cultural desert. This she could counter within the family by her music and conversation, by the books and by the stories she told. When her husband died in 1873, she created another family milieu in the successful school which she then opened at Springfield to teach the young ladies of Sydney the graces and accomplishments of a gentlewoman. His mother's influence counted for a good deal in Gilbert Murray's childhood memories; later in life he and Hubert would happily spend whole mornings enjoying their mother's spirited conversation. The loss of his father removed a dominating figure, but his mother's personality was equal to facing the world without much money, equal to providing and planning for her children and especially for Gilbert for whom she was most ambitious.

At first Gilbert was sent to day-school in Sydney. Of those school-days he retained no memory, except of the rather fine playground and equipment. In 1875 he was sent to a boarding school run by Southey, kin to the poet, in the little country town of Moss Vale in the bush country over the mountains, halfway towards the old Murray properties. Gilbert's memories of those days were very vivid. Southey was a classical scholar, a Demy of Magdalen College, Oxford, who had gone down without taking his degree in consequence of the debts he had run up. His teaching was not especially skilful but it was not bad. Under him, Gilbert began to learn Greek and Latin grammar, to receive in fact a grounding in the classics at least comparable to that of a contemporary English prep school. His enjoyment of this learning was marred by Southey's unfairness in penalising breaches of discipline: hands in pockets meant taking off marks from academic performance. This kind of unfairness reduced Gilbert to tears, but even so it was less unpleasant than other aspects of the school. During his first two terms, Southey's remained at Moss Vale, surrounded by the Australian bush. While there, a bullying stableman made life miserable for Gilbert by encouraging acts of petty vindictiveness among the boys and positive cruelty towards animals. Boys not only stoned each other, under the stableman's orders, but also stoned birds to death. Such cruelty made a deep impression on young Murray, to the point of producing extreme mental anguish and physical revulsion. He was himself involved in fist fights which the stableman encouraged and felt at times so miserable that he thought of committing suicide by hanging himself from a tree. His intention was distracted by another boy's kindness, and then by his interest in the life of the bush. Nevertheless, however unhappy he was, Gilbert was physically and mentally tough enough to stand it. His mother, when he first left home for boarding school, had wisely consoled him at parting by the gift of half a sovereign with which, she said, he could come home at any time, no questions asked. He never used it.

After two terms Southey's moved to the larger and neighbouring town of Mittagong, the stableman vanished, and Gilbert began to enjoy both learning and the company of his school friends, some of whom, like the Goodenoughs, came from other prominent Sydney families. He enjoyed the bush, even when he had the very frightening experience of getting lost in its lonely vastness, and imagining all kinds of terrors as well, as is common, losing his bearings. For, sensitive though he was to bullying or unfairness or cruelty to animals, young Gilbert Murray displayed a remarkable degree of detachment from his surroundings. The solitude of the bush was not something that frightened him out of a fairly cool assessment of what he ought to do when he found himself lost.

Southey's confirmed in Gilbert Murray a process begun by his father. His family background had encouraged not only learning but independence of Authority and the cultivation of what his father called 'manly' virtues. What impressed Gilbert about his father's qualities was his physical stature, his strength not only of character, so far as it was obvious to the children, but of body. During a family walk, when a boar showed signs of attack, Sir Terence had replied to shouts of 'Run, Pups', 'But, my little fellow, don't you see that it would be ridiculous for me to run away from a pig?' Courage, and a bold front born of dignity: this was a direct memory which stayed with Gilbert. So did the ideal of physical strength and of readiness to use it in the right cause; he was never brought up to despise the use of force. He recalled that his father used to tell a story about one of his convict labourers whom he had discovered to be stealing his books and selling them for grog. Terence had laid the man senseless with a blow, and then had feared that he had killed him. 'That, my boy, was a great lesson to me. After that I always took them by the throat.' An educated, liberal gentleman Gilbert might be brought up to be, sensitive to cruelty and injustice, turning a bold front to the world as manly virtues required, taught from an early age how to shoot; but he was not a nervous, dependent child. Sir Terence's household reared children who were taught to be self-sufficient. Family loyalty and affection were strong; the Murrays thought of themselves as a 'clan'. Gilbert greatly admired Hubert, his elder brother who was achieving during Gilbert's early years the first of his formidable successes at school as scholar and as athlete. Gilbert was fond of his half-brother Aubrey and half-sister Evelyn, although less so of Leila who was severe with her younger brothers. But he was close to none of them in the sense of being dependent upon them for companionship or intimate with them. When his father died, Gilbert did not recall any penetrating grief, although he remembered his father with affection. Although close to his mother and warmly affectionate, again he was not dependent. He showed as a child the same intellectual detachment as did his brother Hubert. His feelings and emotions were disciplined, as manly virtues required, by the face he presented to the world.

That world suddenly changed in 1877. Lady Murray had made enough money from her Springfield school for young ladies, selling out at a good profit, to be able to take Gilbert from Southey's and to England. The voyage provided the boy with another adventure he liked to recall. At Suez, during some deck games, a little girl pushed him from the ship's rail into the harbour. During his fall, Gilbert remembered how properly to enter the water, and after he had pulled himself out, he took himself back to the cabin, went to bed and rang for port which he remembered that he had heard was good for such occasions. There his mother found him, composed and recovered, when she rushed in after hearing the news. In Rome, after they had left the ship at Brindisi, she and Gilbert went to the papal audience of Pius IX at which, Gilbert was told, he had freely interrupted His Holiness and had been rewarded with a papal blessing. The incident reveals a self-confident child. It also reveals what Gilbert later suspected: that his memory was distorted by time. Distorted, too, by his looking back in old age to explain the man he had become: *ego ille qui quondam*.

In retrospect, his Australian childhood seemed important to Murray. He often employed the image of 'a little boy in the bush' when he looked back to the origins of a life crowned with fame and honour. It is a trick of memory. Gilbert Murray grew up in big cities. There is no evidence that he ever visited any of his father's former properties in the bush, although he had or thought he had a clear memory of the beauty and the charm of Winderadeen. His close acquaintance with the Australian bush really came from his two years at Southey's, especially the first two terms spent at Moss Vale, for Mittagong, to which the school moved, was not a small bush town by the late 1870s. Plainly his schooling, especially the early horror of it at Moss Vale, made a vivid impression upon the child, but it represents an intensity of emotion, not a considerable period of time in his childhood. No doubt it was the origin of his hatred of cruelty, for when he had earlier been taught to shoot, the normal and casual killing of birds by his father left no record of any distress; Sir Terence took shooting for granted, so long as it killed as distinct from wounding.

The interview in Rome with Pius IX, however, affects a part of Gilbert Murray's life which was equally important to him. He ascribed to his childhood the origin of the fierce anti-organised religion, anti-clerical sentiments that he entertained and often expressed in later life. The priests of his father's Catholic Church, he said, taught that his mother was damned, while his mother's Anglican ministers damned his father. There was certainly bitter sectarian strife in New South Wales in the period of Gilbert's Australian childhood, but between his father and mother within the family there was none. Sir Terence's Catholicism entailed neither infant baptism nor regular religious observance by his children, although as a precocious child among his father's books Gilbert made himself acquainted with the Book of Common Prayer and the Bible. The Murray parents, in deference to the wishes of relations and the suggestion of a priest, allowed the Catholic baptisms of Hubert and Gilbert, but no regular religious observance followed.

Gilbert almost certainly heard of the sectarian strife and bitterness in the colony — indeed with his father's political career in New South Wales where the Loyal Orange Lodge was so strong a force, he could scarcely not have heard of it. But within his personal and family experience, religion had not been forced upon him. His father, indeed, was once described by the Catholic Archbishop Polding as one of 'the unattached', a man who professed himself to have as much right to make a religion for himself as Martin Luther. To his Will, Sir Terence added a Codicil after the case of *Hawksworth v. Hawksworth* in 1871 in which the question of an infant child's religious upbringing led to a court determination that, having been baptized a Catholic, she must be brought up as one in her dead father's religion. He specifically left the spiritual direction of his children to his Anglican wife, free from any control by his relations or by the Catholic church which he 'highly respected' but whose doctrines he had 'but very partially accepted'. On his deathbed, he refused the offices of a priest. Within the family, therefore, Gilbert had neither direct experience nor personal memory of religious intolerance or coercion nor even experience of the restrictions of Sunday religious observance. The presence of

Lady Murray and her son at an audience of Pio Nono (well after the public liberal outrage directed at the First Vatican Council decrees) certainly does not suggest fierce anti-religious sentiment in childhood.

Gilbert Murray himself offered another explanation of his strong feelings against organised religion which had little to do with his own direct religious experience. The roots of this indirect revulsion against Christianity were indeed to be found in his childhood. It was the cruelty to animals which had revolted him to the point of contemplating suicide in those two terms at the Moss Vale school. The miracle of the Gadarene swine set off a moral rebellion in him; it seemed, as he later put it, 'monstrously cruel to drive — or be indirectly responsible for driving — a lot of unoffending pigs over a precipice', the behaviour, he thought, of very wicked boys, the kind of boys who tortured animals and loved bullying. This was the real legacy of his Australian childhood at school in the bush. And it was an enduring legacy. In his unfinished autobiography more space was devoted to the cruelty at Southey's than to any other single topic. As an older man, his nerves could be shattered for the day by seeing a cat run over in a London street. It was not an intellectual rejection of a sense of God so much as an emotional reaction to Biblical cruelties and to the behaviour of many of those who professed the Christian God of history that was the origin of Murray's strong aversion to religion. In his Australian childhood it began as an emotional reaction to cruelty. The rejection of organised religion and its dogmas came with his later education.

So, too, with that other great theme of his life: Liberalism. Gilbert Murray traced the origins of his liberal political convictions to his Australian childhood. He found them in his father's beliefs, attitudes and actions. But Sir Terence was not a man of consistency; rather he was an impulsive, generous-hearted advocate for those he thought to be underdogs. His son recalled his father's relations with the aborigines who worked on or lived near the Murray stations. Gilbert could have had no first-hand memory of these, although he certainly heard his father talk of the black people with sympathy, and he later (after 1892) read his father's commonplace books which further revealed this sympathy. As a child he heard his father's stories of friendship with coloured people. With, for instance, Cakobau, styled King of Fiji, who had ceded the islands to Queen Victoria in 1874. Cakobau, wrote Gilbert Murray in his fragment of autobiography, was an acquaintance of Sir Terence, and had told him that human flesh tasted like pork but that white men spoiled their flesh by eating too much salt. A good story of a not uncommon type around the South Sea islands, but, as Terence Aubrey Murray related it to his son, quite untrue. Cakobau came to Sydney only once, two years after Murray's death; and Murray never visited Fiji. Still, Gilbert grew up in a family ethos that generated sympathy for the underdog — his brother Hubert displayed the same traits — and was filled with righteous indignation against wrongs, even if his father was not consistent over the righteous causes he embraced: Sir Terence, for example, having supported the abolition of capital punishment, nevertheless declared that his fellow Irishman, the would-be assassin of the Duke of Edinburgh in Sydney, should be 'hanged as high as Haman'.

Gilbert Murray's Australian childhood was important to him in later life. He often recalled it, to himself and to others. But the making of his personality owed more to his English education, to the intellectual training and conviction he acquired in England after he had left Australia. His Australian childhood shaped his emotions, fired his indignation about life, remained an affectionate memory and a yardstick for his achievement. Yet, upon his only return to Australia for a brief visit in 1892, he was a slightly contemptuous and disapproving stranger.

2 AN ENGLISH EDUCATION

Gilbert Murray and his mother landed in England in 1877. At first they stayed with her relations in London which made no favourable impression on the boy. The house in Phillimore Place, Kensington, seemed small, full of people who wished to be called Uncle Bill or Aunt Harriet instead of just plain Bill or Harriet. There was no garden worth speaking of. Above all there was no sun, only much gloomy cold; there was no light, and no feeling of space. Gilbert was bored and made no secret of his unfavourable impressions by a certain amount of 'colonial blow'. Nor was his boredom relieved at first by school. After a year at a Dame's school in Brighton, a public school had to be found for him, if his mother's ambitions were to be fulfilled. Her first choice was Malvern where she took Gilbert to sit for the entrance examination. Her son reacted against the uncongenial atmosphere of the school. An invigilating master bullied him. 'Do you want a gradus?' 'No, thank you.' 'Why don't you want a gradus?' Gilbert omitted to tell his mother of one final paper that remained to be taken, and the Murrays left, greatly to his relief, before he had completed the examination. So Malvern was ruled out. But Lady Murray was not able easily to afford the fees of a good boarding school. She had opened another school for young ladies, at No. 1, Observatory Avenue (now Horton Street), Kensington, which became the kind of home for Gilbert that he had enjoyed in Sydney. But even four years later things were only going *tout doucement* for his mother. The failure at Malvern and straitened family circumstances nevertheless had a very happy result for Murray. It was cheaper for him to go to school as a day-boy and there was a good school in London which took him as one: Merchant Taylors. He liked the school from the first. At the entrance examination itself, the interviewers had been gentle to such an extent that the boy had concealed some of his knowledge in case he should be thought to be showing off, a psychological trait which persisted later in the school when Murray found that his love of Greek verse led him to spend so much time upon it that he was too embarrassed to tell an enquiring master just how much.

At Merchant Taylors, under the headship of Dr Baker, Gilbert Murray enjoyed his school-days. Baker himself was a good teacher, with great enthusiasm and a feeling for style in literature, if not a precise scholar. And he could communicate his interest to those whom he taught, inspiring them to attempt the kind of Latin verses he himself wrote with spirit. Gilbert described him as a 'stout, dark clergyman, rather bald, amiable looking' who had 'always been very nice to me although we differ on every conceivable point'. The other masters the boy also liked, although he found the Hebrew teacher (who taught that language to those doing classics) rather dull. Henri Bué, the French master who had translated Lewis Carroll into his own language, was particularly kind to him. But the master who made the greatest impression, who indeed became a lifelong friend, was Francis Storr, the senior master of the modern side. Storr was a good classical scholar who took the Sixth for English essays. He had a great effect upon Gilbert, not simply because he opened up still further the world of imaginative literature which Gilbert had began to enter as a small boy, but because of his Liberalism. Murray went up the school rapidly, into the Head Form at the age of 15 so that he spent three years under the teaching of Baker and Storr. In those years, he later recalled, he awoke to the problems of philosophy, politics and religion, and confirmed the views which he later believed had their origin in his Australian childhood. John Stuart Mill was, at school in England, supplemented for him by Herbert Spencer and Comte. Shelley, Tennyson and Keats were supplemented by Swinburne and William Morris, as well as by the verse of his mother's kinsman, William Schwenk Gilbert. To Comte, he remembered, he was introduced not by a teacher but by one of his contemporaries and fellow Monitors, F. S. Marvin. His Aunt Fanny sometimes took him to Congreve's Positivist service in Lamb's Conduit Street. What Murray obtained from this English education was an intellectual rejection of cruel religious superstitions, and an acceptance of a moral law about the duty of man. He never really changed those views, for this period in the Head Form at Merchant Taylors was the time in which he thought over the great issues and made up his mind. Even at Oxford, where he found Mill and Spencer to be disregarded by his teachers, he still held firm to his belief that, however inconsistent Mill might be, his Utilitarian principles enabled a man to judge rightly in practice on every moral and political question.

Still, what Merchant Taylors did for Gilbert Murray was chiefly to give him an excellent classical education. This work the boy loved, especially Greek verse translation at which he excelled in competition with another bright contemporary, John Maynard. One achievement in particular he remembered because it was his first introduction to a man who became one of his closest Oxford friends: Arthur Sidgwick, Fellow of Corpus Christi College, Oxford. Sidgwick examined the school in Greek and gave Murray the sensational mark of 100% for his knowledge of the *Agamemnon* which both of them in fact knew by heart. At school Gilbert learned the pleasure which comes from the precision of the dead languages and the fascination of metre; and because he was able to read into the classics the values he had formed independently, the discipline strenthened the romantic, liberal spirit which came from his family background. Education for him was a pleasure. His school-days show no anguish of spirit or of mind.

Nor do they show very close friendships with his contemporaries. As a Monitor he shared a table with a few contemporaries, but even with his fellow Monitors he formed few close ties. With Marvin he continued to correspond for years, but not very intimately, usually when called upon for a reference or testimonial. With Maynard, the only other name he recalled in his memoirs, even this association did not survive. Still less did it survive with others at the Monitors' table, who only occasionally wrote to him when there was an Old Boys' dinner or when some honour was conferred on Murray himself. The friendship which did survive was that with Storr, the master, an older man whom Murray respected and admired. In this, Merchant Taylors set the pattern of his friendships in Oxford.

The quality of Murray's classical education showed itself in examinations. He won a school scholarship to St John's College, Oxford, a Tercentenary scholarship for composition and a Pitt Club exhibition. Held jointly, they made him at university financially independent of his mother, except for board and lodging during vacation. (She was already bearing the expense of her elder son, Hubert, who had won a Senior Demyship at Magdalen College, Oxford, in 1881.) Gilbert had no memory of any worries about money after he went up to Oxford. In any case he added to his scholarship stipends by two feats which established his Oxford reputation. Dr Baker had, before the boy left school, encouraged him to sit for the Hertford scholarship awarded to undergraduates in their first two years. Believing Murray to be excellent in Latin composition, the headmaster had arranged for his pupil to go to Cumberland, there to spend a month with Sargent, co-author of a famous text on composition, in the holiday before Murray went up to St John's in October 1884. Gilbert stood for the Hertford in his first term and won it. At Oxford, his tutor, a brilliant and eccentric man, T. C. Snow, thought he should also try for the Ireland, which was open as well to third- and fourth-year men. Gilbert Murray pulled off the remarkable feat of winning the Ireland and the Hertford in his first year, although under his headmaster's influence at school he had recently concentrated not upon Greek but upon Latin. This remarkable success, recalled Murray later, settled his profession for him. That particular memory has more than an element of hindsight, but the double success certainly established Murray's reputation as the outstanding classical scholar of his undergraduate generation. Benjamin Jowett, Master of Balliol, said so. Nettleship, Corpus Professor of Latin, who had lectured to him in Latin prose composition, agreed and added: 'his intellect is rapid and acute, his literary taste singularly pure and fine.' D. B. Monro, Provost of Oriel, described his undergraduate career as 'one of the most brilliant possible'. This brilliant start was consolidated by later successes. In 1886 he won the Gaisford Greek Verse prize, with a rendering of a passage from Shakespeare's Henry IV, part ii, and the Chancellor's Latin Verse prize on the subject 'Olympia'. The following year he gained the Gaisford Greek Prose prize for 'Messalonghi Capta'. He took a good First in Classical Moderations, and then a First in Greats in 1888. One of the examiners described his papers to a mutual friend as 'wonderfully good'. When he took his degree in 1888 he competed for a prize fellowship at New College in an examination at which that formidable and subtle scholar, D. S. Margoliouth, remarked that he would set such papers as would stretch even Murray of St John's, a comment not welcomed by most of the other candidates. But Gilbert's was not merely a local Oxford reputation. Richard Jebb, with Jowett the foremost English classical Greek scholar, called Murray 'the most accomplished Greek scholar of the day', meaning not scholarship in a strict, textual sense, but in fluency and facility in the language. Walter Headlam of King's College, Cambridge, whose own brilliance Rupert Brooke was later to lament in words very like those Headlam himself applied to Murray, wrote: 'many people can translate a thing into Greek or Latin as well as you want it done; but yours have the great merit that the originals are what might have been written by a Greek.'

Apart from his own ability and his previous education at school, Murray's success came also from some singular good fortune in his tutors at Oxford, at a time when the teaching of classics there was not at its high-water mark. T. C. Snow was a remarkably learned man, thought by Murray to be 'a bit of a genius'. In any one who, like Murray, had a taste for scholarship, he inspired not only intellectual effort but affection. His class in comparative philology, wandering as it did through early Icelandic as well as Homeric Greek, communicated his own passionate interest to his students. D. S. Margoliouth, the brilliant son of a Jewish rabbi turned Christian minister, was then lecturing on Pindar because the metre fascinated him. Murray, too, was fascinated to the point of reading, under Margoliouth's direction, Eustathius' commentary on Homer. With Robinson Ellis, a learned Latinist and a noted eccentric, whom A. E. Housman described as having 'the intellect of an idiot child', Murray also had a close association, although not so close as that with Snow and Margoliouth. Robinson Ellis had, as Bowra once wrote, a fine, old-fashioned scholar's taste for impropriety, and he would occasionally nonplus Murray with such questions as: 'Murray, are you interested in incest?' To which Murray politely responded: 'Yes, in a general way.' Ellis's curious interests, which later in his life became less amusing than repellent, did not offend the undergraduate Murray although they prevented a close friendship. Ellis took Murray with him as a companion during several vacations to such watering places as Bognor, Whitby and Saltburn, where his dislike of the ordinary decisions of life amused his younger companion. Murray nevertheless had a high opinion of Robinson Ellis's learning and an affection for one who had recognised in him a classical 'communion of interests'. Such sympathy was important in Murray's personal relationships. With his distinguished tutor in philosophy, Samuel Alexander, a fellow Australian who was Murray's only countryman to precede him as a member of the Order of Merit, Murray felt respect but developed no lasting friendship; he could not accept his philosophical dismissal of John Stuart Mill.

The greatest joy of Oxford was nevertheless Arthur Sidgwick, the man who had examined him at Merchant Taylors. Sidgwick's lectures appealed to Murray because of their feeling for the Greek language, their love of poetry and the beautiful voice in which they were delivered. Sidgwick said of himself 'in erudition I am naught', but he taught Murray the lesson of making the classics live, of moving his audiences not merely by what he said but also by the good looks and diction of a great actor who had, like Murray himself, read and re-read Greek poetry until it became known by heart. With Sidgwick Murray felt he could talk freely, and not only about the classics which occupied much the larger part of his undergraduate life. For Sidgwick was a whole-hearted Liberal and not, like Snow, a Christian, nor, like Margoliouth — *questo bel animal feroce* — a somewhat alien presence, but a sympathetic person 'who always knew what you meant'. Sidgwick in many ways was a father to Murray, as Gilbert openly recognised when he looked back at his Oxford undergraduate days. Nevertheless, even in a father he looked for qualities and opinions which matched his own, like the Greek gods whom, after Durkheim, he came to believe were made by worshippers in their own image.

With the Greek gods and their worshippers one other great influence upon Murray at Oxford became evident. Andrew Lang was no longer in residence at Merton College. He was a man of letters and a neighbour of the Murrays in Kensington. But his published work upon comparative religion, upon the anthropology of Greek society, made a great impact on the undergraduate Murray. Lang's *Custom and Myth* which overturned current philological assumptions was published at the same time as Murray arrived in Oxford. When George Bernard Shaw later called Gilbert Murray 'a collector of religions', he pointed to one of the latter's enduring interests, attributable to his reading and admiration of Andrew Lang. And not only of reading Lang. As an undergraduate, Murray, with all his brilliant classical success, admired the career of a man of letters such as Lang, and he began, even before he had taken his degree, to write a novel of his own, *Gobi or Shamo*. Lang recommended its publication to his own publishers. His intellectual influence upon Murray at Oxford was quite as important as the personal and professional friendships made at university.

Most of Gilbert Murray's Oxford friendships were with dons, with men older than himself. Such was that with Charles Gore. Gore was a devout Christian who always seemed to be in communion with a world beyond this, a man who exercised from his position as head of Pusey House an immense influence on the spiritual life of the university. A man, too, who sought out brilliant undergraduates like Murray. Gilbert found his companionship delightful and Gore, sharing Murray's radical temper in politics while drawing a clear line between orthodox and unorthodox opinions in religion, saw a distinguished potential convert to Christianity. He and Murray both believed in reason as against tradition. Gore invited Murray to join him on holiday in the Dolomites, the first time that Gilbert saw Switzerland and the mountains which he later came to love so well. Both of them enjoyed it. Gore thought Murray had done 'a domineering old prig like me' so much good, while Murray found a saintliness in Gore which he long afterwards said had softened his harsh views on religion, or at least softened his anti-clericalism. Christianity, said Murray to Gore at the time, attracted him as a life, its spirit had appeal, but he did not respond to the latter's attempts at conversion. Gore told Murray that he found it hard to tolerate that a man of Gilbert's character and quality should not be a Christian. He argued with him for the historical faith of the Gospels, and pleaded that he should read the Greek New Testament more. But Gilbert did not yield. Their friendship was unaffected, and Gore grieved when Murray left Oxford in 1889, but the barrier of religion always remained in their relationship. Gore might have been a 'father figure', but, unlike Sidgwick, not one made in Gilbert Murray's own image.

The 'father figure' quality of his Oxford friendships which Murray himself later mentioned should not be pressed too far. Snow and Sidgwick, although older and established figures, were among the most remarkable figures in the Oxford of Murray's day. Gore and Margoliouth, not so much older than Murray, were the two men whom Mr Gladstone called remarkable when he visited Oxford in 1889. For, it was not simply fatherly authority or assurance that Murray was looking for, but intellectual attainment and style, especially when that style had a theatrical quality. Since he was 'in some ways disappointed with Oxford', he sought out the exceptions who possessed them. He also looked for sympathy with his own interests and views, which meant that the important element in all of these friendships had a marked political quality. His friends were Liberals. Among his own contemporaries the few with whom he became friends shared his radicalism. Three of them stood out: Leonard Hobhouse, Walter Ashburner and Herbert Fisher. None of them came from his own college but the two former shared his active political interest, and the third, by his own account, was influenced by Murray to share it. In 1885, after the rejection of Gladstone's Home Rule Bill, they played a leading part in forming the Oxford Home Rule Union, in which cause Murray made one of his few speeches at the University Union in opposition to Lord Randolph Churchill. To the cause of Ireland, a matter both of family feeling and of Liberal conviction, Gilbert added opposition to militarism in Europe, warning the Union of the dangers in a speech he made on a motion of his own choosing. Ashburner agreed; as he wrote during a visit to Germany a few years later: 'I think that this claptrap young Emperor [of Germany] and all that he represents are perhaps the most painful thing [*sic*] in existence.' But with these contemporary friendships, as with the older ones, the political sympathy upon which they initially rested was not in itself enough. These were also the clever young men of Oxford, and they too had style. It was Ashburner's wit which attracted Gilbert, and the self-mocking quality of his American friend's humorous questions: 'Why is it that all the vulgar Americans come abroad while the good ones stay at home?'

Murray's friendship with H. A. L. Fisher was different. He had observed him at lectures, sitting back, listening, and then jotting down a few precise notes. The sight filled Murray with envy and admiration. But he did not know Fisher very well as an undergraduate, although Fisher was very much influenced by Murray's Liberalism to the point of supporting Gladstone over Home Rule, and he returned Murray's admiration, later acknowledging in him the most brilliant classical student of the day at Oxford. After their final year they visited Italy together; they both sat for prize Fellowships at New College and were elected together on the same day. The papers which Margoliouth had intended to stretch Murray were also well within the capabilities of Fisher, for he too was one of the most remarkable undergraduates of the day. Nevertheless, the small circle of clever contemporaries, amongst whom Gilbert Murray formed the friendships he made with those of his own age, did not constitute an Oxford equivalent of Cambridge Apostles. These brilliant young men of Oxford formed no society or dining club; they did not speculate for sheer intellectual pleasure, for all of them had the much more high-minded purpose of doing good in the world. They were young men to whom Mr Gladstone was a hero, and politics or public action, not personal enjoyment, was their goal. When they talked or debated it was a prelude to action. Laughter there might be, but, as Gilbert Murray said of Gore, in the midst of the gaiety there was always the feeling of a higher world than the ordinary material one.

This seriousness of purpose affected Murray's life within his own college. Looking back, he thought that the ideal of an Oxford education was to work hard in the mornings, to play a game between lunch and tea — he himself played cricket, making 40 in the Freshman's match, played rugger when he was wanted and rowed without distinction in the Torpids — then work again after five and in the evenings. But even the exercise was a duty, as was his joining the military unit, the Oxford Volunteers. So was his participation in college life. The St John's College Debating Society often debated political questions. Soon after he came up in 1884 Gilbert Murray spoke there on two occasions in opposition to motions that the British Empire should be federated, and that the military spirit in England needed fostering, although he was not a pacifist and, as an Oxford Volunteer, was quite prepared to contemplate the use of force in a just cause. His interest in the Society was not sustained. He took no part in its debate which favoured a Conservative victory in the election of 1885 nor in that deploring Home Rule nor in that disapproving of Gladstone's Irish policy. In March 1886 he opposed the motion which deplored the preponderance of democratic principles in English politics. Later in the same year he was elected to the Committee of the Society, but he resigned before the following meeting. Perhaps one reason was the invincible conservatism of members. On every occasion on which Gilbert spoke, he did so in opposition to the motion and on each occasion he was on the losing side. When the house was not conservative and moderately serious, it was frivolous, but with the kind of after-dinner humour alien to Murray. He can never have felt at ease in that Society, most of whose members when they came to debate had dined and perhaps wined too well, and not only were Murray's minority politics but he also added to his political principles those of temperance which derived partly from a general revulsion at Australian drinking habits and partly from a reaction to his father's and his brother Hubert's taste for drink. Gilbert's final undergraduate speech at St John's opposed a motion that, while favouring the spread of temperance principles, total abstinence could not be approved. He lost again.

Much more to his taste, both for the tone and the level of discussion, was the College Essay Society. Founded at the beginning of the Lent Term 1884, Gilbert was almost coeval with it. The society was small; it met in the rooms of one or other of its members to hear a paper by one of them or by an invited speaker and to discuss it. The group met in Murray's rooms during his first term, and in May 1885 he read his first paper to it on 'Pure Malevolence'. Next year he read another on 'Daphnis and Chloe', and in his final year one on 'National Education'. Unhappily the papers do not survive nor any record of the discussion. In this society Murray played a considerable part. He was unanimously elected Vice-President in 1886. From time to time it met in his rooms. For some of its meetings he secured speakers from beyond the college. His old master Francis Storr came to talk on 'Schoolmastering as a Profession' to an audience which included Arthur Sidgwick as an invited guest. Hobhouse, from Corpus, was invited to read a paper on that great Liberal hero, Mazzini. In such a society, which listened to and discussed Liberal and progressive views, Gilbert Murray felt at home.

Still, it was not a large part to play in college life, nor yet within the life of the Union and other university societies, although Murray won a reputation as a Liberal spokesman. Indeed, in the *Oxford Magazine* which described the Home Rule meeting of 1888, the fifth verse of a poem by 'Larry O'Toole' was devoted to him as an Irish-Australian. His main concern was the hard work and long hours at his classics, not only their philology but the absorption into his memory of the literature itself which enabled him to produce the brilliant results that made his reputation. He had, as he said later, little time for anything else. As a result his health suffered from overwork. He saw his brother Hubert at Magdalen from time to time, but they were not close. Hubert moved in an athletic, hard-drinking set, among men who were neither his own nor Gilbert's intellectual equals, and when Gilbert ventured into that hearty circle he might face Hubert's *farouche* sense of humour. 'Don't you know X?' he once asked Gilbert, who had expected to be introduced to one of his companions. 'Lucky dog,' he then remarked in answer to his brother's 'No,' and then left him to resolve the embarrassment. On another occasion, upon Gilbert's entrance into his rooms, Hubert put his arm round his shoulders and said to his associates, 'This is my brother Gilbert. He's the quiet bugger.' And this, beyond his own small circle of friends, was what Gilbert was at Oxford: quiet and, as one of his mother's pupils in London recalled, a shy young man who, during his vacations at home, slipped past the giggling group of girls on the stairs.

Yet Gilbert had more in common with Hubert than this Oxford relationship suggests. In later life those who knew them both were struck by the physical resemblance between them. What they normally saw in Hubert was a rather more uncouth Gilbert. Hubert Murray was a man who shielded his emotions and his reactions behind a bored, arrogant-seeming exterior. Gilbert's exterior was different. Physically there was a great likeness in their features, although Gilbert had a slimmer grace than his very big brother, and he also cultivated a charm of manner which his brother did not often choose to exercise. At Oxford Gilbert developed that famous, almost excessive, courtesy and consideration, that shy-seeming modesty. Behind this civilised and serene appearance, the young Murray could be as formidable a personality as his brother, whose frame and build were more overtly powerful, and within the circle of his friends his strength of character and conviction carried weight. The brilliance of Murray's public reputation at Oxford cast an aura over him, but, even to those who did not know of his record, this man of slim athletic grace of movement, with a beautiful speaking voice, a fine head with clearly cut profile, a firm jaw and slightly Byronically cut hair, gave the impression of serene convictions and luminous intelligence. However considerate of and sympathetic to others, and however courteous in discussion, Murray's own convictions seemed unshakeable. He gave the impression of a strong, integrated personality, quietly confident of his talents which had been confirmed by his Oxford successes and by the maturing of those political and intellectual convictions which he had, in a more romantic, less intellectual way, felt as a small boy. The impact on others was considerable. Some, as Gilbert himself later thought, reacted against what they saw as invincible priggishness. Others, as a guest at his wedding said, expected the wise and learned professor but they found as well 'a young Apollo'.

3 A WHIG MARRIAGE

Oxford did more for Gilbert than bring out and discipline his personality and talents, or reveal his brilliance. It also introduced him to his future wife. In the early summer of 1887 he went for a picnic with Arthur Sidgwick, his wife and their children on the Cherwell. While one of the children was trying to make the river blue with a box of paints, Gilbert who was watching found himself addressed from behind by a severe female voice: 'I hear you are a teetotaller, Mr Murray.' 'Yes, I am. Do you disapprove?' Mrs George Howard, the lady who had addressed him, did not, for she was President of the British Women's Temperance Association. She was also Rosalind Stanley, a daughter of Lord Stanley of Alderley and wife to George Howard, heir to the Earldom of Carlisle. On that picnic she questioned Gilbert closely about politics, about Home Rule and the emancipation of women as well as about temperance. He gave satisfaction and, since Mrs Howard collected clever undergraduates of the proper radical Liberal opinions, was invited during that summer, with other of his Oxford friends such as Leonard Hobhouse and Walter Ashburner, to Castle Howard, the great Yorkshire seat of the Earls of Carlisle. And at Castle Howard, in the summer of 1887, he met Mary Howard, George and Rosalind's eldest daughter, the Shelleian heroine of Gilbert Murray's poetic imagination. He fell in love at once. 'You have surprised me,' wrote Fisher on hearing the news. 'We were both agreed that a wife addicted to Primrose Leagues, High Church, alcohol or any other of the vices inherent in our upper classes' would be an impossibility. 'Still, though I knew you would stick to your principles and choose wisely, I was not prepared for your rapidity.'

Nor was the Lady Mary, as she became when her father succeeded to the title. She hesitated. She had been brought up in an extraordinary family. George Howard was not simply a member of one of the great Whig aristocratic families which had played, and still played, an influential part in Liberal politics, but a Pre-Raphaelite artist of some talent. Taught by Costa, he was the friend of Edward Burne-Jones and William Morris, of Swinburne and the Rossettis, as well as host to such continental radicals as the visiting

Mazzini whom Benjamin Jowett, Master of Balliol, met at his friend Howard's London house. George Howard was a gentle, humorous, courteous man who was nevertheless capable of anger. He regarded his wife Rosalind's treatment of their small son as wrong and did not hesitate to say so to his formidable lady. But his chief interest was always in his art. Not only in the pictures which he painted — of his wife and children at Naworth Castle, another family seat, or in Italy which he knew and loved well — but in the decoration of the house he built in London at No. 1 Palace Green, for which William Morris designed the interior and Burne-Jones did the Cupid and Psyche frieze. The same two artists redecorated the chapel at Castle Howard itself, providing a later model for *Brideshead Revisited*. Howard's artistic Pre-Raphaelite tastes were impressed upon and absorbed by his children. When Gilbert Murray, on that first visit to Castle Howard, asked one of the boys who was his favourite painter, the child answered with not the slightest affectation: 'Benozzo Gozzoli', — a painter whose work, especially that in the Medici palace in Florence, was particularly admired by the Pre-Raphaelites.

By 1887, when Gilbert Murray came to know the Howards, the Earl was absorbing himself more and more in Italy and in his painting, for a rift had developed between himself and his wife. Ostensibly the cause was politics. Rosalind and George Howard took different sides over the Home Rule for Ireland question which so bitterly divided the Liberal party. The Earl went with the Unionists while his wife, much more radical in temperament, followed Mr Gladstone. It is related by Arnold Toynbee that, during the Home Rule debate, Mrs Howard, on the terrace of the House of Commons, was warned by an acquaintance that by her vehement support for Home Rule she was dividing her family. 'What is that to me?' was her answer. It is a revealing one, for it demonstrates the force of her personality, her placing of political principle above family or personal comfort. But the estrangement with her husband was not solely due to politics. Kate Stanley, Rosalind's sister, who saw the Howards at an earlier period in their married life, already recorded the differences of temperament which led Rosalind to stigmatise her own son and thus cause her husband to sulk angrily. Her energy and force of character had already begun to dominate her family. She took over the management of the Carlisle estates while her husband followed his artistic career. She reduced the very considerable debts, said to have had their origin in the payment of Charles James Fox's gambling losses by a former Earl, and she put the Howard property into the sound condition which made the Howards of Gilbert Murray's day rich. For Rosalind Howard had inherited something of her own mother's formidable character.

Lady Stanley, a daughter of Lord Desborough, was a woman of great self-confidence in her own judgement, in her own intelligence and in her positive (although not, in her grandson, Bertrand Russell's, judgement, subtle) opinions. When her daughter Rosalind's friend and secretary, Leif Jones, once remarked to her during the Home Rule bitterness that he could not understand how a woman of her intelligence should not be convinced by the arguments for Home Rule, she stared and, after a pause, said: 'Mr Jones, I cannot abide a fool.' Not even within the family. Bertrand Russell long remembered that, when he had read none of the books about which she asked him, Lady Stanley then announced to the drawing room at large: 'I have no intelligent grandchildren.' Rosalind was not her mother's favourite daughter — that was Kate, Russell's mother — but Rosalind's own character had many of the same traits: the same confident, dogmatic opinions which finally tolerated no disagreement on any of the principles which she held to be self-evident: Home Rule, women's rights, temperance. To these principles, family and friendship were ultimately sacrificed.

Bertrand's sensitive Russell soul, he stated in his autobiography, shrivelled in the face of these hearty Stanleys. Perhaps George Howard's did too. But Gilbert Murray was made of sterner stuff. He knew Lady Carlisle before the full force of her personality had completely clouded over the family relationships, before, as he put it, her 'masterful nature was exasperated by troubles and ill health'. When he first went to Castle Howard he was inspired by her milieu, as were many other eager, idealistic young men. It was also fun. The great Vanbrugh house, filled with a splendid collection of pictures, bubbled with conversation about politics, about the ideals and the purposes of life. He came into contact with a wider world, with famous men and women. There was cricket in the hot summer with the villages round about. The conversation might be 'deficient in subtlety', he told Bertrand Russell, but it was 'magnificent in its force and directness, ranging over all fields of politics and ethics'. Gilbert Murray admired and respected Rosalind Howard, while she saw in the brilliant undergraduate whose opinions matched so closely with hers, a young man of great talent and promise, of strength of character and purpose who, as London society parodied her daughters' marriages, could be a middle class son-in-law who would stand up for her when political convictions separated her from her own sons. The Countess did not hesitate about Gilbert Murray when her daughter Mary did.

Mary Howard was a slim, graceful girl, beautiful in the opinion of some who knew her, for whom she seemed 'to carry a fire in her face'. Ardent, high-principled, she possessed some of the same passionate, self-confident force of her mother. In that Howard household, devoted to the emancipation of women, she was nevertheless not formally well-educated, although she spoke French, German and Italian fluently and as a matter of course. She was well grounded in certain books, such as Mazzini's *Duty of Man*. Her mother had early introduced her to her public duties, leading her to speak for the causes the Countess herself held dear to groups of working women and to temperance bands, in one of which Mary and her sister, early in their teens, in fact took the Pledge. Like her mother, she dutifully read the parliamentary debates and carefully studied the Factory Acts so that she could take her part in the Liberal Women's Association over which Lady Carlisle presided for so long. Very much under her mother's influence, protected by the domination of that personality which ruled the Howard family, Mary was very hesitant about marriage to Gilbert Murray. Her mother might try to persuade her, but Mary herself still had doubts. After three weeks' acquaintance she was accusing Gilbert of weakness and aimlessness and a want of clear ideals. He defended himself:

> You have under-rated my sober qualities as much as you have over-rated my brains . . . I have never, even for you, tried to seem other than I am . . . I have other ideals beside the winning of your love . . . I was a soldier in the service of man before I entered yours. But the others are ideals of duty only, this is of happiness too. Deny it to me and I shall do my life's work much the same as before; that will engross me again as it did before I met you; only half the force would be gone and all the brightness.

The only way, replied Gilbert, to remove her doubts was for him to let her know him better so that he could dispel her complete misreading of his character. She agreed. During the next two years Murray spent many weeks with the Howards at Castle Howard or Naworth Castle, the other family seat in Cumberland. When Mary accompanied her father to Switzerland in August 1889, she had indeed come to know Gilbert better. She had read the manuscript of his undergraduate novel *Gobi or Shamo*. She had picked *edelweiss* for him in the Swiss mountains forgetting that he would not like the flowers to be plucked from their roots. And her hesitations slowly vanished, for both of her parents approved of the suit.

But love was not marriage. Even with family approval, a potential Howard son-in-law required some position and some income as well as prospects. Gilbert could not propose until he had established himself. He had indeed won his Fellowship at New College in 1888, but this gave him only £200 p.a. for seven years. His first thought was to establish himself as a writer, a man of letters. His undergraduate novel was recommended by Andrew Lang to his own publishers and went into several editions by 1890 (but it made no great income for Gilbert). Writing was plainly not enough for marriage to Lady Mary but, even before the novel actually appeared in print, Murray had gained an established position with a considerable income. In 1889, at the tender age of 23, he was elected Professor of Greek in the University of Glasgow, in succession to Richard Jebb, a post which carried with it the then very considerable income of £1,300 p.a., a large house in The College, and the very considerable dignity of a Scottish professor. Neither the salary nor the house could match the grandeur of Castle Howard and of Naworth Castle, but they certainly enabled Gilbert Murray to maintain the Lady Mary in something like style. The Howards, in any case, themselves lived without obvious luxury which the Countess regarded as a betrayal of duty and an unwarranted self-indulgence. Her daughter, too, was to have a considerable dowry in transferred capital and an annual allowance, with the Countess making later gifts of large houses in Surrey and in Oxford and such frequent gifts of money that Gilbert sometimes forgot to thank her for them. Marriage was now possible, but would Lady Mary accept?

Gilbert had continued to woo her by letter after she returned to England from holiday in Pontresina:

> I long to see you again even if you should strike me dumb with your coldness . . . If you ever do love me I shall rejoice in all

things but if you do not love me they are worse than poison. Do not be afraid: I believe I am the one man in the world who can watch over you and make you happy and give a full life to your marvellous character to live. You cannot have a full life till you are with me — not that I should ever try to make you one jot less devoted to your mother, for I love her too — but because you will have a wider sphere with me and have all your energies free. O my angel, I know that I can help you — I can make your life wider and stronger . . . I am fevered and worn out with yearning. Do love and trust me when I come back. There is nothing to fear; there may be Paradise to gain if only you will give yourself to me as I have given myself to you utterly and forever.

When he revisited Castle Howard, he proposed to the Lady Mary in the Old Library on 15 October 1889, at 9.30 p.m. after dinner, an occasion she often recalled to him although at the time she still hesitated. Her sister Cecilia had tried to dispel her doubts, not now so much doubts about Gilbert as uncertainty of her own feelings and character and, above all, fear of the strange, alien world which lay beyond Castle Howard and the family circle dominated but also protected by her mother. Gilbert's appeal to her, in terms of romantic devotion, had also to reassure her that marriage would not exclude her mother, while it would free her for the part she might play in life. Mary still hesitated, but finally accepted. Once she had decided, her passionate nature broke out. Gilbert became 'my own, own knight'; while she was staying at the seaside resort of Scarborough, she imagined him walking over the waves to meet her and carry her off:

You who have braved so many storms and have subdued my fortress and made me yours at last . . . glorious marriage will not take away my great deep love for my mother and sister but deepen it, and that you will love with me I have no manner of doubt . . . you will influence me every day as I grow to love and understand you better and better. Our love is not for ourselves alone but for humanity.

Nevertheless, during the short engagement that Lady Carlisle preferred for them, there were storms for both of them to brave. The long period of doubt and hesitation had tormented and tired Mary Howard. Immediately after the engagement she had to be sent with her sister to Scarborough, on the east coast of Yorkshire, not far from Castle Howard, to recover her strength. She felt sadly weak, in need of Gilbert's patience, reassurance and protection:

> I think the uprooting and the long doubts and questioning of myself before I came to know I loved you and then the being so tired afterwards — all these things have made me rather fearful, so that silly nervous fancies and doubts of myself and the sufficiency and truth of my love have been able to trouble me.

But the holiday at Scarborough helped to restore her nerves. Gilbert's love letters and poetry reassured her still more by November: 'your little bird will be the most joyful, peaceful, safe little bird in the world, I can have no manner of doubt.' She knew that her mother had no doubts. Gilbert quoted in one of his letters the Countess's view that he had 'woven' his life 'inextricably into ours: we have gathered you to ourselves in tender love and profound union of soul'. Whatever the weakness that the Lady Mary occasionally felt during the engagement, her doubts faded, especially when she was caught up in the details of the wedding, of the shopping and of the planning of her future household, under the firm guidance of her mother who organised the ceremony, ordered the trousseau and arranged the drawing room of the house in Glasgow. Thus reassured, Mary contemplated the marriage as a perfect union: 'I love you as a believer would love her Christ. It seems too good to be true, the life that lies before us . . . Oh my peerless Galahad, my maiden knight, I love you.'

As Lady Mary's doubts and hesitations were swept away and as whatever weakness she had felt vanished in the arrangements to be made, Gilbert Murray's own nerves began to shake. He felt during most of the engagement like a 'limp rag'. He was anxious about the reception of his first book, the novel *Gobi*; worried about his Inaugural Lecture in Glasgow and the criticisms which it incurred because of his lack of any reference to his distinguished predecessor, Jebb; dejected about his new professorial duties and the quality of his students. At the same time he faced both his fiancée's demanding need for reassurance and her will to organise life for them both. His doctor in Glasgow told him that his limp, dejected states were 'all worry — most people get ill like me when they are going to be married'. He felt nevertheless that at 23 he had lost vigour and freshness from years of excessive strain and overwork.

In this low state he was as much troubled by nervous fancies as the Lady Mary. She showed a masterfulness that he sometimes resented: 'You are a hard task mistress;' 'You have always taken the lead instead of me.' This feeling came in part from the practical details of the wedding and setting up house. Gilbert felt harried by the painting and decorating of The College house, for the painters and the plumbers made it impossible to read; and by delays while Lady Carlisle and her daughter looked for exactly the right chintzes to match wallpapers and paints. He felt constricted when his fiancée asked him: 'What do you need a tailor for? I want to choose your things.' He was embarrassed by some of the consequences of Howard riches: a gift of a handsome gold watch which he loved but felt so guilty about that he buttoned up his jacket in order that his colleagues might not see so gorgeous a present. He was nervous about the great wedding planned at Castle Howard by Lady Carlisle: some 80 girls in green and white outside the house, the estate labourers lining the gallery inside, the Harrow band which was to play at the ball on the wedding eve. 'It will be a miracle if we are not both laid in an untimely grave by the exertion of the dance and the wedding. Do for heaven's sake rest before that miserable dance.' But when he made the mistake of asking his prospective mother-in-law if they could not 'escape' by an earlier train, he discovered that he had no choice but to accept the plans made for him. Mary had at first tried raillery: 'You dear noodle head . . . the idea of disturbing yourself about the ball — you will not be ill-treated and I shall not overtire myself. Do not be a fidget.' But when the Countess declared herself hurt by Gilbert's reaction, a sterner note came into Mary's letters to her betrothed:

What grieves me most is the thought of her eager loving plans being dashed and spoiled, all her pleasure taken out of what she in her unselfish way had taken such pleasure in planning. Besides, it would be bad to think of poor working men robbed of their treat for this . . . It was selfish, dear, was it not, to forget that we both had our duties on that day?

Gilbert at once became humble and contrite; he had hurt Lady Carlisle without in the least intending to. Nevertheless, he reflected that 'our life won't be cloudless; no human life has ever been'. Regretting that such letters had made Mary uneasy, he declared: 'I think I understand what you say. You want me to be something like what your mother has been.' This, indeed, was what his fiancée said she wanted, yet she herself reflected the Countess's own masterful personality in what she assumed about her place in the relationship with Gilbert: 'I cannot be really unhappy or dis-illusioned with our professorship.'

Such misunderstandings came from pre-wedding nervousness on both sides which magnified what were in themselves trivial things, nervousness intensified by the serious, high-mindedness they both professed in the love they so constantly declared to each other and which they expected would conquer all, like 'some dream too sweet for earth'. Still, there were lighter moments. Gilbert sent many poems and a lock of his hair — not easy since he was beginning to go bald; Mary then wanted a crystal locket in which to keep it. They discussed whether Mary should retain her courtesy title after marriage, and, with Lady Carlisle's strong opinion in favour, decided that it would be affectation to drop it, although Mary herself thought that it would be truer and simpler 'if you let me bear your name and no other'. But the Lady Mary Murray she became when they were married in the chapel at Castle Howard on 30 November 1889. Gilbert had been teaching in Glasgow until the previous day. He then caught a train to the nearest Yorkshire railway station where he was met by the dog-cart, and arrived at the house when the ball was already in progress to dance down the hall with his fiancée. They were married the next day at 10 a.m. by Benjamin Jowett, at Lord Carlisle's invitation, because Charles Gore, whom Murray wished to have, had been unable to perform the ceremony. The newly married couple spent their honeymoon in Italy before returning to Glasgow to their house in The College, in which they were to live for ten years, before moving first to a house in the country near Churt and thence, in 1905, to one in the Banbury Road, Oxford.

The Lady Mary had seen marriage as 'perfect unity, utter love'; 'the perfect joining of two people must have something in common with the mystics and Christ; it must take self away'. And so, at first, it did. She adored Gilbert with all the passion and force of a Howard woman. She thought of her husband with 'tenderly pas-sionate longing . . . It makes me cry, I love you so much.' High-minded and serious of purpose she might be, insistent on honourable public behaviour, but she had no horror or revulsion from a passionate, physical relationship with her husband, nor from expressing such a relationship in her letters. Whatever the uncompromising moral standards she, like her mother, upheld, a licit private relationship held no coy reservations.

My own darling, My Beloved, My precious treasured husband. It is lonely going to bed and seeing only one corner turned down . . . my tender lover — husband. I think of you tonight alone in our bed — that dear bed where you first made me *all* yours — body as well as soul — when you gave me through that marvellous, spiritually mystic, physical though it be — mingling of our bodies my precious unborn baby — my marriage gift from you, my knight — oh sweet — we have had wonderful nights there and elsewhere . . . the passion which has blended us into one has grown in the blessed nights when I have lain in your loving arms, heart beating against heart, bare breasts pressed together. They blaspheme and wrong the beauty and holiness of love who say that in a passion like ours there is aught ugly or wrong . . . let the passion and fondness grow yet more . . . let us help each other to make his or her life an intense flame of passionate, loving service, seeking truth and beauty and bearing them to those who do not know them.

No reservations: but the intensity of Lady Mary's passion for her husband was never a matter of selfish enjoyment, of self-absorption in the love by which she felt carried away. Always there was the thought that this rapturous joy was competitive and self-less; 'I tell you that my love will wrestle with yours to be the greater', until their souls became one and were purified and purged of all wrong, 'till we can lay them without fear at the feet of the One Unknown God and let them die together in the service of humanity'.

A love of this intensity and high-mindedness was what Gilbert Murray in his wooing of Lady Mary had pleaded for and promised to her. And he evoked it in his wife. But he himself was of a cooler, much more cerebral temperament than the elemental passions of his Howard wife. He returned the adoration in the first years of marriage, in language that matched Mary's own, although it was less uncontrolled.

My own darling, why do you ask me to believe in you? I do believe in you and I not only believe but know what a pure, high souled, true hearted queen I have given all my heart to. And I feel sure that you and I, with average and good fortune, will do good work in the world.

The quality of their love he did not doubt, especially as he compared it with that of other people. Talking, on his journey back to Australia in 1892, to Lady Allen, he learned of her marriage, in which she was engaged at 14, married at 15, bore her first child at 17 to a husband 18 years older than herself: 'I think she never loved him in the passionate absorbing way that Puss and Poss love.' 'Puss' was Lady Mary, 'Possum' himself. In animal endearments — Lady Mary was a 'silver-tailed kitten', Gilbert 'Thomas Dog' — Murray almost seemed to put his declarations of love and devotion into the third person, at any rate to avoid the direct language of love, the 'meum, tuum sense' with which 'lovers in the act, dispense'. He recognised his love for Lady Mary, after two years of marriage, by reference to other people and other times. On his visit to Australia, he was 'seized by a feeling that this was really my home, the aromatic breath of eucalyptus made a tingling in my veins . . . Little one, the more I approach the place that was my home as a child, the more I feel that now you are my home, and I have no home except where you are.' And the more, when he contemplated his brother Hubert's marriage, he knew how different was his own. His brother's wife, Sybil, was patient, tactful and loving 'but companion she is not'. Companion, in Gilbert's eyes, Lady Mary certainly was. He told her the details of each day because he did not like having 'interests and memories apart from you'. Yet he valued the times when they were apart for a little while 'because they make me value you more'. Where marriage was, for Lady Mary, an absolute union, for Gilbert it was relative: his and Mary's union in relation to others. The difference, springing from their temperaments, later made for strain and tension, although they were always agreed that their marriage was not for themselves alone but for Humanity.

Until 1896, Gilbert and Mary exchanged declarations of love and devotion in very much the same language as they had used during their courtship. On 16 April 1894, his wife declared:

dear love, I see that Swift had to blame poor Esther for irreverence in saying she worshipped and adored him . . . but nothing seems to express parts of the love I give you so well . . . it seems to me that I loved you all the ways that ever any one loved. If my wifehood and my woman's passion for you were taken, there would be complete trust and sympathy and confidence and reverence — the deep friendships [sic] which are mine towards you could not be taken away but they are made more part of me, are more bound into every fibre of being by the passionate love which can only be given to a woman who is blessed with the love of the truest, purest, knightliest lover-husband in all the world. Sometimes it seems to me as though the force with which I was held by my great love for you, my complete dependence on you were almost a revenge for my slowness in loving completely and sometimes I am afraid you will weary of it and of me.

This was written to Gilbert while he was on his way to visit Greece and while Mary coped with their daughter Rosalind's diphtheria in Glasgow. He was worried by such terms as 'worship', but he replied with letters that overwhelmed his wife by 'their gentle loving goodness' and their 'fulness of interest of every kind', so that she felt she could never repay her husband for the strength and wisdom and life he offered her. No one, she believed, could love with a more whole or devoted heart than she, but she also believed that love was not enough, that her husband would really like to see her 'strong in body and mind and wise and persevering'. The doubts lurking in that expression of love and devotion were never completely allayed by Gilbert. When, in the spring of 1895, he was in Glasgow and Mary was attending Liberal women's meetings in London with her mother, he reassured her that she was 'so full of thought and interest in your subject and have such power of sweet and clear expression that you can not but speak well and with charm. So says the cranky and difficile hound.' He was, he said, 'so lonely without you', but he did not then match the fervour of his wife's language of love. In the same spring, when Mary was at Naworth with the ailing Countess, Gilbert was not becoming accustomed to bachelordom: 'I want you as much as ever.' His wife missed him, wanted him, loved him. In March 1897, while on holiday with his professorial colleague, Andrew Bradley, at the Bridge of Allan, Gilbert declared: 'I *do* love you, quite certainly and undisturbed.' But undisturbed, by mid-1897, their love was not. The passionate and absorbing love of the early years had faded; obligation, to each other, to their children and to others, began to take its place.

On the Lady Mary's side, there were doubts about her ability to fulfil all of the obligations she imposed upon herself. In late 1890 she had already found it necessary to tell her husband that 'if there was anything in her that seemed to him wrong or foolish' he should point it out and 'you must not ever let me drift into being idle and not still seeking my own work'. She felt the temptations of laziness and was grateful for Gilbert's teaching her all that she was willing to learn. But she was never confident that she was a good wife. By 1894 she believed that her behaviour was a burden to Gilbert, that she was 'stupid and fidgety and irritable and pettifogging', and she feared that he would weary of her. She promised she would 'try to learn and to work and to be serene and always cheerful for your sake and to repay you a little; much I cannot repay you for you give me much more than I can ever give of strength and wisdom and life'. For all of Gilbert's sweetness towards her, she felt she made but poor return. She did not, for instance, persevere in learning Greek. Her intellectual companionship was largely confined to their reading aloud together in the evening: Turgenev, Dickens, Ibsen. Of course Lady Mary listened to her husband reading his own poetry and plays and she read his works in draft, but she was never confident that her opinion or criticism had any value, except in the practical details of publication or production. She was confident that Gilbert's book on ancient Greek literature would be brilliant and very sorry that it had to be compressed: 'I don't think we'll write any more for series.' When the book was actually published and she held it in her hands, her reaction was: 'big, isn't it, and very good in print'.

In spite of Gilbert Murray's suggestion, when he first went to Glasgow University, that his wife should help him to do the easy, mechanical work of Greek prose corrections, Lady Mary could never enter into his life of teaching and scholarship. And of other aspects of her husband's life — his literary work, his involvement with the theatre — she was jealous, although Gilbert encouraged her to attend rehearsals because she was 'so nice to everybody', and was grateful for her help when, in his absence on the continent, she went to talk to Mrs Patrick Campbell about the production of his first original play *Carlyon Sahib*. To one who had seen marriage as a complete mystic union, the knowledge that there were important parts of her husband's life which were closed to her bred a sense of failure and inadequacy which, to one of Lady Mary's temperament, were particularly hard to bear. She felt that she was not upholding her high ideals; her strong sense of duty was unfulfilled, perhaps unfulfillable; and she blamed herself, even while she was jealous of those who could engage her husband's interests in worlds she could not share with him.

Gilbert Murray was inclined to blame himself for his wife's unhappiness, although he early recognised their temperamental differences. As early as November 1890 he was telling Lady Mary not to bear other people's grief, to which she replied that she had little facility for really feeling other people's troubles but her 'sympathy could take away something of the feeling of loneliness'. She added that it was impossible to count those one loved as 'other people'. The Lady Mary's emotions were deeply involved in any activity she undertook, in any persons to whom she believed she had obligations. The result was a constant feeling of being over-burdened, of being harassed, while her duties and obligations continued to multiply: to her family, to her servants, to her public and political work and her hospital committees, to any one in need who came to her attention, but above all to her mother. In the mid- and late 1890s, Lady Carlisle's family troubles became bitter; she suffered, Gilbert thought, 'almost beyond human endurance' because of the political rifts which separated her from her husband and her sons, and she lived behind 'a wall of personal suffering'. In 1892 the Countess had a serious illness, another in 1893 and again in the following year. In May 1896, Lady Carlisle told her daughter that she expected to die, and Mary felt a great obligation to be at her mother's side. Lady Carlisle believed that her illness was 'nerve storms', but when her daughter spoke of returning to her husband, she broke down and cried. Her daughter had no choice but to stay; to leave would be shirking the claims of duty, even though she was herself on occasions 'not totally pleasing' to Lady Carlisle. However tired or weak Mary felt, however much the Countess's nervous storms played upon her own nerves, she continued to do what she knew was her duty — travelling to London to the National Women's Liberal Council, corresponding with temperance workers, with Lord Bryce on the Factory Acts and the condition of female labour, while governing her own household and servants (who often fled from her overpowering concern) in houses that she disliked. Serenity vanished as she exhausted herself mentally and physically, while at the same time blaming herself because she was not a good wife, that her marriage had not achieved that 'perfect union' she had foreseen.

Such a temperament as the Lady Mary's had a complicated relationship with physical stamina. Physical weakness, or at least an acute sense of it, there certainly was. She had looked forward to bearing Gilbert's children, but actual childbirth itself, in the state of medical knowledge in the earlier 1890s, with memories of the high infant mortality rates of her grandparents' and of her parents' generations, was a great strain upon her. Mary Murray was 24 when her first child, Rosalind, was born in October 1890. Two other children followed: Denis in March 1892, Agnes in June 1894. Rosalind was born in her grandparents' house at Palace Green in London, where Mary had gone in order to get the best medical attention available, in the opinion of the Carlisles. As was customary, she fed the child herself, and, as was also customary, spent some weeks in bed after the birth. After a fortnight, she used a bath chair to go out: by 13 November she was allowed to walk downstairs, although she must be carried up. Three days later she travelled north to Naworth Castle and thence to Castle Howard where she spent some weeks building up her strength, although she believed that she was still not strong when she returned to Glasgow early in 1891. Gilbert, in the midst of the university teaching session, had had little part in events, although he had joined his wife for Christmas. Apart, however, from the physical strain upon Lady Mary, her first baby daughter caused her to worry. Lady Mary was convinced that the child was delicate, in need of constant medical attention, so that, although a nurse took a great deal of the physical burden, the mother's nerves were on edge with anxiety. This anxiety increased with the birth of her second child. After Denis was born her health deteriorated. After the third, Agnes, was born she felt in great need of a rest. Thinking it utterly silly to go on being ill 'for no reason at all, and to the worry of those who love her', she nevertheless felt by 1894 that her nerves were all to pieces so that 'I can scarcely help crying all day'. In January 1896 Gilbert persuaded her to spend her mornings in bed with temporary beneficial results, but Lady Mary, after her third child at the age of 28, was always liable to exhaustion, bad nerves and sick headaches. To her this was a confession of weakness, a failure not only as a wife but as a mother, for which she blamed herself.

That sense of weakness in a relationship in which she wished ardently to be strong, became the more intense when two further children were born to the Murrays: Basil in June 1902, Stephen in 1908. Lady Mary was, with both of these boys, at an advanced age for childbearing, and the physical strain which she had always felt — quite apart from the emotional consequences of childbirth — was the greater. By the end of 1901 she was, in her husband's judgement, 'desponding: she won't rest and she won't let me or Miss Glaholm, the nurse, do things for her, unless at the end of an exhausting struggle'. By February 1902 she was still weaker; she seemed to Gilbert to be 'quite broken down, incapable of moving'. A year after the birth of her fourth child, her health collapsed to such an extent that she had to go into hospital, although she resented being called a 'nerve patient'. She could have letters from Gilbert about her children, but none on other topics. After Stephen was born, the Lady Mary, in hospital at Sidmouth in May 1908, had suspected heart trouble but finally concluded that she was just 'flabby and weak'. She was expected to rest between lunch and tea, to have breakfast in bed, but she still thought she could manage the house, read aloud once a day and look after the children's health. Her doctor was then a well-known osteopath, Christopher Wheeler, whom Lady Mary at first judged to be a materialist who had no belief in the power of mind over body but who, in her later belief, 'mended' her. By October 1908 her physical health was much recovered, but she felt that her illness had left her with no imagination, no idealism, nor understanding of art.

Perhaps I shall emerge some day; at present I feel crushed by Mother's and your personalities, by the extent to which I disagree with you both, by the feeling that there is something in my opinion (I have too little faith to dignify any of my opinions with the name of belief) — I'm not strong enough to make anything of it.

Lady Mary had diagnosed one of the roots of the trouble. Before marriage she had persuaded Gilbert that she wanted him to be something like her mother, but she came to resent the dominance of both, to feel her own intellectual helplessness in the face of it, especially when her mother rebuked her for failing to appreciate the worth and work of her husband. When, in late 1902, Lady Carlisle rebuked Mary for not appreciating his Euripides translation, she achieved a marked effect; her daughter, half-asleep with fatigue, took to her bed and read Gilbert's versions of the plays. 'Her dreams', her husband told the Countess, 'must be awful.' Yet, it was not just the insufficiency Lady Mary felt in the face of her

mother and her husband that troubled her marriage; it was also a
feeling of betrayal that her husband had, or needed, any relationship outside that with herself. She sensed, even if she had never
read Gilbert's letters to Lady Carlisle, that her husband had a
special relationship with her mother which she could not match.
She knew, because her mother told her so, that the Countess
thought Gilbert 'wonderful', 'marvellous'. She may not precisely
have known that her husband told her mother 'that there were few
things of any personal importance to me except you and the process
of constantly referring in my mind to your sympathy and
encouragement'. The Countess's letters were among Gilbert's most
cherished possessions because she more than anyone, he wrote to
her in May 1894, had

> seen me whole and knew (as far as I knew it or any one can know
> it) what I was always aiming towards, in teaching Greek or
> talking politics, or writing learned books or plays; and you have
> steadily and always encouraged me. I cannot thank you enough
> . . . In discussion I once said 'if any one does understand what
> you mean, then you love them — instantly and for ever'. Mary,
> if I remember, was displeased with me, no doubt rightly. But I
> feel this to be true. I should owe you all this, even if you were a
> perfectly prosperous human being with a serene life and leisure
> to think of other people all day. When I think of the wall of per-
> sonal suffering that you have to pierce through first, before you
> can begin to see inside other people, I am filled with wonder.
> Ever your loving Gilbert.

It was to the Countess, rather than to his wife, that Gilbert Murray
revealed his thoughts and aspirations. Where, in his letters, he
recounted to Mary the details of each day, Lady Carlisle he treated
as a confidante, his *Carissima Socius*, and to his wife this seemed a
reproach which never left her.

Some reproaches never left Gilbert, because his relationship with
Lady Carlisle was not the only one that seemed to his wife to
exclude her. Burdened as she felt with children, with servants, with
the houses in which they lived at Glasgow, Barford and Oxford,
with family and public duties, inadequate as she felt to enter into
the whole of her husband's interests and activities, the Lady Mary
was particularly sensitive to Gilbert Murray's relationship with
other women who could offer him what she could not: intellectual

companionship, gaiety and a certain kind of beauty.

One of the guests at Murray's wedding had described him as a young Apollo. Combined with his impact as a university teacher, dwelling on the beauty of Greece and of Greek civilisation in his beautiful voice, physically graceful and unfailingly courteous, Gilbert Murray, still in his mid-twenties, always attracted devotion from the women he taught. He devoted himself to his teaching, sharing Lady Carlisle's and his wife's strong views about women's rights. In 1896, for the first time, four women enrolled for Honours in his Greek class at Glasgow. At first they exasperated him because they would not do their work, but what Murray later called 'their instinctive wish to please' and his to 'protect and help' soon established a closer relationship than usual between teacher and taught. No doubt, believed Murray later, they felt the admiration he had for them. One certainly knew: Janie Malloch. She was an attractive, lively, intelligent girl who went on from Glasgow to Oxford although her heart was 'really in romance and adventure'. She married in October 1898 another romantic who was also a pupil of Gilbert Murray, Noel Brailsford. Janie at Glasgow offered Murray the companionship and devotion, the communion of academic and intellectual interest which by 1897 Lady Mary felt she herself could not give. She became jealous of Janie, especially of the love poetry which her husband wrote at this time, containing such phrases as 'easy to betray'. Gilbert reproached himself for causing his wife any unhappiness, but Lady Mary saw anything less than a complete union in marriage as a form of betrayal.

In 1899 Gilbert's health deteriorated to such an extent that the Murrays had to leave Glasgow, and they went to live in a somewhat pompous house at Churt, near Farnham in Surrey. Lady Mary had always felt an alien in that dour Scottish city but, with the near proximity of London to their Surrey home, Barford Court, she also felt alien to some of the circles in which her husband now moved in the capital. Janie Brailsford was, in any case, also in London with her journalist husband, and common radical causes brought Gilbert into her company. So the estrangement between the Murrays continued. In May 1900 Lady Mary was greatly upset by this friendship of her husband's, while he, who had gone in June on holiday to the Continent, resented his wife's acting as a police-woman: 'the chief thing I should ask is that in facing any possible future phase of the matter I may be entirely free. I want to act consciously on my own judgement and responsibility and not to feel you are "forbidding things".' Yet Gilbert did not think there was anything in the situation which 'need give us a moment's uneasiness. My love for you is rooted in the rock.' Lady Mary, however, saw things differently; she thought that, because her husband was unhappy and uneasy for reasons over which she had no control, they were better apart unless he had some condition of mind or body which she could help, although she 'would come at an hour's notice if you needed *me* really'. This was the point upon which she always needed reassurance, why she deeply resented any other of her husband's relationships that implied she was not needed for her own sake. Gilbert resented the restraints this placed upon him, although he asserted that his wife's anxiety was based upon a misunderstanding. He was prepared, by the beginning of July, to make a break with the Brailsfords; he 'professed to treat friendly relations as possible, though I was beginning to see in my own mind that they ought to cease'. During this separation in the summer of 1900, Gilbert Murray blamed himself for causing his wife unhappiness and, while resenting her dominance over his actions, was able to reassure her that it was '*you* I wanted, simply you; not companionship or comfort in general'. He had become alarmed: 'I cannot think what would happen to me if you were either to die or to get thoroughly indifferent and hostile; do not admit in your mind the possibility of becoming hostile or indifferent'. His wife talked to their friend and former colleague at Glasgow, Andrew Bradley, and to her sister Cecilia, both of whom reassured her; the latter adding that Mary was 'a little donkey at times'. When Gilbert also reassured her of his love — 'how much I love you and how I will try to be a good husband to you and a good father to the kittens' — the estrangement was over. By August 1900 Gilbert Murray was enjoying a bright and happy life among his children in Surrey, 'sick with dismay' when he thought about the recent past, and declaring to Mary: 'you are the dearest wife and the best mother that ever was.'

Still, neither Gilbert nor Mary changed their characters after this reconciliation, nor did Gilbert's involvement in work from which Mary felt excluded change. In 1897 she had already resented the intimacy of what she called her husband's 'dramatic and fashionable friends' who used his Christian name, at a time when Gilbert was writing plays and mingling with theatrical and literary friends. When they went to live in Surrey, the theatre became an even more important aspect of Gilbert Murray's life. Within a few months of his return home in 1900, Lady Mary was 'quite horribly disappointed you are to be away so long and so constantly now'. By mid-1901 she was beginning a series of apologies for the cross words she used to her husband, crossness she explained by her feeling of weakness although she thought that no excuse for her behaviour. During her fourth pregnancy, however, in late 1901 and the first half of 1902, her discontent with herself and her husband increased. When he went to Italy in February 1903 to consult Euripides' manuscripts for his edition of the Greek text, Lady Mary was jealous even of the companionship of Jane Ellen Harrison, a Cambridge Greek archaeology don whose work was close to Gilbert Murray's own, whom he described to his mother-in-law as 'like a middle-aged Club bachelor', but who, he had to reassure Mary, was not in love with him. This kind of suspicion, in her low state of health, was a legacy from that earlier estrangement, the keener when the object of that suspicion was one who was part of her husband's classical world, the keener still when the lady in question was an actress.

The Lady Mary had no suspicion of Mrs Patrick Campbell; indeed when she met her during negotiations over Gilbert's first play and heard the actress's life story from her own lips, she came away 'her sworn friend'. Not so, however, with Penelope Wheeler. Mrs Wheeler, the wife of Dr Christopher Wheeler, was an actress whom Murray met during rehearsals of his English version of Euripides' plays at the Royal Court Theatre. Her performances, according to Dame Sybil Thorndike, tended to be over-dramatic, a lisp was an impediment to her career, but she was a striking personality who charmed Gilbert. On 21 May 1905 he wrote to Lady Mary 'I think it is a good thing (Please, this is not bite but an un-bite) for married men sometimes to see . . .', but the next page is missing. Such openness pleased Lady Mary no more than her suspicions of clandestine behaviour, and her husband had to reassure her that 'I am your own and no one else's', and that he had had 'no communication with any strange ladies in any way'. Nevertheless, the old resentment persisted that his wife acted as a policewoman, was forbidding things, was making him helpless and of no use to her, and he continued to enjoy Penelope Wheeler's company during rehearsals — and also that of her husband Christopher Wheeler, a man described by Dame Sybil as 'a saint', who was very fond of Gilbert.

In her fifth pregnancy in 1908, the Lady Mary's unhappiness because of her husband's friendship with, and enjoyment of the company of, vivacious women, went beyond Penelope Wheeler to include her own childhood friend Margaret Burne-Jones who had married J. W. Mackail, a classical scholar, poet and civil servant, a friend of Gilbert Murray's for almost 20 years. In the spring of 1908, Gilbert, with his eldest son and both daughters, was on holiday at Rottingdean with the Mackail family, and they were joined on 24 April by another childhood friend of Lady Mary's, Frances Cornford (née Darwin). Three years earlier Lady Mary had wondered whether, upon his first meeting Frances, Gilbert would find her fascinating. She would, wrote Mary, 'always tend to be neurotic — a little bit mannered and sometimes quite plain, but I rather love her'. Not, however, in 1908. She was troubled by the company in which her husband took his holidays, and one of her letters, said Gilbert,

> leaves Mr Dog a little helpless. I mean, as to Puss's mistrust of radicals and playwrights. You know, dear one, you are in the same boat with me. You were as much Ibsenite as I ever was, and though conservatives and suchlike thought we read Ibsen entirely for the sake of the impropriety and spoke of 'Ibscenity', you know quite well that it wasn't true. Why should you turn and suspect people now? I don't think you would if you were quite well.

In hospital at Sidmouth, Lady Mary was not well and she was suspicious. She was jealous of that April holiday and still more jealous of the holiday Gilbert planned to take in the summer at Kynance Cove with Rosalind, her nurse 'Bombie' and the Wheelers. Her husband offered to avoid the Wheelers, if that was her wish, and he wondered why he was not nicer to her, but always 'hurting and disappointing you'. He could reach no satisfactory conclusion about this, but he wondered if it was not mostly that

> we did not make a real imaginative effort to understand each other twenty years ago. The differences are so slight and yet they seem never to be got over. But I do love you, Puss, and I try to be good to your kittens, so far as in me lies.

His wife was not reassured. She refused to join the summer holiday party: it would not do; it would take time to get used to Penelope Wheeler 'even, you see, if it was all my fault and not hers. I can't forget the harm my unhappiness about her did Baby and me; I hope that remembrance will grow less vivid in time, but I don't suppose I should rest well in her company till it has.' She did not, however, refuse her husband's suggestion that Christopher Wheeler might see her in hospital; and from him she gained some reassurance, not only about her health but about her husband, although she still deplored what Penelope represented: 'this apotheosis of freedom and the dramatic profession — so entirely at the cost of an excellent husband — seem to me, well, ridiculous.'

To Gilbert, it did not seem ridiculous. During this summer holiday he felt rather like Dumas with the ladies he called '*mes enfants*'. He was sure that his wife would, under happier circumstances, like Penelope — 'such a frank and kind and young-hearted person' — and he declared that he was not falling into a desperate passion, nor yet becoming bored, both possibilities Lady Mary had foreseen. Penelope, said Gilbert, had spoken with more admiration of Lady Mary than he had ever heard her speak of any one, 'all of which was very pleasing to Dog though Puss would say thank you for nothing'. Penelope Wheeler undoubtedly charmed Gilbert and became a confidante — she was told at once of the offer in 1908 of the Regius Chair of Greek at Oxford — and she was one of the party (Ernest Barker was another) with whom Gilbert Murray took another holiday in the autumn of 1908 and again at the Villa Splendide, Alassio (where Rosalind was being medically treated) at Christmas. Lady Mary had sufficiently overcome her jealousy by that date to insist that her husband return home 'first class' so that Penelope should have the extra luxury which she herself always refused.

None of these relationships were 'affairs' in the modern sense; rather were they romantic devotions. Murray himself explained them to his wife:

I love you very much and with the whole of me as my life long friend and my wife . . . the sort of imaginative love which shoots here and there through my friendship for Penelope or Margaret or, I might even say, if it does not sound odd, for Rosalind, makes me only feel how much deeper and wider my love for my wife is.

Gilbert believed that his behaviour had been

> all right, but of course I do become charmed by a certain kind of beauty . . . beauty mixed with something else always; and though I feel that I love you now perhaps more than ever in my life, I realize that other emotional friendships do come drifting across my heart and that such things could not happen to you and would seem to you a kind of treason if they did. I don't feel any element of treason in them myself. If I did, the whole thing would become revolting to me. I feel as if I should like to bring them to you and show them, rather proudly and expecting sympathy — as the cat at Barford used to bring us young rabbits' heads as a mark of sympathy . . . I have written too much about this and made it seem more than it is.

To the Lady Mary, these differences were always more than they were to Gilbert. She was a passionate, active woman of ideals unrelieved by a sense of humour or a sense of joy in life (one of her Stanley relations before her marriage had referred to Mary's 'joyless' nature). Gilbert, who held equally strong convictions, was nevertheless capable of detaching himself from his emotions and, with his sense of humour and wit, he also achieved what his wife never did: serenity. Both of them came, after 20 years of marriage with its tensions and misunderstandings, to recognise and to accept these differences in each other.

Even during their estrangements, they had never failed to accept that they had a duty to each other. A major part of that duty was their sickness and health. Because Lady Mary felt that she could not completely share Gilbert's scholarly and theatrical life, she laid the more stress upon her duty to his physical health. As an undergraduate he had overworked. As a young professor he worked still harder in the uncongenial climate of Glasgow. The symptoms which had plagued him during his first months there, during the engagement, did not vanish with marriage. The devotion he felt to his wife, the pleasure he took in their household and the decoration of his study, in the small details of domestic life with his bride, could none of them give him the rest that he thought he needed. In July 1890, Gilbert, at his wife's insistence, began the habit of taking a holiday by himself, on this first occasion at Pontresina in the Swiss mountains, in order to recover from overwork, while his wife, then towards the end of her first pregnancy, stayed with Lady Carlisle. But in the following year, Murray's health was more seriously affected, and he was obliged to enter Smedley's clinic at Matlock in Derbyshire for treatment for what Dr Hunter diagnosed as a liver condition, although he also diagnosed that overwork and excessive intellectual activity had exhausted his patient's system, the symptoms being catarrh of the stomach and gouty tenderness. The cure which the physician at Smedley's prescribed was a strict diet to cut out all fatty or rich foods, plenty of rest, a variety of baths and a long sea voyage round the world. Unless this was done, said the doctor, Gilbert Murray would become a confirmed invalid. The advice about diet was taken but Murray did not feel that he could undertake the sea voyage until, towards the end of 1892, he became sufficiently ill to take leave of his wife, his children and his university post to sail back, for the first and only time, to his native Australia.

The sea voyage itself was of no particular benefit, his doctor's advice notwithstanding. On the voyage out he suffered from headaches, sickness and fatigue which he ascribed variously to food poisoning and to hot weather. He admitted to irritability with some of his fellow passengers. On reaching Australia in November 1892 he did not like the life of 'rich, unfeeling' Australians which stuck in his throat. Nor, although he found his brother Hubert, then Crown Prosecutor in New South Wales, 'shy, farouche, fascinating', did he approve of his heavy drinking with such people as Edmund Barton, later to be the first Prime Minister of federated Australia, and Armstrong, later a judge. Nor again of his brother's suspicious knowledge of Catholicism. He saw in Hubert's marriage a contrast with his own, for Sybil Murray was not the companion, unlike Lady Mary, that a wife should be. Nor did he like the shock of being told by an old friend of his father's, what he had, he said to Mary, half suspected, that his father drank to excess. But the visit was a break in the pattern of Gilbert Murray's Glasgow life. He returned feeling stronger, although his wife thought he looked no different, to a reunion with the Lady Mary in Italy, marred by the illness there of Lady Carlisle whom her daughter had to look after. After the university session of 1893–4, and a visit to Greece in April of the latter year, Gilbert was again in the hands of the doctors.

This time the consultant was Buzzard, a famous London physician, who told Gilbert that resignation from Glasgow, which he had been contemplating when his health again collapsed, would be quite wrong, that he would regret leaving the university to his dying day. What he needed, said this specialist, was regular work, the more the better, so long as it was not 'original work'; there must be early hours, no dieting but plenty of food, with a Mantilla sherry at dinner, although Burgundy would be catastrophic. The real disease, said Buzzard, was neurasthenia, but he had no doubt that Murray would get well. Gilbert himself, taking another holiday in Switzerland with the Verralls at the year's end, felt strong enough to undertake a Euripides lexicon and to plan his history of ancient Greek literature. But in 1897 new symptoms appeared: cramp, eczema and hayfever; he was feeling 'very seedy'. In March he told Mary that he had experienced a slight but unmistakable rigor, and a cyst in his right eye had burst. He also suffered from a good deal of vague toothache, feeling 'flabby and tired'. Another doctor diagnosed him as 'very much run down in every way'; his stomach was 'wrong'. The treatment: holiday, rest and wine — a prescription Gibert did not accept. In May he had the cyst in his eye removed while in London, away from his wife whom he thought would be angered by his having the operation. In March of the following year he was again in hospital in London for a period of six weeks' treatment prescribed by Dr Eccles which Buzzard thought admirable for his condition. The treatment was severe. He might neither write nor dictate, nor receive letters other than those 'of friendship'. He was again placed on a strict diet. His spirits were low; his stomach distended. After the six weeks of diet and massage, the doctor prescribed, as an after-cure, a cycling holiday in France. During this excursion Murray's teeth started to break and hayfever afflicted him every day. In fact, as the patient thought, the treatment seemed to have done him little good and the doctors seemed unable to get to the root of the trouble. Indeed, one of the profession in Glasgow in 1898 reached the conclusion that Gilbert Murray's life was in danger and advised resignation. When Murray acted on this advice, however, and actually submitted his resignation, the doctor declined to give a certificate to this effect in support of his diagnosis.

Certainly people of Lady Carlisle's generation were accustomed to frequent illness and early death which, as their correspondence shows, was never far from their minds, a preoccupation which naturally enough carried over to their children of Murray's own generation. Without a modern pharmacopoeia, diagnosis and treatment were still very much a hit or miss business, and since most of Murray's doctors could make neither certain diagnosis nor a consequent precise treatment, it is impossible now to be certain what his disease or diseases may have been. Later gossip speculated about general paralysis of the insane and other serious conditions, but the diagnosis of one contemporary physician was neurasthenia, a term which might cover almost anything, and of another, in retrospect, Scrivener's palsy. Since Murray lived to be over 91, and until a late age possessed the strength and agility for quick walking and mountaineering in the Swiss Alps and tennis, it seems very unlikely that there was anything seriously wrong with him, although there is no doubt about the symptoms which plagued him: hayfever, weak eyes, cramp in the hands, bad teeth, headaches and a delicate stomach and eczema.

Still, whatever the diagnosis, the state of Gilbert's health was of particular concern to Lady Mary. Whatever her own feelings of weakness or feebleness, she had no doubt that her principal duty was to look after her husband. In April 1898, scarcely a month after her own doctor had found her 'not too strong', she was telling her husband who had apologised for the trouble his ill health had caused: 'don't say you have been a nuisance to me, it cuts me to the heart.'

Duty in sickness or in health was not, of course, only to each other. Their marriage, they had agreed, was not for themselves alone. Their duties naturally included their children whose physical, mental and moral well-being they took very seriously. The children's health preoccupied Lady Mary. She worried when her first-born, Rosalind, screamed at feeding time, although she believed extra feeding necessary since she thought the baby had been starved. With her second-born, Denis, she worried about his being constipated and was cross with the nurse who failed to give the baby regular enemas. The preoccupation was natural enough to a new mother who remembered the infant mortality rates of her parents' day, and it was justified when, in 1894, Rosalind caught diphtheria, then a dangerous illness which might, had it not been a mild case, have been fatal: 'we might have lost our little maid since she is delicate.' Lady Mary's anxieties concentrated upon her elder daughter. In 1897 Rosalind had pneumonia, a fever and what Gilbert called to Lady Carlisle 'rheumatism of the heart'; thereafter there were undiagnosed symptoms which finally led to the girl's establishment at Alassio for treatment for what one doctor in 1905 believed to be the preliminary symptoms of tuberculosis, although another could find no traces of the disease and believed, after a thorough examination, that the child had a trace of pleurisy which was not serious. The Lady Mary was not satisfied: the doctor had not stayed to talk about the case 'as I expect and require . . . a doctor should stay until all has been said that has to be said', and his verdict that a month at Alassio would be enough to set Rosalind 'right' she thought simply 'foolish'. Her daughter was kept at Alassio until, in two or three years' time, she could lead 'a *fairly* normal life' as the first doctor had predicted. But Lady Mary worried that Rosalind's nurse 'Bombie', who had come out with the Murrays, was not 'weighty enough' to look after her because she was 'so very unintellectual and the reverse of clever', while the choice of a girl-friend for her daughter was an anxious matter: one could not have anyone who would be 'bad for a sensitive girl beginning to read Keats and Shelley'. Rosalind's illness remained mysterious. The Murrays continued to 'pour away money' on her establishment and treatment, but by Christmas 1908 Gilbert believed that they were getting their money's worth, and could say to Lady Mary that

she does seem, in a slow and doubtful way, to be really conquering her disease, whatever it is. If it were not for this eye trouble, which is a tiresome symptom, I should feel that she was getting near the edge of the wood. (Like all other symptoms, it is ambiguous; Basso and Boon both say that it comes either from rheumatism or tuberculosis or anaemia, and as usual cannot say which.)

Still, the Murrays took no risks. Rosalind remained abroad, separately visited from time to time by each parent, protected by the establishment they created for her, until she was 18 years old.

Rosalind Murray's upbringing, tinged as it was with the natural anxiety of parents about the first-born child, nevertheless set a pattern of parental behaviour for their other children. None of the others, until the youngest, Stephen, was born in 1908, was thought to be so delicate as Rosalind, but each was the object of physical and moral concern. Agnes's teeth and tonsils exacted the same anxious parental concern as Rosalind's symptoms. The boys' physical health was never so much in doubt; they were each provided with a nurse — in Denis's case, two — so that the Lady

Mary's duty was to supervise the nurses and to choose, in emergencies, the doctors whom she also wished to supervise. Yet, important as the physical care and health of the children was, the Murrays' greater preoccupation was their children's moral education.

By morality Mary and Gilbert Murray understood the austere standards of high-minded, later nineteenth-century radical virtue, not the more conventional morality of the Christian preparatory and public school. The moral behaviour of their children was tested by their sense of obligation and duty to parents and to others, by their early acceptance of radical political principles and causes, by their willingness and ability to learn, combined with, in Lady Mary's view, healthy, physical activity. Although the children were brought up with nurses, maids and cooks to staff their parents' household, although they were regularly taken to the great Carlisle houses — Castle Howard, Naworth, Palace Green — under the watchful eye of the Countess, they were not expected to acquire any taste for luxury or high-living, any more than they were expected to display religious tendencies. Both Murrays carefully watched for such ominous signs in their children from an early age, but their actual contact with daughters and sons was not extensive when the childrens's basic needs were looked after by servants. It was a matter for particular comment that, when a nurse fell sick, Gilbert Murray himself took the two-year-old Rosalind for her afternoon walk. In May 1896, when Lady Mary was staying with her mother while Gilbert was in Glasgow, she told her husband that 'it was very sweet and good of you to have the children so long', but she did not wish him to see them at all in the morning 'beyond a good morning', and certainly not to have them for more than half an hour in the afternoon: 'they should not weigh against your all important work'. Nor did they, while the Murrays remained in Glasgow. Gilbert took no great pleasure in his children in those years. Not until he retired from the Scottish university to the English countryside did he at last detect, in his fourth child Basil, the charm of babyhood which he had not found in any of his earlier ones.

Gilbert's relations with the first three of his children were not close during the years in Glasgow. He had on occasion felt some affinity with Rosalind, but with Denis in whose discretion and affection he felt no confidence he was on 'stand off' terms, while Agnes was far from agreeable: '*un peu exigeante* and selfish'. But the children went to kindergarten and then to boarding schools at the age of seven. With this remoter relationship by correspondence, punctuated by the occasional closer contact of holidays, and later through the classical tuition he could then occasionally give them, Gilbert came to have a better appreciation of his children.

Not necessarily, however, a more favourable appreciation. After he left Glasgow, he and Rosalind were staying at the Grand Hotel Caux sur Montreux on Lac Leman in April 1899. His daughter's family nickname was 'Gosling' — Goose. From the hotel, on 16 April, he caused Rosalind to write to her mother: 'I am such a goose, you could not believe it unless you saw it, you never saw such a goose.' Gilbert added to Mary that he feared that there was some truth in this, because he believed that Rosalind certainly wanted showing her place some day, that he and the Lady Mary would have severely to discipline their daughter. The reason for this view was not only the Jacobite romanticism he had earlier detected in her conversation, but also Rosalind's obvious preference for the grandeurs of Castle Howard, Naworth and the Earldom of Carlisle. At Rottingdean in the spring of 1908, when she joined her father, Denis, Agnes, and Frances Darwin, Gilbert discovered that his daughter had after all some conversation: she defended self-denial and monasticism very well. Her father's affection for her markedly increased, but then his younger daughter Agnes resented both his attention to, and affection for, her elder sister. Rosalind in conversation with her father pleased him by praising the wisdom of her mother's upbringing of the children, although she then confided to her father the grief her nurses had been to her because of their vulgarity. Murray still suspected his elder daughter's tastes: in looking for houses she was 'less useful as a critic because she likes spacious halls and retainers and two hundred acres of forest and ravine'. Rosalind caused him 'pangs by defective Liberalism'; she also, although 'sweet-tempered when overruled', was not energetic and she had a disturbing taste for luxury. She might, Gilbert feared, take a facile, pleasure-loving view of things, with not much moral enthusiasm. Yet, he was not sure that this lack of moral enthusiasm was a great loss; in his own early life it had been mixed up with a lot of hypocrisy and censoriousness and lack of sympathy. Still, he regretted his daughter's predilections, the more so because he put his love for Rosalind on a level with the sort of imaginative love he felt for Penelope Wheeler and Margaret Mackail. His elder daughter, then 18 years old, would someday need a good influence of a kind 'different from ours': 'you and I', he told the Lady Mary, are both too stern for her, 'too averse to pleasures and the motor carrish side of life on the one hand, and to sentimental religion on the other'. Rosalind, nevertheless, was an intellectual companion to her father and for that he could forgive much. When at 18 she wrote her first novel, *The Leading Note*, he was, amidst criticism, impressed. When in 1909 she wrote her second, *Chloe*, he exclaimed 'what a clever creature that goose-child is'. It was even cleverer of her, in the next year, to begin to fall in love with a young Fellow of Balliol, Arnold Toynbee. Apart from the love of a father for a first daughter, Gilbert Murray approved of Rosalind's imagination; it redeemed the lack of formal education, and it compensated for the romantic, aristocratic view of life natural to the granddaughter of the ninth Earl of Carlisle.

Agnes, the younger daughter, attracted no such love and affection in her early years. In June 1897 her father had found her far from agreeable, although three years later he came to believe that she gave him the greatest pleasure of all his children. This was not a sustained opinion. As Agnes grew up, her father thought that although she struggled with herself she was really rather stupid. At the age of 14 she was 'more like eleven', and was resentful of the attention and affection he gave to Rosalind without the latter's asking for it, while she herself was rebuffed. This, Gilbert told his wife, was Agnes's own fault, for she insisted on intervening in all conversations about poetry and 'always stupidly, so that one does not encourage her': 'I sometimes feel I don't love her enough.' His relationship with his younger daughter had in fact always been a playful or whimsical one. The letters which he wrote to her after she was sent away to school at the age of five, bore such greetings as Miss Agnes Murray, Madam — and continued with the pretence that he was writing as if he were a small dog. More usually she was his 'own very dear small Bags', or his 'dear Small Pussy-Cat Agnes Slippers Jemimakin Murray' who, when unhappy at school away from her parents and, feared Gilbert, in danger of becoming as much a stranger as Denis, was nevertheless told: 'I hope school is nice — it is sure to be by this time.' He prescribed her reading *Villette*, but only displayed real interest when Agnes began to write poetry of which he could be critical: 'I think you ought not to try things of that length and difficulty until you can give your whole time and energy to them.' To Agnes this seemed, especially by contrast with the parental appreciation of her sister's novels, yet another rebuff. When she herself wrote a story at the age of 17, her father told her that it would not bear criticism; it was quite immature. Still, Agnes's literary efforts and his earlier doubts about her intelligence led Gilbert to suggest that she should read English for her degree at Somerville College, Oxford. He thought that she should take Pass Moderations rather than take a Third in Honour Moderations because the pass work was limited, rather easy and known by rote where Honours might be too hard and end in hysterics. Agnes did not take her father's advice. When she went up to Somerville she read for Honour Moderations and in 1915 took a Third, a result attributed by Lady Carlisle, who regarded her granddaughter, provided she did not have friends who smoked, as a heroine of woman's achievement, to an ineffective classical teaching at school. Gilbert Murray predicted a more respectable degree for her in Greats. She never took it, but Agnes's was the best formal academic performance of the Murray children.

If Agnes suffered from her father's preference for Rosalind, the boys suffered from his preference for his daughters over his sons. No boyish nicknames were the equivalent of 'Gosling' and 'Bags'. The eldest, Denis, was a puzzle to his father. In 1896 Denis was asking most of the time after his absent mother. By the following year, Denis was described by his father as 'really a nice boy', although he 'cried for very little'. The Murrays tried to shield their first son from bad influences. Lady Mary forbade military toys such as a popgun, toy soldiers, a torpedo boat, gifts, however, which her husband could not prevent being given, so he soothed his wife that such things were unavoidable, and in any case that a boy could not be made peaceful by excluding guns and swords from his ken. By 1905, however, Denis was in his father's opinion both willing and trustworthy; he had 'outgrown really'. The boy was sent to Winchester, but the Murrays were not altogether happy with that school. In August 1907 Gilbert felt obliged to write to the Rev. F. P. David who had displayed what Murray called 'sectarian objections' to Denis's presence: he and his wife felt that it was difficult, in that Anglican milieu, to count on any generous sense of co-operation in what they themselves saw as the proper moral training and general education of their son. Gilbert was still more worried when, during the family holiday at Rottingdean in April 1908, Denis told him of the obscene conversation of two older boys, with one of whom he had been thrown into intimacy when they were together in the school infirmary and with whom he was then accused by the school authorities of associating too much. Denis was at pains to defend himself against any wrong-doing, and the two older boys were in fact leaving his House, but the incident intensified the worried concern the Murrays felt for their son. Still, they looked for encouraging signs in him. He was, Gilbert thought, good-tempered and even rather unselfish; indeed he seemed 'rather clever in many ways'. Like Lady Mary's own brothers he would, his father told his wife, 'come out with strength of character when he gets older'. By the end of the year it was possible to believe that the 'change we have expected is coming and his real intelligence is beginning to come out'. Yet Denis, as his father feared might also happen in the case of Agnes, now at school at Connamur in Ireland, had become a stranger to his parents and even less suited than his sister to reading classics at Oxford. Denis sat for Pass Moderations in 1911 and, showing his father his Latin prose after he had sat for the examination, caused Gilbert to wonder how the examiner could possibly let him pass. The examiner did not. Gilbert had read some Homer with him for three hours before his next paper, but it made no difference, and in July 1911 Denis was withdrawn from Oxford with a view to becoming an apprentice engineer.

The two younger boys, Basil and Stephen, were the children of early middle age, when Gilbert was coming to feel that he and his wife could be sufficient for each other. Whatever doubts the Lady Mary or Gilbert had about the effects of their austere discipline in the upbringing of their first three children, they nevertheless brought up the last two in much the same way: nurses, servants and separate establishments which, in the day-to-day business of parenthood, kept the children apart from their parents. Yet, the moral and educational supervision of the parents remained, to be exercised in accordance with those high principles from which neither of them departed. Gilbert and Mary Murray might, in later life, wonder if they could have averted the disappointments which their children caused them, but they never doubted that the ideals at which they had aimed were right; and they were always optimistic, looking for every sign in their children that, as Hubert Murray once reassured his brother, it would come out 'alright in the end'.

Beyond their own family, the Murrays always recognised their duties and obligations to others. At the beginning of their marriage, that had meant Gilbert's colleagues and students at Glasgow University. Their large house in The College was often filled with guests: the Sidgwicks and the Fishers from Oxford days, Glasgow colleagues such as Andrew Bradley and the Adamsons, and, above all, students to whom, the Murrays believed, such hospitality was new. John Buchan, Janet Spens, Helen Rutherford, Dorothy Murray, Janie Malloch and Noel Brailsford were all regular visitors during their undergraduate years. To these guests the Murrays dispensed plain hospitality. Although Mary and Gilbert on very rare occasions took wine or liquor for health reasons — the former a little brandy when she was faint, the latter a little claret at dinner when he was very exhausted — they were abstainers, and no guest was offered wine or liquor. Presently they also became vegetarians, but in the Glasgow days they ate meat: a typical daily menu in 1890 was partridge with bread sauce for luncheon, rabbit soufflé for dinner and, for breakfast the next day, plaice and the cold remains of the partridge. Late in the 1890s both of them abstained from flesh foods, after dieting was prescribed for their respective illnesses, but the real reason was their growing conviction that meat was the product of a cruelty to animals which they could not tolerate. Still, unlike drink, meat was still provided for their guests and the servants. The Lady Mary, who had so much trouble with servants, was pleased with them when they ate meat no more than once a day but instead preferred tea and bread and cheese, although this wasted a great cupboard full of Harrods' Celebrated Inferior Cocoa, Jam for the Use of Domestic Servants and Economical Coffee, which, Gilbert jokingly told his mother-in-law, might instead be given to the less respected class of guest. The Murrays' hospitality was in fact a good deal better than this suggests; even when, at Barford and later at Oxford and Boar's Hill, they themselves ate nut cutlets or some other vegetarian dish, there was always a joint or other meat for their guests. In his Oxford days, Gilbert would ask his guests: 'will you have some of the corpse, or will you try the alternative?'

Plain living and high-minded thinking: not an unfair description of the Murray household. Their hospitality was generous but those who were offered and accepted it were expected to make a return in the constant flow of conversation, to make a contribution to what was in effect a radical *salon*. Political compatibility there must be. Neither of the Murrays was at ease with Conservatives or illiberal or politically indifferent guests. In later life Lady Mary was known to say: 'if you don't believe in Progress, out of this house you go'. In the Glasgow years, this imperiousness, so reminiscent of both Lady Carlisle and Lady Stanley, was more muted, but those regularly invited to the house must be politically sympathetic. Thus Gilbert's Liberal colleagues at Glasgow came, but not, for instance, Ramsey or Kelvin. Noel Brailsford was a welcome student, but John Buchan, even then a Conservative, was suspect. To such hospitality the Murrays added, for those in need, outright gifts in money or in kind which on occasion exhausted their own resources until they were replenished by Lady Carlisle's own generosity. Gilbert sometimes remonstrated with Mary over her beneficence: 'you have given away all your cloaks; what will *you* wear?' Although agreeing with her in their own self-denial, he was occasionally prepared to use their money for themselves; he once bought first-class train tickets instead of second when his wife was very exhausted after Basil's birth, an action which reduced the Lady Mary to tears because of its self-indulgence.

The marriage of Lady Mary and Gilbert Murray lasted until their deaths, within a few months of each other, nearly seventy years later. Their household on Boar's Hill from the end of the First World War, became an Oxford institution. That there were strains within the marriage should be obvious. Their temperaments, as they recognised, were different. The upbringing of the children caused difficulties. Gilbert's other relationships almost led to a breakdown. With the decline of the once great Liberal Party, political disagreements troubled the Murray's relationship. Nevertheless, whatever the difficulties between them, the sense that their marriage was for others as well as themselves and the Lady Mary's conviction that her husband's work, whatever it might be, was so important that it must be supported above all else, held the marriage together, a union which seemed to observers beyond the family to be an unshakeable and natural alliance in the good causes of Humanity and Progress.

4 A SCOTTISH CHAIR

Gilbert Murray's marriage was made possible by his election to the Chair of Greek at Glasgow University in 1889. His duty as professor was the first important work which his wife saw as her duty to put before anything else. Murray's election to the chair at the extraordinarily young age of 23, in Scotland where education was a serious matter and a university professor a man of great status and dignity, was seen by his fiancée as public recognition of his brilliant talents, but others saw it differently. Labouchère, deploring the appointment of Andrew Bradley to the Chair of English in the same university, continued: 'Even this outrageous job is surpassed by the appointment of an utterly unknown young man to the Chair held by Jebb and Lushington.' Labouchère was writing Conservative political invective, and ignoring the fact that Richard Jebb himself had been a young man upon his appointment at Glasgow, a university which had not infrequently appointed younger men who then made their reputations in its service. It was in any case untrue that Gilbert Murray was 'utterly unknown', and his own later description of himself as having 'a local reputation' and having 'written nothing' was unduly modest. Sir Richard Jebb himself knew of Murray as the most accomplished Greek scholar of his generation, while some of the Oxford dons who supported him for the chair were men whose reputations were national. When Benjamin Jowett, Master of Balliol, told the Glasgow electors that Murray was the most distinguished undergraduate of his time, this was testimony from a national figure and therefore more than a local reputation. Murray's Oxford teachers — D. B. Monro, Provost of Oriel, Henry Nettleship, Corpus Professor of Latin, and Margoliouth — all testified to his brilliance as a scholar, but their testimonials also emphasised that this was more than technical excellence. As Nettleship said: classical education in Murray's hands would not be 'a mere engine of literary culture but a general training of the character and affections'. Nor was it wholly true that Murray had published nothing. His Gaisford Greek Verse prize and his Chancellor's Latin Verse prize entries had both been published by Blackwell in Oxford in 1886, as was his Gaisford Prose prize in the following year; and in the year of his election to the chair he had published a philological article on the Greek elegiac poets. Nevertheless, if Murray's later self-assessment of his achievement by 1889 was unduly modest, it is obviously true that he had no major reputation beyond his brilliant undergraduate career, that his appointment really rested on great promise.

Labouchère's attack upon the appointment, although it seemed to rest upon scholarly grounds, was nevertheless a politically motivated one, an attack continued by the *Scotsman* for some years in foreseeing the day 'when the young fool who now sits in Lushington's chair has succeeded in emptying his classroom by his blue ribbon and red neck-tie principles'. It was Murray's political views as a radical Liberal which were being held against him in a Conservative stronghold. The Principal of the university, John Caird, himself a Liberal, warned Murray not to make a parade of his views. Gilbert was surprised when he was in fact elected to the chair. He could never remember who suggested that he might stand for it, but the testimonials he then collected encouraged him to do so. As was customary, these had to be printed and distributed to the electors. The candidate then had to call upon each of them. Gilbert spent a few days with Jebb in Cambridge, bought a top hat, and set off for Glasgow to canvass each elector for his vote. In the course of this, Murray told Lord Carlisle, it appeared that the Baillies were willing to admit his knowledge of Greek, but one of them had pointed out a significant omission from his testimonials: none had said that he came of a respectable family. Gilbert asked his future father-in-law to supply the want, and the Earl obliged. Murray, he said, was a gentleman in every sense of the word: by birth, by education, by nature. He had high moral aims in life and lived up to them without ostentation. Gilbert found the whole business of canvassing the electors to the chair for their votes 'degrading', but he nevertheless called upon all except two, to whose bedells, he said, he had nevertheless 'grovelled'. The other candidates had all been round before him, and he had heard that Lord Lytton, the chairman of the electoral board, had written in favour of another candidate. Nevertheless, the quiet, cultivated, courteous young man, with his air of earnest conviction and obvious enthusiasm for the benefits of Greek in education, struck a chord with the electors. What to some of Murray's own contemporaries sometimes seemed priggishness, to the electors seemed appropriate to the demeanour of a Scottish professor.

Murray was not altogether pleased by his election. It meant

leaving Oxford and a life which he liked for the very different atmosphere of a big, northern industrial city, of which the climate was notorious. Nevertheless, the post, with its large income, large house and servants in The College, and recognised status, made possible his marriage to Lady Mary Howard. She could not, she said, 'be really disappointed with our professorship', although she found the society of Glasgow as alien as did her husband. In retrospect, Murray thought that his years as a Scottish professor had caused him to miss his youth; he had stepped straight into middle-age beneath the dignity of his post and the hard grind its duties entailed. But his later judgement is somewhat coloured by hindsight. Their life at Glasgow was still relatively leisured. The university's teaching session ran from November to April, and outside that period the Murrays were often at Castle Howard or Naworth or Palace Green, in one or another of the great Howard houses, or on the Continent. The session, it was true, fell into the worst time of the year for black, freezing fogs, howling winds, gloomy light and cold. The first lecture of the day was at 8 a.m., which meant early rising and breakfast at 7.15. There was none of the opportunity for games, in the Oxford pattern, in the afternoons. In fact Murray came to like this regime, and the hard grind which he later came to think had robbed him of his youth was the result of his own enthusiasm, not only for his professorial duties which occupied less than half the year and were in any case supported by an income and servants which removed the mechanics of living from his ken, but also for his own literary and public work which he and his wife believed to be the important duty of a gentleman of talents.

Teaching was not new to Murray. As a Fellow of New College he had tutored Oxford undergraduates, but at Glasgow there was no such tutorial system of personal attention to each student. Murray tried to combine this Oxford system with what was the main teaching duty of a Scottish professor, the lecture. It was the combination of the two, of Murray's own volition, that entailed the hard work which he later blamed for his loss of health, vitality and youth. When he arrived in Glasgow in October 1889 his first task was to enrol the students. He and his one assistant, Murdoch, sat in the professor's room. Before Murray there lay a plan of the classroom in which he was to lecture, and a stack of tickets. When a student came in, he or she was given by Murdoch a form to be filled up which was then handed to Murray who assigned by ticket a place in the classroom while the student was paying his fee in cash to Murdoch. On that first day, 20 students came; on the second, 150. After several days of enrolment something over 350 had passed before Murray, whose pockets were stuffed with bank notes which he had then to carry to the bank. He was advised to carry a cudgel when he did so, and preferably to take a bodyguard. This rough quality of life was reflected in the students. Many of them were a good deal older than the professor himself, and some obviously lived and worked in very hard conditions, far removed from those of an Oxford college. One man actually gave an address seven miles from Glasgow and when the assistant asked him 'I suppose ye'll take the train?' got the answer 'Na man, I walk'. The experience of enrolling students added to Murray's nervous tension, for he had already heard of the Glasgow tradition of student rowdiness and unruliness in class, of the difficulties which some of his colleagues had in keeping order. G. G. Ramsey, the Professor of Humanity (Latin), told his new colleague of his own early difficulties, of his actually buying a ticket back to London in order to leave the place. Even Lady Mary Howard repeated to her fiancé stories of student demonstrations which she had heard from a Scottish minister whom she met while on holiday in Switzerland. To her Gilbert confessed that he 'dreaded' meeting the Middle and Senior classes.

The first class Murray met was in fact the Junior, the first-year students. They numbered 70, but as newcomers they were timid. Even so, the new professor found the task of assigning places to them in the classroom and setting their first work 'an awful strain, much more than I thought possible', since he did not dare to make a mistake nor to show any hesitation in case he lost control of them. His main work, on that first day, was 'policing, very degrading'. 'How I look back to my New College men.' But this early apprehension, reflected in the story that one night, on a journey by rail sleeper from Glasgow, a clergyman in the other berth was startled from sleep by Murray's suddenly sitting up in bed and thundering 'Silence. I must have absolute silence passed.' When Murray met the Senior class for the first time at 8 o'clock in the morning of 11 November, he passed a very pleasant hour with them on Homer's *Odyssey* Book xii. Then he returned home to breakfast. After breakfast he took the Middle class which was 'alright', although the prescribed text was Xenophon which was, in Murray's opinion, boring. The following day he began to believe that 'the work will really be very interesting after all'.

Certainly he threw himself into it with all his strength. He had felt misgivings about succeeding such a man as Jebb who 'of course knew ten times as much Greek as I do', but he never hesitated to improve on Jebb's system. One very important lack, he felt, was that the 'poor wretches' had never done any unseen translations because it took too long for the professor to correct them. Murray proposed, with his wife's help, to spend some five hours a week correcting unseens, work of an easy, dull, mechanical nature, he said, but of inestimable value to the Glasgow students who had never received this kind of individual attention before, certainly not from a man who was not only giving them technical instruction but at the same time trying to open up to them a new world.

The real instrument of Murray's success as a teacher at Glasgow was not the tutorial — which he undertook well beyond his expected duties — but the lecture. The contrast with Jebb was great. The latter's delivery had been flat. Murray, to the contrary, cultivated a dramatic, theatrical quality, all the more effective because it was delivered without histrionics or gestures but by voice control and timing. Something of this quality had been obvious to those who heard him speak at Oxford. Thoughtful, suggestive, finished, logical: those were the adjectives then applied. But in Glasgow he had to hold the attention and try to capture the imaginations of students all too ready to reduce a lecturer to incoherence. In Glasgow, too, Murray had to lecture not only to a potentially disruptive class but in competition with the weather. Competing against a howling wind Murray had to sing some of his sentences in a high key and then drop his voice to a low note when the noise of the gale fell at intervals. His tenor voice had a beautiful musical quality, but Glasgow was a hard school in which to learn the arts of capturing an audience. For many of his students, however, his lectures were the chief memory they retained of their university days because he captured their imaginations in a way that perhaps only Andrew Bradley among his Glasgow colleagues could equal. Although the general standard of the students was naturally not so high as at Oxford, and the teaching, even to the Senior class, more elementary than advanced, many students responded to Gilbert Murray's personality and scholarship. The *Scotsman* notwithstanding, he never emptied but rather filled his classroom. Noel Brailsford and John Buchan, Janie Malloch, Helen Rutherford, Dorothy Murray and Janet Spens were among his pupils who later distinguished themselves, but during the rest of his life even some of the students who became ministers of religion wrote to record their pleasure and profit in the years Murray had taught them at Glasgow. Still, there were others who had reservations. MacCallam Scott and Menzies never took to Murray, whom they regarded, together with Lady Mary, as priggish strangers from an alien world; they vastly preferred his assistant in the mid-1890s, Ronald Burrows.

The arts and skills of a lecturer, of an actor *manqué*, might serve to capture an audience, but what finally held the students was the content of what Murray taught and still more the earnest faith in which it was delivered. For, as he proclaimed in his Inaugural Lecture, he believed that the teaching of Greek — which 200 years ago had provided a good education — had become narrow and bad. From the cultivated standpoint, why should a boy spend all his time upon a comparatively small branch of knowledge? In doing Greek, did he not ignore history, geography and his own literature? Was his mind not stunted and strangled? The strength of this kind of attack, Murray declared, 'I would not if I could, attempt to baffle'. What use is a dead language for business? It leads only to schoolmasterships. This second kind of attack, said Murray, was the exact opposite of the first, because, instead of calling for a better education, it called for no education at all. Classical education was indeed, he asserted, deplorably narrow 'in the sense in which it is obtainable in public schools', but the French solution for this, the method of the Encyclopaedia, was perhaps even more disastrous than what it replaced, because it substituted a vague general knowledge for specialism. Of course a man needed more general knowledge — of grammar, of arithmetic, of great books and — in future — of evolution, of physics, of chemistry, of political economy and of history. But this essential general knowledge was not in itself of much educational value. It was mastery of a single subject that gave stimulus to the mind and afforded glimpses of the enormous range of human knowledge. Murray's moral: all departments of knowledge were equally honourable and deserving of study, but not all could be studied by the same people. 'Some few subjects ought to be studied by everybody: I do not think that Greek is one of them.' The Greek language was one of unusual difficulty, but knowledge of ancient Greece shed floods of light on history, political philosophy, ethics, logic and psychology. 'Greece, not Greek, is the real subject of our study. There is more in Hellenism than a language, although that language may be the liveliest and richest ever spoken by man.' Language helped the rest of the study because without it there were needed special gifts to win the spirit of Hellenism, but language itself was for most purposes subsidiary to the wider study: Greece. And Greece had something unique to offer. 'Once in the history of all mankind a unique people in the course of six hundred years passed through almost all the stages of development we know in the rise and fall of the nations of the world.' Poets, philosophers and moralists, soldiers and explorers, the Greeks were 'the one nation that grasped and assimilated the teaching of Christ . . . Every form of social life was known to them — there was no political experiment they did not try.' Pleasure-loving yet iron-souled, cynical yet idealist, there was 'no subject of human knowledge they did not touch, no thought too abstruse, no moral height too arduous'. The stories that aroused them most were those of self-sacrifice. If, therefore, we are to choose some period to educate our youth, for those minds naturally attracted to it 'the study of Greece is an education as full and as satisfying as lies within reach'.

Any inaugural lecture in those days was a manifesto of purpose: how the professor saw his field; what he proposed to do. Murray gave some offence with his. To his immediate audience in Glasgow, he gave offence by including not a single reference to his distinguished predecessor, Jebb, and by the appearance of a radical, Liberal approach to his subject which not only ignored the past but seemed to break with it. A Scottish professor was there to teach students who had a vocational end in view. Greek, until recently one of the seven compulsory subjects which made up the Glasgow curriculum — the others were Latin, Mathematics, Logic, Moral Philosophy, Natural Philosophy and English — was a passport to schoolmasterships and to the ministry of religion. As such, it was a means to a practical end, a job, and to seem to subordinate it to the understanding of Greece was an intellectual luxury which had no immediate appeal to most students and their parents. In attacking the way in which Greek was taught in schools, Murray introduced a worrying uncertainty into what had seemed a matter of assured, if mechanical, learning at school which should simply be continued at the university. Indeed, where at school pupils were taught, almost by rote, to be able to construe and to scan a set text, at university (including the Oxford of Murray's own day) the same preoccupation with the text itself was the dominant approach. The content of the text, as literature or as poetry, as political philosophy or as history, was not a matter of great concern. When Murray proclaimed that it was what the texts could reveal of Greece, not Greek itself, which was the principal object of his teaching, he seemed to be a radical in a Conservative stronghold. When his Inaugural Lecture was in print, he could remedy his omission of any reference to Jebb, but his attack on contemporary teaching of the classics remained, to earn for him the hostility of those who believed that when a Greek text would construe or scan it was enough.

Moreover, the vision which Murray revealed of Greece itself aroused suspicion. The textual scholars believed that it went beyond the evidence of the texts they so carefully studied; it might be 'brilliant' — not a complimentary adjective — but it was 'unsound'. To pious Scottish listeners, the assertion that the pagan Greeks alone grasped the spirit of Christianity was anathema. To many, the idea that a remote period was, as Murray claimed, relevant to the present was unacceptable. Nevertheless, the shining vision of perfection which Murray revealed had an imaginative appeal, especially to the impressionable young, and there is ample testimony that many students at Glasgow responded to Greek and Greece as taught by Gilbert Murray. As one of them said to Lady Mary: 'I cannot think of any higher work than the revelation of light and beauty which Mr Murray gave us students in his lectures. Those hours in the honours class were like peeps into shining Athens from out this murky city.' Or as another told Murray himself upon his retirement from Glasgow: 'we may get someone who will appear at lectures with never-failing punctuality, but it will be long before we get another who will so give himself to his class or lend such a charm to its work.' Not everyone responded to the charm — to some it was affectation — but many did.

Murray's Inaugural Lecture, apart from setting out his programme and his method as professor, also reveals two themes which he was to develop in his later work. Marvellous and beautiful as the Greek achievement was, it was the result of progress throughout 600 years, of evolution or development from primitive beginnings to the glory that was fifth-century Athens. As a Whig, using that term to describe his radical Liberalism, Murray had a firm belief in Progress in human history and, like other Whig scholars, the theory of evolution supplied a scientific basis for a belief which was implicit in the Utilitarians whose philosophy he believed enabled a man to judge rightly on every moral and political question. The theme of Progress, based on assumptions about evolution, ran through Murray's life. But he plainly did not believe that Progress and evolution operated automatically, without human striving and endeavour, and he did not believe that Progress could be traced in a direct, unbroken line from the past to the present. In his Inaugural Lecture he referred to the 'stages of development we know in the rise and fall of nations'. The language is evolutionary. The idea of Progress is there. But so is the assumption that, in human history, both are cyclical; there is a cycle of rise and fall, growth and decay. Murray did not assert or even imply in 1889 that this cycle is inevitable. Indeed, his listeners could have drawn the conclusion that the study of Greece was relevant to a modern education because from the Greek experience could be drawn the inspiration and the lessons which would preserve modern, progressive, liberal civilisation. What was missing from Murray's views in 1889 was awareness of the threat from barbarism to the achievements of civilisation.

The themes of Murray's work as a Hellenist are clear enough at the beginning of his career in Glasgow. They run through all of his later works. The precise form of his work, however, grew out of his undergraduate teaching. In November 1889 Evelyn Abbott, Senior Classical Tutor at Balliol College, Oxford, had invited him to edit the Greek lyric poets for a series of texts proposed by the publishers, Rivingtons. Murray enthusiastically accepted, believing that his special knowledge of Greek dialects could be useful. Nothing came of the proposal, in the event, but his lecturing duties at Glasgow convinced him of the need for Greek texts suitable for teaching purposes. In June 1893 he himself proposed such a series, to be known as the Glasgow Critical Texts, to be published by his friend, the Glasgow publisher Maclehose. A printed letter was sent round to a number of Greek scholars and teachers, asking them to consider the scheme as it was outlined to them in the publisher's circular. What Murray intended was a series of carefully revised texts, with the briefest possible critical notes at the foot of the page, since students were often discouraged by piles of notes. The texts should also contain the *scholia*, the ancient commentaries on the Greek texts, with references added in the case of quotations. A student, Murray explained, who read Aristophanes with the help of the *scholia* got nearly all that the fullest modern edition could give him or her. He also proposed to include the ancient lives of the various poets, and in some cases to add a special introduction, in English or in Latin, which would be printed before the text. Those to whom this letter was sent were asked to give their opinion of the general scheme, to state whether they would be prepared to give a trial to these books in their classes, and to indicate how many copies they would be likely to take.

The replies were not encouraging. Almost all of those asked agreed with the idea that schoolboys and undergraduates should use the complete texts of a single author, rather than the text of a single book or play, and that these texts should be annotated as little as possible with explanatory notes. But most also felt that printing the *scholia* was a bad idea, the schoolmasters in particular thinking that boys would not use the *scholia* and that if they were to be printed at all it should be at the back of the book or separately. One or two people opposed the whole idea. T. C. Snow, whom Murray greatly respected, did so; Margoliouth opposed the inclusion of the *scholia*; Sidgwick, himself an assistant master at Rugby for many years, thought that teachers would not use the texts; Verrall was doubtful. What, nevertheless, finally forced the abandonment of the scheme was not the adverse or reserved opinions of those closest to him but the practical objections. The circular letter had asked about the vital matter of sales. The existence of the Teubner series was not in itself fatal, for they did not provide, as W. R. Hardie pointed out, a plain text, and anyway they were on bad paper, their print was unpleasing and the texts themselves were too arbitrary and conjectural for a standard series. The Oxford Classical Texts series, however, was already under way. Macmillan's, too, had long contemplated a series of texts with a new typeface they had already prepared; both would sell for a lower price than was proposed for the Glasgow ones. By November 1894 Murray had dropped his idea because he had had no clear and convinced support. By that date, too, he had had another idea.

In 1894, while he was preparing his lectures for the Honours class, he became more and more interested in the Greek playwright Euripides, especially in the play *Hippolytus*, which inspired him to write a diatribe on the real greatness of Euripides as playwright, as a master of subtle and poetic language. This Greek author, he thought, had been generally misunderstood because he was so mistranslated. What Murray proposed was a new Euripides translation of his own, faced by the Greek text, preceded by an introduction and followed by literary and philological appendices. During the summer he asked Lady Carlisle to invite the Verralls from Cambridge to Castle Howard so that he might talk to them about the idea, in company with T. C. Snow and two of his own women students from Glasgow. And he took another, more important step. He wrote in Greek to Ulrich von Wilamowitz-Moellendorf at Göttingen, the foremost Euripidean scholar in Europe who happened also to be, as Murray himself was in his own recently completed original prose play *Carlyon Sahib*, a devotee of the Norwegian dramatist, Henrik Ibsen. The contact thus established with the German scholar not only confirmed Murray's lifelong interest in Euripides, but confirmed his particular view of that playwright as a man who had a vital message for Murray's own contemporaries.

When the session began at Glasgow in November 1894 Murray's work with the Honours class on Euripides seemed so very interesting that 'I seldom feel the need for anything outside it'. The class obviously took an interest in this author so generally thought to be a bore — 'a tissue of depressing commonplaces' as Hubert Murray once told his brother — so that Gilbert Murray felt greatly encouraged in his pursuit of Euripides. 'I think I see something in him which people lately have not seen. I almost feel that he expresses my own feelings and beliefs: rational, liberal, humane, feminist.' But Murray did not quite know how he should go about the task he had set himself of rescuing and restoring Euripides to his proper eminence by means of a lexicon which would personally be 'an immense help and resource, supplying that outlet for hard and original thinking and honest drudgery which my lectures do not entirely supply . . . I shall go to Göttingen sometime and see Wilamowitz.' Murray never went to Göttingen — indeed, despite Maurice Bowra's assertion, he never met Wilamowitz until the latter came to Oxford in 1908 — but he opened a correspondence. Unable to 'speak his *patois*' Murray wrote in Greek and Wilamowitz at first replied in kind:

> A letter in Greek calls for a Greek reply — though I must say that in my opinion the best practice is for each to write in his own language . . . it is surely always true that a man can express his thoughts more clearly and exactly in his own tongue than in any other.

Wilamowitz encouraged Murray, welcoming the idea of a text of Euripides: It would be 'most useful to Greek scholars. No one is preventing you. Bergen is dead, Berthold gave up. Stoppel is not up to it'; and he went on to give practical advice and guidance about the making of a lexicon. He enclosed some of his own notes on Euripides' *Phoenissae*, offering also any other of his material which would help, and undertaking to read the proofs. The proofs, however, when they finally came to Wilamowitz, were not those of the proposed lexicon but of the volumes of Euripides plays which Gilbert Murray later edited for the Oxford Classical Texts. His interest in Euripides, originally kindled by his undergraduate teaching in Glasgow, had survived the failure of the Glasgow texts proposal, of which the only result, Murray later said, was an invitation from the Clarendon Press to edit for the Oxford series. On 26 June 1896, P. L. Gill invited Murray to undertake the edition of the whole of Euripides' works, a proposal Murray eagerly accepted since his idea of a lexicon had already implied the making of a Greek text in his mind. In the summer of 1897 Murray was hard at work upon the edition which took 'every scrap of my brain', but ill health forced him first to suspend work and then to postpone it, until after his retirement from Glasgow.

Teaching undergraduates at Glasgow directed Murray's scholarly attention to textual work as the necessary foundation of his faith. It also prompted him to provide a textbook to speak out his message. The courses which he had prepared and delivered impressed upon him the need for a survey of Greek literature as an indispensable teaching aid, but he also felt that such a book could usefully be addressed not only to scholars but also to the general public. In May 1895 Edmund Gosse invited him to contribute such a book to the history of literature series that he was editing for Heinemann. This was not, wrote Gosse, to be a series of texts but of books of graceful and permanent criticism. Murray accepted the invitation saying that he hoped to have the volume ready within three years. Gosse insisted that 1897 be the date, and in fact Murray finished the manuscript within a year.

The book grew out of the lectures he had prepared at Glasgow which had had to cover the whole range of surviving Greek literature. It grew out of them in another way too, for the book is really the spoken word upon paper, something written not to be read in print but to be listened to. Murray asserted in his preface that 'to read and re-read the scanty remains now left to us of the literature of Ancient Greece is a pleasant and not a laborious task' and he set out to convey that pleasure to his readers. The textual scholar might react, as did Henry Jackson in Cambridge, with the words 'insolent puppy', but the general reader appreciated a popular exposition.

The book was a remarkable *tour de force*. Written at a time when a good deal of recognisable modern scholarship was available but before new material was being discovered in significant quantity, it surveyed the whole field of ancient Greek literature — poems, histories, plays, philosophy — by the light of contemporary scholarship from the continent as well as from England. And it did so with imagination. As Murray said in his preface:

> For the last ten years there has been hardly a day when Greek poetry has not occupied a large part of my thoughts. I have tried — at first unconsciously, afterwards of set purpose — to realise what sort of men the various Greek authors were, what they liked and disliked, how they earned their living and spent their time.

He hoped to save students from the error of supposing that the Greeks were all alike. 'In reality it is their variety that makes them so living to us.' He dismissed the images so often entertained of the 'serene' Greek, the 'aesthetic' and the 'fleshly' Greek; they were phantasms. 'There is more flesh and blood in the Greek of the anthropologist, the foster brother of Kaffirs and Hairy Ainu' but even this Greek was only the 'raw material of the man we want'. What was the Greek Murray wanted? Within the necessary compression of the book, he was chiefly the Greek of Athens and the Attic period, but Murray traced an earlier moral growth towards that society which was the only one in history so near to 'the highest side of our own': the society of Euripides and Plato. In looking, therefore, at Homer, the author saw a gradual working over of poems from what he called legendary poets, the clan of the *homeridae*, to the last working over in which the treatment of Helen and Andromache, of Hector and Achilles, showed a moral growth. In these stages of growth, assumed by Murray, Pindar became an early beacon of enlightenment and progress, although his life had had a great flaw: he was the servant of sacerdotal tradition and of racial prejudice. Socrates became a daemonic, semi-inspired man whose positive doctrines amounted to little, whose criticism was destructive, often unfair, yet who was nevertheless deeply honest; but so were his accusers who were responsible men not villains. These earlier Greek figures, nevertheless, were the harbingers of that Athenian flowering which was the Greek Murray wanted.

The Greek poets and playwrights also had an ancestry. Gilbert Murray, a great admirer of Wilamowitz's introduction to his 1893 edition of Euripides' *Herakles*, found the origin of tragic drama in the goat-song of the Dorian North Peleponnese which had then merged with the speech poetry of Ionians. In origin, the chorus of a Greek play was the essence of tragedy but this role of the chorus dwindled as a dialogue between individual actors grew in importance. Comedy, Murray believed, had a different origin — the mummings of rustics at vintage or harvest feasts — but at the time he wrote his book, however, comedy did not really interest him. It was tragedy that he found fascinating. Half-way through his book he arrived at Aeschylus, whose *Oresteia* he believed to be not only that playwright's highest achievement but probably the highest of all Greek drama, because of its splendour of language and its lyrical magic, especially in Cassandra's scene with Agamemnon. Still, even Aeschylus was only a precursor of the sophistic movement: an enthusiastic democrat of an early type who could be praised because he was anti-sacerdotal. Sophocles, by contrast, was a rich, pious, good-looking, pleasure-loving man who had, asserted Murray, no great message to convey, who remained safe within the limits of convention and who was quite helpless in trying to represent blasphemy. Sophocles lacked the elemental force of Aeschylus just as he lacked the speculative range and subtle sympathy of Euripides who was, for Murray, the epitome of the sophistic movement foreshadowed by Aeschylus.

Why was Euripides so great? Because, answers Murray, while representative of his age, he was in apparent hostility to it. He found the curse of life in political and social complications. He showed an iconoclastic spirit towards the Homeric gods. He was the apostle of clarity of expression. He created wonderful portraits of women in his plays in which he refused to idealise any man and championed the woman. He was hostile to the supernatural which he satirised with merciless realism in poetry which made him the greatest master of imaginative music. What followed Euripides was therefore necessarily an anti-climax. It was Aristophanes. He was indeed a great writer, but he often opposed what was best in his own age — for instance attacking Euripides — or advocated the best on the lowest possible grounds, although still, Murray recognised, with high spirits. Aristophanes' dramatic construction was careless. His politics agreed with those of Plato, a brilliant young aristocrat who, changed by Socrates' death, was one of the saints of history. Plato's thought, wrote Murray, was indeed inconclusive, not so much a system as a spirit, but he achieved a uniform level of loftiness. Nevertheless, the Greek achievement ended with the death of Demosthenes. Before that, wrote Murray, Greek life was unique; afterwards, it was 'ordinary first rate', like the Roman or the French or the Italian. Athens had dulled her faith in her own mission and in human Progress, and the final extinction of ancient culture, with its rational, humane, untheological ideals, came with the death of Julian to whom the label 'Apostate' was attached by the Christian church. Murray's book concluded:

> The search for Truth was finally made hopeless when the world, mistrusting reason, weary of argument and wonder, flung itself passionately under the spell of a system of authoritative Revelation, which acknowledged no truth outside itself, and stamped free enquiry as sin . . . The intellect of Greece died ultimately of that long discouragement which works upon nations like slow poison. She ceased to do her mission because her mission had ceased to bear fruit . . . And the last great pagans . . . [were] content to rouse mere echoes of that old call to Truth, to Beauty, to Political Freedom and Justice, with which Greece awakened the world long ago, when the morning was before her, and her wings were strong.

This concluding paragraph encapsulates most of the themes which preoccupied Murray, not merely in this book but throughout his life: rational enquiry and debate as opposed to superstition and revelation; the pursuit of political freedom and justice, of Truth and Beauty, the highest side of civilisation, as a duty to Humanity.

Murray's *History of Ancient Greek Literature* reveals more than the major themes which continued to run through his later work. It reveals the approach to scholarship which he took throughout his career. He was, he wrote to Lady Carlisle in 1900,

> averse, as you know, to mere learning. But I think that a large history of Greek literature would not only exercise all my powers in a very full way but also might be of value to 'humanity' . . . Greece has a profound and permanent message to mankind, a

message quite untouched by 'super-naturalness' and revealed religion; it is humane and rational and progressive, and affects not Art only but the whole of life . . . I have got a faith and a message . . . and I want to speak them out . . . Greek literature contains the germs of almost everything, so you can treat of almost all tendencies in treating of it.

Plainly Murray, in taking this view of his own work, did not reject scholarship, in its narrow sense of the production of reliable texts of the Greek literature, properly edited and annotated. Indeed, the constitution of good texts of the literature was basic to his own purposes. Equally plainly, however, scholarship, in that narrow sense, was to Murray a means to his end, which was to further the understanding and appreciation of Greece, not Greek, with the further aim of bringing its message to bear upon his own contemporaries, and especially upon the young who were his students.

Murray had declared his purpose in his Inaugural Lecture. He worked out the consequences in his first book. As an interpretation of Greece, Murray offered his readers a vision of the remote past which had an appealing coherence and unity. He also made the past come alive for his contemporaries by his evocation of a sense of its beauty. Even the analytical mind of Bertrand Russell was captivated by the interpreter of Greece. But Russell, too, was a Whig and a radical. Murray read the Greek past by the light of the present; an approach which worked in two ways. He discovered an affinity with his own views in a Greek, Euripides, and then he identified those views with what was most progressive in Greek society which in turn became a message for his own. Euripides became a proto Whig or radical Liberal. As a scholarly approach the dangers are obvious: the past is distorted into a reflection of the present; what becomes important is what is important to us, not what was actually important to the men of the past themselves. It was not a danger which was then obvious to Murray. He was not, after all, a professional historian, but even had he been, his dominant contemporaries in historical writing — Stubbs, Freeman, Froude, for example — were themselves, whatever their contemporary politics, Whig historians who saw the past in relation to the present. Murray's model, as an amateur historian, was Grote whose *History of Greece* (1856) stood in the Whig tradition — he was the mentor of Freeman — and whose work he saw himself as continuing because Grote 'always had in mind Humanity and

Progress while writing about Greece'. Murray's model in classical scholarship, Wilamowitz-Moellendorf, was aware of the danger. In 1908, in words which Murray himself translated for the University of Oxford, Wilamowitz said:

> We all know that ghosts will not speak until they have drunk blood; and the spirits which we evoke demand the blood of our hearts. We give it to them gladly; but if they then abide our questions something of us has entered in them, something alien which must be cast out, cast out in the name of truth.

Significantly enough, when Murray came to quote — indeed to misquote — these words, as he did several times, he ended the quotation by giving the blood of his heart to his Greek ghosts from the past. He did not take to his heart, and repeat, the warning: something alien of us has entered into them which must be cast out, and Wilamowitz himself once wondered to Murray if he did not see things in Euripides which were not really there. The defects of Murray's account of Greek literature as history, however, are irrelevant to his purpose in delivering a message from Greece. What had happened in ancient Greece was a spectacular rise from primitive savagery to the highest achievement of civilisation. What had also happened was civilisation's decline and fall. What had brought Humanity and Progress to its end? Murray's answer to that question has already been quoted, but it was subsumed under the title which he gave to his last chapter: 'The Failure of Nerve'. This was a phrase borrowed from J. B. Bury, a Cambridge ancient historian, but it was the heart of Murray's message, the faith he wanted to speak out not only as a student of ancient Greek literature but as a Victorian progressive. To maintain rational, humane, progressive, liberal Victorian society, it was important that his contemporaries' nerve should not fail. Ancient Greece pointed the moral.

Gilbert Murray's own nerves shook as he awaited the reception of his first book. He was nervous, as he told Lady Carlisle on a later occasion of publication, because it was 'as if you had taken out a bit of your heart and exposed it in a shop window'. He had had copies of the book privately sent to leading classical scholars and he waited anxiously for their replies. His family, of course, reassured him. Naturally Lady Mary thought the book did justice to her husband's brilliance, while his brother-in-law, Charles

Roberts, the Lady Cecilia Howard's husband, himself an Oxford classics don, wrote to say 'I don't think I know any book which so well succeeds in seeing through the scholarship into the literature and through the literature into life.' Murray appreciated still more the opinion of a friend who was also a distinguished literary critic, his professorial colleague at Glasgow, Andrew Bradley. He, thought Murray, was always chary of praise and never given to flattery on a point of literature. Bradley took Murray for a walk to tell him how very good the book was, an opinion which caused Murray to think that he had achieved a success in the book's effect on popular opinion and especially in its influence upon the young, upon feeling in England about Greek literature. He had the satisfaction of knowing that he had said what he had felt about the things in his mind as a teacher at Glasgow and that these things had an audience wider than that of his classroom. Moreover, when the established classical scholars acknowledged the book their judgements were more kindly than its author expected. The first to comment was Rutherford, whom Murray regarded as one of the three or four leading Greek scholars and who was 'so discriminating and real and so exceedingly generous'. Monro, a 'unitarian' (i.e. one who believed in one poet, Homer) said that he had read the book with very great pleasure. Others among Murray's friends were more reserved. Herbert Fisher was cool; Arthur Sidgwick friendly but doubting Murray's account of Sophocles. J. W. (Jack) Mackail thought the book extraordinarily adroit on so difficult a subject, but it left him, he said, with the feeling he had had before he read it: there was no such thing as Greek literature.

These private opinions caused Murray to fear that the reviews would not be favourable because he had controverted the views of the best scholars and had ventured into lions' territory with the Homeric question. Nevertheless, Verrall warmly reviewed it for the *Classical Review*, for he was also a controverter of scholarly opinions and a friend of Murray's. The book was not in fact generally hailed as brilliant by the scholars, but for teachers of Greek in schools and universities it provided a survey of the Greek literature, the only one of its kind, which was still being recommended to students in the 1920s and was republished, in a third edition, in 1956, the year before Murray's death. It achieved the kind of success its young professor and author aimed at in his Glasgow classroom: reaching students and, beyond them, the general educated public.

In one sense it is unfair to judge this first book of Murray's as history or scholarship. It was, as Edmund Gosse had required in his series, literary criticism which could be judged in its own terms, on its innate literary quality and analysis, detached from Greek historical and textual scholarship. Naturally, as a professor of Greek, Murray wished to stand well with his peers, but he wanted to do more than that. Even as an undergraduate he had ambitions to be a man of letters, a recognised if not always respected and rewarded profession. Murray's undergraduate novel of 1889, *Gobi or Shamo*, attempted to set his feet on this path. It was an adventure story in a successful Victorian mould. A young Englishman discovers in an old manuscript in an Aegean island an account of the discovery of a lost Greek colony in Asia. With a small group of companions he sets off to find it and after some adventures does so. The Greek colonists preserve an interesting society, exotic but somehow familiar, which is threatened by the revolt of its primitive subjects. The visitors must therefore escape and, after further adventures, return to their own society reflecting upon their strange and dangerous but improving experiences. The theme is a familiar one. Robert Louis Stevenson in *Treasure Island*, Conan Doyle in *The Lost World*, Rider Haggard in *King Solomon's Mines* — to name only a few of the best known — all used it. But in the young Murray's hands the excitement of strange adventure was overlaid by the characters of his story who were moral stereotypes rather than convincing individuals, a point Lang made to him in respect of one of the major ones when he read the book in manuscript before it went to the publisher. The potential excitement of the theme, and its potential appeal to readers, was frustrated by the author's wish to use the pristine beauty and virtue of Greek life as a moral object lesson to his Victorian contemporaries. The preacher spoiled the novelist. The book ran into three small editions by 1890 but it achieved neither great success nor reputation for its author. Its chief interest, in relation to Murray's life, is that it shows both an early knowledge of and interest in primitive religious cults and his awareness that these both underlay and could threaten an apparently established civilised society, even one with superior technology, as well as a higher morality, at its disposal.

Murray's ambition to be a man of letters was not much affected by the small success of his novel. He never attempted to write another but, from his professorial work with Greek dramatists who wrote in poetic metre, he was led to playwriting himself. When he was obliged by his health to take leave from his post in 1892 and to take the sea-voyage to Australia, he was at work upon an original play: *Carlyon Sahib*. Again there was the Victorian preoccupation with exotic societies, in this case Indian. Again there was the preoccupation with a moral issue: the pro-consul who has defended civilisation against primitive revolt by committing a dishonourable deed. Carlyon's public honour and reputation rest on his successful defence of civilisation. His private dishonour, in the original version of the play, was that he had poisoned a drinking well in order to let infection spread among the native rebels. What is the pro-consul, retired full of fame and honour, to do when a young journalist's investigations threaten to reveal the guilty secret? Use his medical daughter to ensure his death upon the operating table? In the event, Murray has the pro-consul himself killed by a native servant whom he had tried to kill after first using him to poison the well. The theme of a super-man, strong enough to break moral laws to preserve his own reputation, who is thwarted by a woman's strength of character and then laid low by an agent of his own immorality was recognisably pure Ibsen, a parentage identified by those who thought Murray's piece powerful theatre and by Gilbert himself who told his wife that he had got the idea from Ibsen's *Per Gynt*.

This second attempt of Murray's to establish himself as a man of letters certainly arose from his increasing acquaintance with the Greek dramatists he lectured upon in Glasgow. But where his undergraduate novel had an appealing theme which was not well treated, his first original play was relatively well treated but had an unappealing theme. The author first sent his work to the Charringtons in 1893. They 'liked it exceedingly' but were too poor to produce it, although Charrington himself prophesised commercial success for it, and his wife, the actress Janet Achurch, plainly thought that in Carlyon's daughter it contained a good part for her. Murray sent it in 1894 to his mother's cousin, W. S. Gilbert, who was glad to commend it to the well-known actor, Beerbohm Tree. 'Schwenck' Gilbert, however, while saying that any producer should be gratified to see the work of so distinguished a scholar, added that, if there were any brains in a play, it would make no money; if it made money, it had no brains. And Murray's play, it seemed, had too many brains, for no other producer thought that it would make money. But in 1895 Charrington sent the play to the well-known critic, William Archer, who as English translator was introducing Ibsen to the English stage. Archer was very interested in what he called 'a great thing in its way'. He did not, however, think it would play as it stood, but he asked to be put in touch with the author so that he could properly explain what needed to be done in order that 'the most original and powerful piece he had ever come across' might be put upon the stage. This was the beginning of a friendship which was one of the closest of Murray's life. He took Archer's advice about the alterations, in particular allowing Carlyon simply to let a natural infection spread rather than deliberately to infect a well. Still, although altered upon expert advice, the play was turned down by Lewis Waller, by Forbes-Robertson and, towards the end of 1897, by Miss Robin. Actors all liked it, for it had the important male parts of Carlyon and the native servant, Selim, and a good role for an actress in Carlyon's daughter, Vera. None of the actors, however, had the money themselves to produce it and none of the producers thought it good box-office. Archer indeed included it in his list for the first year's productions of his proposed National Theatre, but Murray, after Miss Robin's refusal, resigned himself never to seeing any play of his performed. Even Archer was not prepared to guarantee the financial success of *Carlyon Sahib*. When it was finally produced on the stage, Gilbert Murray had left Glasgow and was much more closely involved in other ways with the London theatre.

His apparent failure with *Carlyon Sahib* depressed Murray and frustrated him, feelings compounded by Andrew Bradley who told him that the play was not good enough for a man of his talent and that such would be the opinion of anyone whose opinion Murray respected. Yet Archer's enthusiasm encouraged Murray to try again. Always, as he admitted, very sensitive to criticism, praise from those whom he respected restored both his faith and his energy. He wrote *Andromache*, a prose play based on the Greek story of Orestes, pursued by the furies because he had killed his mother, Clytemnestra, in order to avenge his father Agamemnon's death. Orestes comes to Phthia where Andromache, widow of the slain Trojan hero Hector, is now slave to King Pyrrhus. Orestes seeks to avenge himself on the King for marrying Orestes' own betrothed, Hermione, daughter of Helen of Sparta. This play was written in 1896. In January of the following year Murray read it to a family gathering at Castle Howard who were all, but especially

Lord Carlisle, very enthusiastic. The Countess thought Hermione too despicable a character to be dramatic, but she was very insistent that her son-in-law ought to put the play on the stage even at her own expense. Bradley on this occasion agreed with the family judgement of a play which he 'admired so much', but Archer and the professional stage were less enthusiastic than they had been about *Carlyon*. This play, too, never saw production upon the stage while Murray was in Glasgow.

Nevertheless, it had one result: it convinced Andrew Bradley, the well-known authority upon Shakespeare, that Murray was a poet, that the play really ought to be in verse; 'a goodish part of it is, do you know that?' In fact one speech in the play was overtly in verse which, A. E. Housman told Murray in 1900, was 'so good that I wish you would write more'. The lines in question were:

O Light and Shadow of all things that be,
O Beauty, wild with wreckage like the sea,
Say who shall win thee, thou without a name?
O Helen, Helen, who shall die for thee?

Gilbert Murray needed neither Bradley's contemporary nor Housman's later encouragement to be a poet. His prose plays had seemed to fail. Another piece of tragic dramatic writing had been begun in 1895: *Leaves of the Sybil*. He planned to have his hero find one from the sheaf of leaves on which the Sybil wrote eternal truths and then to follow that single leaf blindly to the exclusion of all the others. Moral: you need a great number of leaves to get a connected view of life. That work was never finished. But he had already begun, in the course of his Glasgow lectures, to translate the Greek plays and to recite — sometimes to sing — his verses to his students in class.

Andromache, which had struck Bradley as really a verse play, was later published with a prefatory letter. Murray said that he and William Archer had cycled over the hills near Rievaulx Abbey not far from Castle Howard in Yorkshire, arguing as to how far an historical subject could be treated loyally and unconventionally on the stage, how to convey 'the force, fire, the depth and richness of character', how to portray living heroes against a background of primitive superstition and black savagery. Archer had wanted the verse and the Greece of the English poets in order to do this; Murray had wanted a nearer approach to his conception of the real

Greece of history and 'dare I say it, of anthropology?' The
primitive savagery in *Andromache* he found in Orestes' blood feud,
but the language he used to describe it came close to the English
poetic language Archer had demanded — for example, when
Andromache and her son Molossus argue over the payment of
compensation for the herd boy whom he has killed:

> *Andromache.* Listen, can you hear that little beating sound —
> down seaward, away from the sun?
> *Molossus.* It is the water lapping against the rocks.
> *Andromache.* There is a sound like that in the language I told
> you of. Old, old men, and those whose gods have deserted them,
> hear it in their hearts — the sound of all the blood that men have
> spilt and the tears they have shed, lapping against the great
> rocks, in shadow, away from the sun.

One can see why Bradley thought the play was really verse. His
opinion and that of Archer encouraged Murray to continue with
what he had earlier begun to do for his Glasgow classes: the translation of Greek drama into English rhymed verse, an activity which
later received strong support from George Bernard Shaw who
asserted in the preface to *Major Barbara* that Murray's translations
were original verse in their own right.

Poetic translation came naturally to Gilbert Murray, quite apart
from his teaching duties and his theatrical and literary ambitions.
So deeply believing in the beauty of the Greek language in the
mouths of its tragedians, it followed that to convey such beauty
poetry was the only possible diction to use in English. He had long
written private poetry for his wife and his mother-in-law. In the
little book which he gave to Lady Carlisle soon after his marriage
he proposed to write a poem on every appropriate occasion. From
the beginning there were renderings from Greek and one of them he
later included in his little volume in the Augustan series:

> She walked in the morning air,
> The sun was happy and high,
> A white rose fell from her hair;
> She saw, but she passed it by.

And I thought: Shall I bow my head
For a thing cast lightly away?
I will stoop for her, I said.
But not for a dead rose spray.

And back in the print of her feet,
I came amid winds and snows,
And I kissed the stones of the street,
But where was the Rose, the Rose?

Most of Murray's translations from Greek poetry were written after he left Glasgow, but this early verse shows the influences under which it was done. He considered Shelley's *Prometheus Unbound* to be the greatest poem in the English language — he was 'stunned' by its beauty — but under Lady Mary's influence he came also to admire Blake. The romanticism, the rich imagery: these were what he sought. From Swinburne, removing the erotic elements — Mr Justice Oliver Wendell Holmes was later to call Murray's verse 'Swinburne and water' — he took the feeling of mystery and strangeness. But the more immediate influence upon him, especially through his wife's family's Pre-Raphaelite connections, was William Morris. Morris had tried to recreate a lost world, not indeed the world of classical Greece but still a vanished medieval world which he admired. Perhaps this explains why Housman found the Greek world of Murray's play *Andromache* so much more medieval than he himself had imagined Greece to be; a world in which characters 'trowed not' and 'recked but little'. In retrospect Morris's emotion, like that of other Pre-Raphaelites, seems so dramatic as to be contrived; Rossetti, another of Lord Carlisle's friends, searched other literature for the 'stunning' word. In any case it runs the risk of most times of emotion: men and women tend to express themselves in *clichés* which, to some contemporaries and nearly always to posterity, sound banal. Murray was saved from the triviality of one, at least, of his models by the fact that he was trying to convey neither his own emotions nor emotions invented by him, but those of characters who had been created for him by Greek tragic poets. His verse had therefore a freshness often lacking in William Morris's and even in Swinburne's own work. Moreover, Murray's verse had a quality not always shared by those he admired: it was written to be spoken aloud to an audience, not simply to be read on the printed page. He intended to have an immediate and direct impact through his metres and his rhymes, through his diction and his imagery, spoken directly to an audience, not to be pondered over after reading. He took the trouble to begin to master the techniques of his poetic craft, but what he aimed at was not only technical skill but also dramatic impact on the stage. Nevertheless, what is acceptable when spoken in the emotionally charged atmosphere of a theatre is not always tolerable when read in the cooler air of the drawing room or library.

The ten years in Glasgow were decisive for Gilbert Murray's career. At their beginning he was speaking of the novels he would write. At their end he had come to see himself as the translator and inter-preter of the Greek world to his generation. He had discovered his dramatic powers as a lecturer, as a poet and as a playwright. But that was not all he had learned. He did not neglect technical scholar-ship, textual work intended primarily for other scholars, as his beginning with the Euripides text makes clear. Nor did he neglect his professorial and public duties. A professor, even in those more leisurely days, had certain administrative duties. Murray never threw himself into unnecessary university committee work nor into university politics as did some of his colleagues, but in what he felt to be his duty on boards and in committee he revealed a cool, balanced and reasonable judgement. He even managed to be on terms with his difficult colleague in Humanity, G. G. Ramsay, a man capable of pettiness and obstruction and unredeemed by a sense of humour. When Ramsay, for example, tried to prevent children from cycling in The College precincts, amongst whom were the young Murrays, and it was pointed out to him that they were the families of professors, he replied: 'they can't all be the legitimate children of professors.' In that Scottish atmosphere, Murray's influence was not as great as it might have been. When he supported the candidature of his friend Herbert Fisher for the vacant chair of History he was unsuccessful: others had already arranged that the choice should be Lodge. What Murray came up against was a Conservative professoriate which, if it did not share the open hostility of the Glasgow press to Liberals like Murray, nevertheless did not allow them great weight in university matters. Gilbert never disguised his Liberal sympathies. He openly campaigned for a Liberal Rector, for women on the Hospital Committee, and he went to hear the German socialist Wilhelm

Liebknecht deliver a public lecture. Nevertheless he duly recited the Lord's Prayer — albeit in Greek — at his first lecture of the day until, in 1896, he abandoned the prayer altogether. Among his colleagues the Murrays had close friendships with only two: Andrew Bradley, a bachelor who suffered from unrequited love and fits of melancholy which attracted Lady Mary's sympathy, and the philosopher Adamson and his wife, neighbours in The College who were somewhat less close to the Murrays than was Bradley. Murray had, of course, many casual friends and supporters. When he announced his retirement in 1899, W. Smart told him that the Senate could ill afford to lose one of its entirely honest and generous members. Dr David Murray and another member of the University Court, Dr MacVail, tried to persuade him not to resign. But the main tributes to Murray, other than the 'high appreciation' recorded by the Senate of his distinguished services, came from the pupils in whom he had inspired not only love of Greece but personal affection for the pains he took and the sympathy he showed. The regret was shared by Liberals outside the university. The Murrays had heeded Principal John Caird's views about public political discretion, but they had nevertheless played some part in the public life of Glasgow, Lady Mary on hospital committees, Gilbert as a Director of the Society for the Prevention of Cruelty to Animals and of the Dog and Cat Home, and both of them in the Scottish Band of Hope Union. Still, through his professorial duties and his literary work, Murray's main achievement in Glasgow was neatly put by S. H. Butcher: 'your time in a Scottish university — far too brief as it has been — will yet have done much for the teaching of Greek and for inspiring a love of Greek literature.' Neither this reputation nor the high appreciation of the Senate, however, secured for Murray a pension from the university, for the doctor who had considered his life at risk would not certify that so young a man was an invalid. In fact when he left Glasgow he was only 33 years old and he had almost 60 years of active life ahead of him.

GENTLEMAN OF LEISURE

Gilbert Murray left Glasgow after the session was over, in April 1899. For the next six and a half years he could be a gentleman of leisure, holding no academic post, very much in the tradition of those other Whigs, the historians Macaulay and Freeman, who were most of their lives private scholars and men of letters. The Murrays went to live in the English countryside, on the Surrey—Hampshire border in a somewhat pompous house, Barford Court, near Churt, bought for them by Lady Carlisle who also increased Lady Mary's allowance by £300 p.a. The Countess would have preferred them to take a house in Wimbledon, but finally agreed with her daughter that a small estate — she added 50 acres of land — might help Gilbert to recover his health and strength. 'If only', he himself told Lady Carlisle, 'I can get back my moral courage and activity and make something out of this passive, vibrating sensitiveness which fills so much of my life just now.' What he really wanted to do was to retrieve the youth he had lost as a Scottish professor. Regrets haunted him, he said in 1901, for his wasted years: 'I should have written poetry and looked about me and tried to get leisure instead of deep grinding.' Now he had leisure. He also had proximity to the great city, London, the Mecca of any man of letters. When he recalled for Arnold Toynbee the happiest years of his life, it was to these years at Churt that his mind most readily turned, the years when his close association with the theatre and poetry and literature made him believe that he could be a man of letters and, above all, a poet.

As a memory, this recollection is coloured by the roseate glow of hindsight. During the Barford years Murray indeed saw his work produced upon the stage, had his poetry hailed as masterpieces, cut a figure in the literary world and in public life. But he also produced most of the Greek text of Euripides' plays, a 'disgusting task' as he came to believe, and a diversion, as Lady Carlisle told him, from his true work: 'there are many learned Greek professors, there are few poets.'

Murray's first real task during these years as a leisured gentleman was the revision of his original play *Carlyon Sahib*. Mrs Patrick Campbell decided that she wanted for herself the part of Vera, the pro-consul's daughter, and she proposed to stage the play. But, like everyone else who had read it, she insisted upon changes. While Lady Mary supervised the settling-in at Barford Court, her husband took his daughter Rosalind to Montreux in the spring of 1899, together with the script of his play. Throughout the rest of April and early May he worked at its revision, by the unsatisfactory method of correspondence and the occasional exchange of telegrams with Mrs Campbell. It was absurd, he complained, 'to write ten lines and only to know four days later if they will do'. He complained, too, that there were 'more hurdles with Mrs Patrick Campbell than I knew'. Nevertheless, he completed the revisions the actress thought dramatically necessary, and came home in May to watch the rehearsals: 'it would not be business to let rehearsals start without me, or to miss anything for love of ease.' *Carlyon* ran for twelve nights from 19 June at the Prince of Wales Theatre. Mrs Campbell played Vera, Nutcombe Gould Carlyon, Bertie Thomas the journalist Ardene, and a rising young actor, Harley Granville-Barker, the pro-consul's one-armed, Indian servant, Selim. It was not a commercial success. Expenses were £300, receipts £180. The public, in contemporary judgements, found it, as Archer had originally done, a 'grim' piece. The play was never revived, although in 1921 the President of the People's Theatre League translated it into Finnish. Nevertheless, Gilbert Murray received private encouragement from those whose judgement he respected. Charrington and his wife, Janet Achurch, who had first shown the script to William Archer, also showed it to George Bernard Shaw who 'admired it exceedingly'. J. M. Barrie saw the first performance and was very taken with it; Carlyon he thought 'more like a man' than anything he had seen on the stage for a long time, while the whole play contained the best acting for a 'first' that he had ever seen. Reginald Golding Bright went further; he was 'very sure' that *Carlyon Sahib* stamped Murray 'as *the* dramatist of the immediate future'. Such private judgements from people who had nothing to gain by flattery were always of great weight with Murray. Mrs Patrick Campbell, although she had lost financially with *Carlyon*, thought sufficiently well of his ability as a playwright to try to insist that she should act in the plays he was then translating from the Greek. Murray, however, like many another dramatist, blamed the actress for the failure of *Carlyon*. He acknowledged, in the text which Heinemanns published at the author's own expense, her 'vivid and helpful criticism', so that the printed play was nearer to the acted version than to the original script, but to Shaw he commented that on stage Mrs Patrick Campbell had not known her lines and had 'refused to act'. Still, the real cause of *Carlyon's* failure was its affinity with Ibsen. Many people, including Frederic Harrison, had a rooted aversion to Ibsen and to all forms of 'Ibscenity', which they regarded as the 'corruption of Art — beastly, morbid, sickening' and to those who followed Ibsen they applied such terms as 'Decadent, Degenerates and Sodomites'.

For Gilbert Murray's career as an original playwright, this division of opinion was ominous. Those of his correspondents who liked *Carlyon* did not greatly care for his second original play, *Andromache*, while those who did not care for *Carlyon Sahib* were moved by *Andromache* which was even less of a commercial proposition. This second play was produced by the Stage Society in February 1901. Edyth Olive played Andromache while Janet Achurch was Hermione. Written as the play was after conversation, previously described, with William Archer, Murray had elected to make the old Greek story boldly 'realistic and rather Ibsenite' whereas the critic had argued with him for 'verse, and the Greece of the English poets'. Archer in the result never thought it playable. Andrew Bradley, when he saw the 1901 production, did not change his opinion as to the merits of the play, but agreed with Shaw that the actors' diction and movements were a 'desecration: almost all the most beautiful passages suffered'. Bradley had, nevertheless, one major criticism of its construction. Murray, he felt, made too great demands upon his audiences by expecting them to grasp and to understand the slightest verbal indications or short speeches. In his view, an occasional long speech was vital. Gilbert Murray in retropect thought his play 'ultra-romantic', echoing judgements which A. E. Housman and Frederic Harrison made at the time. The latter, seeing the Stage Society performance, agreed with what both Bradley and Housman (who described himself as moved by the performance he saw) had earlier said: the Greeks were never so romantic or so sentimental as this and the play should really be in verse. No matter that some of Murray's friends and colleagues thought *Andromache* a fine achievement. Walter Ashburner pronounced it 'very, very good'. Jane Ellen Harrison, the Cambridge classical archeologist, said 'this is exquisite'. Herbert Fisher could not go to bed after seeing the performance without writing to say 'how very beautiful and perfect I think it'. But it reached no wide public. *Andromache* was performed only once more, and that upon the amateur stage. Both the failure of this second play and the private encouragement to write more in verse, came when Gilbert Murray was constituting his Greek text of the whole of Euripides' plays. As he made his Greek edition, he began systematically to translate the text into rhymed verse in order to restore Greece to the English stage, just as he had in Glasgow tried to bring it before his students.

Murray consciously set out to restore Euripides' reputation as a dramatist whose recent standing was low, his plays regarded as a tissue of commonplaces, unplayable upon the English stage. The tragedians Aeschylus and Sophocles were generally deemed to have more dramatic power, although scarcely more often played. A comedian such as Aristophanes was generally believed to be better theatre. The first play Murray translated in full was in fact one of Aristophanes — the *Frogs* — but comedy, with its elements of rustic bawdiness, was never suited to his high moral purposes and to the pursuit and encouragement of the higher things of life. As an exercise in translation, Gilbert was pleased enough with the *Frogs*, but Euripides, not Aristophanes, was the man after his own heart. In 1901 he translated *Hippolytus*; in 1902, the *Bacchae*. He read parts of his translations to various gatherings. In February 1901, when he read some of *Hippolytus* at Newnham College, Cambridge, Bertrand Russell was so overwhelmed that he dated the beginning of his close friendship with Murray to that occasion. After George Bernard Shaw heard some at the Fabian Society, he was moved in 1902 to order Murray to send his work off to the printer at once: 'every university professor is an ass . . . You think that because Gilbert Murray the poet is not an ass, Professor Murray cannot be one . . . Send Euripides by the next post to the printer. Mind, by the next post. I am *durchaus* serious.' Murray accepted both the praise and the advice. The two Euripides plays, together with the *Frogs*, were published, the first of many slim green volumes of his translations, by George Allen in 1902. Three years later the *Trojan Women* and *Electra* appeared. The rest followed in the years after he had left Barford. By the 1920s, over a quarter of a million copies of Murray's Euripidean translations had been sold — more than twenty thousand of each play. He had indeed reached a wide audience in print, and the foundation of that success was laid in these years in the countryside at Churt between the spring of 1899 and the autumn of 1905.

Nevertheless, the initial enthusiasm for and continuing success of his poetic translations in print was not Murray's first objective. What he intended was that his verse translations should be played upon the stage, not simply read in books. His own original plays in production, whatever their commercial fortunes, had taught him something about stagecraft. His attempt to recreate the Greek world for his students had given him a view of Greek theatre. His translations were therefore made with their staging always in mind, and it is worth remembering that, whatever changes in poetic taste have meant for his sales to the reading public, there are very few actors who have played in them who have not regarded them as good theatre, in the sense that they are playable upon the stage.

In the spring of 1904 the New Century Theatre, formed by William Archer and others in order to bring Ibsen before English audiences, chose Murray's *Hippolytus* for four matinée performances at the Lyric Theatre. Harley Granville-Barker produced and himself declaimed 'in a wildly exciting fashion' the Henchman's speech in Murray's translation:

'Twas by the bank of beating sea we stood,
We thralls, and decked the steeds, and combed each mane
Weeping; for word had come that ne'er again
The foot of our Hippolytus should roam
This land, but waste in exile by thy doom.

The verse and the manner of its delivery marked a complete break with the formal style of speech, copied from the French neo-classical theatrical tradition which was commonly employed on the rare occasions that classical tragedies were actually performed in England. Henry Irving had expressed an interest in playing the part of Hippolytus but could not do so in the event, so Ben Webster played the role to Edyth Olive's Phaedra. The success of the performance astonished Murray. As he used to recall: 'the first day there were about fifty people in the house. The second day perhaps a hundred. On the third the house was full. On the fourth I found a crowd stretching down Shaftesbury Avenue and thought I must have come to the wrong theatre.' Harley Granville-Barker was convinced of the commercial possibilities. When, later in 1904, he formed with Vedrenne the management of the Royal Court Theatre, in Kensington, *Hippolytus* was included in the matinée programme, together with Shaw's *Candida*. In October 1904 the

Greek play was again put on, but its success on this occasion was not so great. Irving was still unable to play, and so a major box-office attraction was lost. The pre-opening bookings were bad. Murray was asked to send tickets to as many people as he knew. With the warm approval of Lady Carlisle, he advanced Vedrenne and Barker £200 before Christmas to help save the Royal Court enterprise, but the commercial success of Shaw's plays at the theatre redeemed their financial situation. Barker and Vedrenne's experience with *Hippolytus*, although its relative failure in October 1904 could be attributed to accidental circumstances, meant that the next Greek plays to be staged in Murray's translation were still to be performed as matinées, despite J.M. Barrie's offer to subscribe £100 towards an evening performance. The *Trojan Women*, with Marie Brema as Hecuba and Edith Wynne-Matthison as Andromache, was staged in 1905. *Electra*, the name part played by this latter actress, with Harcourt Williams and later Henry Ainley in the cast, ran in January, February and March 1906. In April of that year *Hippolytus* was revived. In 1907 came *Medea* at the Savoy Theatre, with Hubert Carter and Edyth Olive in the cast, after Barker and Vedrenne had left the Royal Court. In 1908 William Poel directed Lillah McCarthy, Granville-Barker's wife, in the *Bacchae*.

These five Greek plays were staged in London at intervals over three years by a management which, chiefly through its productions of Shaw's plays, made a considerable impact upon the contemporary London theatre, in retrospect a revolutionary one. The Greek drama did not command so wide a popular audience but it nevertheless attracted sufficient support, and achieved a certain *réclame*. In February 1906, for instance, six performances of *Electra* earned £587 18s 3d, of which Murray's share was just over £44. The *Trojan Women* in the previous year did less well than *Hippolytus* but it brought in £438 10s 3d. Gilbert Murray, as playwright, had an agreement with Vedrenne which gave him 5 per cent of the gross takings from 700 seats at eight matinées, and 7½ per cent above that figure. From the performances in early 1906, his income from the theatre averaged £10 per week. The appeal of the plays was indeed sufficient to encourage later productions of others: *Iphigeneia in Tauris* in 1910; *Medea* repeated in the same year. In 1911 Murray's translation of Sophocles' *Oedipus Rex* was staged, after the Censor's initial refusal to allow it to be done in 1910, and in 1912 Max Reinhardt, fresh from a triumph with Hofmanstahl's *Oedipus* in Berlin, used Murray's version of Sophocles' play at a spectacular theatrical occasion in London, with Martin Harvey as Oedipus and Lillah McCarthy as Jocasta, at the Covent Garden Opera House. When Martin Harvey made his farewell appearance on the stage in 1936, Murray's version of *Oedipus* was the play he chose for the occasion.

Dame Sybil Thorndike recalled that, when, as a young actress, she returned from four years' tour in the United States, the impact of the Vedrenne-Barker 'new theatre' was 'startling'. And Murray's translations of Greek drama were a part of that impact. The initial sensation was in London, but Annie Horniman believed that what Barker had done at the Royal Court could also be done in the provinces. Dame Sybil's husband, Lewis Casson, had played in the Euripides' plays in London; he and his wife now helped to take them to the provinces. This was very much to Gilbert Murray's taste. Euripides and his message would reach a still wider audience. In 1907 Lewis Casson produced *Hippolytus* at the Gaiety Theatre in Manchester; in 1908 he repeated the play for an annual meeting of the Classical Association in Birmingham. Penelope Wheeler who played Phaedra in this production formed her own company to tour the provinces with a repertoire of Murray's versions which continued to be performed in public theatres, in college and school dramatic societies and, during the First World War, to the troops in France. In the United States, university theatres and Little Theatres began to perform the plays, and the *Trojan Women*, produced by Ellen van Volkenburg and Maurice Browne, was used as part of a campaign for peace in 1915. In terms of an audience, of using Greek tragedy in the cause of Humanity and Progress, Gilbert Murray could be satisfied that the plays he first translated at Barford had begun to reach thousands of people, most of them 'Greekless'.

The actual production of the plays, in Murray's translation, went beyond his years at Barford, but the original work was done there in order to convey the profound and permanent message Murray believed Greece to have for his own day. This must be 'true to the spirit of Hellenism'. For this reason, Gilbert while he lived in the country took an active part in the production of his plays, well beyond the normal role of author. Dame Sybil Thorndike, 60 years later, had an actress's sense of shock that an amateur should ever direct the professional stage. Barker, she believed, would never have allowed it. Nor did he. On one occasion in October 1907, when Barker was very overworked and late at the theatre, Murray had felt obliged to conduct the first part of a rehearsal of *Medea* at the Savoy. This had very much offended one of the professional actors. Nevertheless, it was to the Greek scholar who was the translator that producer and players turned, in this revival of Greek tragedy, for expert guidance on diction, movement, costume and staging. The producer, more exceptionally, consulted him on the right casting to achieve the true effect. Gilbert Murray's involvement with the theatre was therefore close. Sometimes, as in October 1904, he complained of the time and nervous energy it took: 'rehearsals and dresses — Booh! I prefer my children and my White Cat.' Yet he enjoyed the part he played in this theatrical world and the professional problems it presented to him.

The actual production of Greek tragedy upon the modern stage encountered difficulties which came from the state of the English theatre at the end of the nineteenth and beginning of the twentieth centuries. Unlike France, where the tradition of Corneille, Racine and Molière had been preserved in contemporary French theatre, there was no such neoclassical theatrical tradition in England. When Greek drama was, on rare occasions, staged in the late nineteenth century, the convention in which it was performed was that of the 'aesthetic' Greek, played with the 'lady-like languor' of Alma-Tadema and Albert Moore. What English convention of performance of Greek tragedy there was, was the antithesis of what Murray wanted. To translate his vision of Greek drama on to the modern stage had its own problems, given the premiss from which he started. Gilbert Murray wanted realism in the production of Greek tragedy, but he did not mean by that a realistic reproduction of what he believed Greek drama to have been in Athens itself. He intended always to translate into an idiom which his contemporaries could understand and appreciate while remaining true to the 'spirit' of Hellenism: not a literal translation of the Greek words nor a transposition of the Athenian stage to London, but an interpretation for the modern theatre audiences. Between the difficulties which Murray encountered from the state of English theatre, and those which came from his own vision of how Greek theatre could be translated to the modern stage, the problems were considerable.

Casting was the initial one. George Bernard Shaw warned him in April 1905 of that danger, before the *Trojan Women* was staged, of choosing safe, dull actors because the ideal could not be got. G.B.S. concluded that there was nothing for it but the establishment of an order of vestal virgins to play the 'higher drama'. Murray did not agree, but he was well aware of the problem. He had hoped that Henry Irving could play in the first stage production as Hippolytus, because on the strength of the actor's reputation a better actress might then be secured to play Phaedra. As it was, Frederic Harrison who saw the original production was critical of the casting: Aphrodite should have been lighthearted; Artemis should have been sublime. J.M. Barrie had a professional playwright's criticism of the diction; he had missed many of the words. Rosina Filippi who acted in one production complained of the untutored actresses she had had to play opposite, and in particular found Miss Gardner's Phaedra 'unpleasant', although possibly 'truer' than that of Edyth Olive whose Cassandra in the *Trojan Women* Shaw pronounced ridiculous because she was too warm and vulgar to be cast as a ravishable virgin. Shaw continued to make suggestions for casting and for stage business. It was his suggestion that Gertrude Kingston should play Helen in the *Trojan Women* and when he saw the play it was she whom he liked best in a 'medium good' cast; she at least had the method of Athens while the others, he said, had the methods of Beyreuth and Bedford Park.

Murray, having his own vision of Greek drama, never wholly agreed with Shaw, but the latter, in pressing the matter of casting, had put his finger on one of the major difficulties of producing Greek drama on the English stage.

In the first four plays to be put on, Granville-Barker, with Murray's advice, tried a series of actresses. Only Edith Wynne-Matthison was generally regarded as satisfactory in the London productions. About the others — Edyth Olive, Janet Achurch, Rosina Filippi, Marie Brema — there were always reservations, in part because Barker and Murray himself were still experimenting to find the right effect. Sybil Thorndike, who played Artemis in the first Manchester production of *Hippolytus*, then came new to Greek drama. The advice she received from Gilbert when she consulted him about the playing of the part was 'I want you to be like an opalescent dawn'; 'enlightening', said Dame Sybil later, 'but exceedingly difficult in performance'. Granville-Barker believed that a director could not take a really leading part as well, so that the question of casting the main roles when he himself was

producer became critical. It was especially critical in the case of
Medea for the 1907 production. Lillah McCarthy, Barker's wife,
very much wanted the part, but she agreed never to talk business
with her husband, and Vedrenne, for business reasons, would not
allow her to play a leading role at the Savoy Theatre to which the
partners had moved from the Royal Court. Barker had initially
objected to Edyth Olive as Medea because he did not think she
could control the play, but he did not like Shaw's alternative
suggestion of Janet Achurch. So, because Edith Wynne-Matthison
was already playing two leading roles, he settled for Vedrenne's
opinion that Miss Olive was the most sensible choice. This
continual search for suitable actresses to play the leading women of
Euripides' plays was a handicap that Murray was never confident
had been overcome, although the prominence that Euripides gave
to women meant that the casting of the female roles was critical.

Even more critical was the matter of the chorus, which had so
essential a role in Greek drama but no counterpart in the contemporary English theatre. The tiny stage of the Royal Court Theatre
was in itself restrictive. As Florence Farr (who had formed The
Dancers in late 1903) put it: a chorus of nine ran a severe risk of
treading on each other if they were to perform stylised rhythmic
movements while at the same time, singly or in unison, chanting the
lines to her own accompaniment of her own music upon a psaltery
which she had borrowed from Mrs Patrick Campbell. Max
Beerbohm, who saw one of these Royal Court performances of
Bacchae, made the same point in the *Saturday Review*: there was
just room for three young ladies to revolve in the middle of the
stage, by taking very great care and keeping altogether, but 'these
were the wild maidens of Dionysus' retinue'! — while four other
'cramped young ladies' at the front of the stage were 'immobile in
attitude of the deepest dejection' although supposed to be singing
songs of the wildest lyric passion. Beehbohm, however, wanted
Greek drama done in Athenian conditions: open air amphitheatre,
costume and masks, very different from Murray's conception. The
chorus, as Florence Farr conceived it, should obviously be one
composed of trained dancers and singers, and in June 1904 she
offered to suggest some names after she had seen the original
production of *Hippolytus* in which she had found the movements
of the chorus to be 'very funny'. Granville-Barker, however, had
other ideas. For the second run of *Hippolytus* he himself chose

the members of the chorus, to Florence Farr's professional disgust, although she conceded that his choice might result in a 'bevy of beauty and talent'. Nevertheless she acted as the leader of the chorus during that second run of the play and then pointed out another difficulty to Murray: that of the chorus keeping up appropriate expressions, while the others on stage acted for two hours. Barker and Vedrenne did not invite Florence Farr to arrange the chorus for the *Trojan Women* nor for *Electra*; they, like Murray, still wished to experiment, although S. H. Butcher privately told Murray that he had liked the chanting chorus, which had made the words both audible and articulate. Florence Farr herself was dissatisfied. She did not believe that she had been allowed the means properly to perform at the Royal Court, and she wished to try out her own ideas in association with Mrs Patrick Campbell by producing the *Bacchae* in a version very different from the style of a Royal Court performance: it was to be 'very archaic'. Mrs Campbell herself wanted dancers to music in the background, with the lines of the chorus to be spoken to a musical accompaniment. Both ladies, when the King of Greece sought a Greek play for a charity performance in London, thought of the *Bacchae*. They then wished to engage barefoot dancers who, to the accompaniment of pipes and timbrels, would do elaborate dances through the other actors on the stage, while Florence Farr alone spoke the thrilling choruses. This was precisely the kind of treatment that Murray and Barker rejected, the kind of treatment the dancer Isadora Duncan too might have provided had her terms not been too high to be acceptable. Lewis Casson, when he produced the plays, used a considerable amount of chanting, both by a single voice and by a trained choir, based on Hebridean melodies discovered and adapted by Rita Thom, combined with a musical effect based on the *hwyl* of the Welsh preachers. He actually employed this in his production of the *Trojan Women*, as an antiphonal dialogue between Hecuba and Andromache. Harley Granville-Barker also tried the antiphonal chant rather than singing. Gilbert Murray himself preferred the choruses to be spoken rather than sung, but he was prepared to experiment with music if it offered a solution to the difficult matter of the Greek chorus on the English stage.

Florence Farr had set to music certain choruses from the *Bacchae* and *Hippolytus* as early as 1903, and Gustav Holst later did a musical setting for a chorus for the former play in 1906, but no one undertook the music for a whole play. In 1908 Granville Bantok, who had written the music for the Classical Association production at Birmingham, was convinced that for such a play as the *Bacchae* a decent choral and musical treatment was essential, and he continued to compose for the plays as did Rutland Broughton from 1915 onwards. In 1919 Vaughan Williams also made a setting for the *Bacchae*. That play, more than any other, attracted composers' attention, as it also attracted the attention of dancers who saw themselves as Bacchantes. Murray invariably received such suggestions politely, and readily granted permission for musical experiments, but he himself had no ear for music. He was in fact tone-deaf. What interested him above all, as it interested Granville-Barker and any other producer too, was the audibility and clarity of the words. He did not object to passionate delivery — as in Barker's own 1904 Henchman speech — but music tended to subdue or obscure his words rather than to amplify them, and he did not need W. S. Gilbert's judgement of 1904 that many members of the company at the Royal Court did not do justice to his verse in order to be aware of the problem. Max Beerbohm had in any case made the point in a review of one 1904 performance at the Royal Court. Four years later it was again aptly illustrated by Granville-Barker, who in suggesting names for a chorus of nine for *Medea* recommended one of them on the grounds that she had a voice like a well-tuned bassoon: 'you must have heard it, she lives within half a mile of Hindhead.'

Neither Barker, Casson nor Murray was ever satisfied that they had found the best way to handle the chorus. Music and singing impaired the words. Dancing might make the whole thing look ridiculous, so easily did it become at odds with the sentiment and emotion of the plays. Chanting and formal rhythmic movement were preferable, but they ran the risks of monotony and perhaps of absurdity. Murray was pleased with Evelyn Hall's speaking of the chorus in Casson's Manchester production because it contained no trace of 'tiresome soulfulness', but his was an austere view which producers and actors did not readily share. For them the temptation was always dramatic effect upon the stage, a temptation which led to great public success, when Max Reinhardt produced Sophocles' *Oedipus* in Murray's translation at Covent Garden in 1912, but to Murray's disapproval. In Greek tragedy he wanted 'more stress on the sense of mysterious sin and less on physical pain . . . the overpowering calm of spiritual tragedy'. The chorus could make the whole thing grotesque. The main point to him was always that the horror of the tragedy should be relieved, and redeemed at the end by sheer rhythm and the beauty of the language.

Rhythm and the beauty of language: these were what Murray aimed at in translating Greek tragedies into English for actors to speak from the stage. William Archer had told him that Greek tragedy demanded to be clothed in 'a formal decorative beauty, scarcely attainable in English without the aid of rhyme'. A very great poet might achieve the effect in blank verse, but that form was so closely identified with Shakespeare and the Elizabethan stage as to be wholly incongruous with the atmosphere of Greece. Because Greek tragedy had no rapid and bustling action upon the stage — that was quite literally obscene, *ob scena* — the impact must be achieved by the 'reinforcement of highly wrought and continuous verbal beauty'. Archer believed that Murray had achieved this. He heard Murray read some of his *Hippolytus* translation in the course of a 1901 lecture before anything was published: 'I felt then and there that he had found a satisfying solution to the problem of re-producing in English the very life and movement of Greek Tragedy.' Archer was speaking as a theatrical critic and playwright, with the actors and the effect from the stage in mind. Nevertheless, Murray's translations were printed before they were acted, and many more people read them than heard them in the theatre. Murray intended his versions to be played, but he also believed them to be poetry, and to be appreciated as poetry. Those who encouraged him to use verse — Housman, Bradley and Shaw, as well as Archer — were those who had heard Murray himself read his own translations. Their response was an auditory one. But poetry is more often read than heard, and Murray, the playwright–poet, was no exception.

When his first book of translation was published in 1902, Lady Carlisle wrote to her daughter: 'All hail, my sweet, to this great day. Isn't he wonderful, that man who came and married you . . . How I do revere him through and through, how I glory in him. The Euripides is a wonder, a miracle of beauty.' This beauty Archer believed Murray to have achieved in the detail of 'his subtly-modulated and free moving verse'. Andrew Bradley, who read the translations in manuscript before publication, thought them 'wonderful', 'extraordinarily good', although he also thought the version of *Electra* a good way below those of *Bacchae* and *Hippolytus*. Bertrand Russell's reaction has already been mentioned. Herbert Fisher declared that he was 'enraptured', and he was echoed by Edmund Gosse, S. H. Butcher (himself translator of the *Odyssey*), Edward Caird and G. M. Trevelyan. Private praise from those with whom he was in sympathy encouraged Murray, especially when it also had public support. *The Times* and the *Spectator* both favourably noticed the published translations in 1902. George Bernard Shaw, introducing Murray to an audience at a lecture to the Independent Labour Party at Clifford's Inn in March, told his listeners that the speaker had written a great deal of very remarkable poetry which he was in the habit of attributing to the ancient Greek dramatist, Euripides. His tribute to Murray's translations as 'original work' was still more explicit in the preface to Major Barbara in 1905: 'The Bacchae came into our dramatic literature with all the impulsive power of an original work.'

Gilbert Murray himself certainly regarded his rhymed translations as poetry in their own right and himself as a poet. He wrote, he said, with the 'dull roll of metre without words' in his ear and he suffered the exhaustion of creative activity. When the first translations were published, he suffered the agonies of a literary man. 'What shatters me, is not anxiety that Andrew Gosse and Edmund Lang should praise me but the mere strain and pain of having taken out a bit of my heart and exposed it in a shop window.' Nevertheless, he still exposed his heart. Some of his verse began to be included in anthologies — for example in the selection by Edward Thompson for one of the slim volumes of *The Augustan Books of Modern Poetry* put out by Ernest Benn, a series which included amongst others Robert Bridges, Edmund Blunden, Rupert Brooke, John Drinkwater, Walter de la Mare and another translator, Edward FitzGerald, whose version of the *Rubbaiyat* of Omar Khayyam had already achieved the status of original poetry. But FitzGerald had created an idiom for his translation from the Persian, whereas Murray took his idiom from the poets, not of his own day, but of a previous poetic generation in England: Swinburne (whose *Atalanta in Corydon* he admired) for the choruses; William Morris for the speeches in the Greek tragedies of Euripides, and later of Sophocles and Aeschylus; and W. S. Gilbert for the Greek comedy of Aristophanes.

To borrow metre and form, however, does not in itself rule out original poetry. Alexander Pope used the heroic couplet which he did not invent. Nevertheless, to borrow diction and imagery as well as metre and form, and to use all of them for the purpose of translation, rules out any serious claim that Murray was a major original poet, although it does not necessarily deny that some portions of his translations are as much poetry as the translations of Milton, Pope and Arnold. For, granted his obvious debts to Swinburne and Morris, there were other less obvious ones. The man who wrote *The Flying Fawn*, as a translation of a *Bacchae* chorus, obviously also knew his Old Testament:

> What else is Wisdom? What of man's endeavour
> Or God's high grace, so lovely and so great?

To fuse, as Murray did, a number of models, if it did not produce a large body of original poetry, yet produced something distinctive. Indeed, it produced poetry, if W.H. Auden's description of poetry as 'memorable speech' be accepted. Some of Gilbert Murray's lines stayed in the memories of those who heard or read them. Elspeth Huxley recalled in the 1920s a district officer in Kenya quoting:

> Oh feet of a fawn to the greenwood fled,
> Alone in the grass and the loveliness;
> Leap of the hunted, no more in dread,
> Beyond the snares and the deadly press!

It may be true that this poetic idiom appealed to those who, like Murray, grew up with the poetry of mid-Victorian England, because it was familiar. It is also true that Murray's 'memorable speech' consisted in a relatively small number of lines remembered from many more passages which were not at all memorable, even though he himself objected to isolated lines, separated from the whole. There was always a considerable element of bathos in Murray's translations, sudden lapses into far less than memorable speech. Still, there is no question that Murray's rhymed translations had an enormous success with those whose poetic fables were formed in the third quarter of the nineteenth century and even with the 'Georgians' in the first decade of the twentieth. Just after the First World War, each of the eight earliest translations had sold well over twenty thousand copies and two of them, *Electra* and *Trojan Women*, well over thirty thousand each.

Fashions in poetic taste obviously change. Murray's verse has been increasingly out of fashion since the First World War. He himself accepted that each generation must write its own poetry, although as one who judged and awarded the King's Medal for

Poetry in the 1930s he could not wholly escape the use of the poetic idiom of his own generation as his standard. Going-out-of-fashion was nevertheless a quite different thing from the actual attack upon his poetry as such. A.E. Housman, who had encouraged Murray's poetry at the turn of the century, was less enthusiastic by 1917. Reviewing volumes 13 and 14 of the *Cambridge History of English Literature* for the *Cambridge Review*, he said of the 1860s that a band of writers arose to launch poetry on a new career, but time had shown that they were cruising in a backwater, not finding a channel to the mainstream:

> In twenty years all heart had gone out of the enterprise. The fashions of that interlude are already so antique that Mr Gilbert Murray can adopt them for his rendering of Euripides; and there they now receive academic approbation, which is the second death.

That was not wholly fair to Murray as a poet, any more than was T.S. Eliot's slightly later judgement that he was 'merely a very insignificant follower of the Pre-Raphaelite movement'.

As a translator Gilbert Murray's stature is much more considerable. Shaw believed as late as 1940 that, from the revolutionary burst of London playwriting through which he had lived, only the Greek plays in Murray's translations were likely to survive. For Murray translated not occasional speeches nor even occasional plays but a major portion of surviving Greek tragedy, and, despite what some contemporary and later critics have thought, he did not unthinkingly accept a particular poetic convention as the vehicle for his great body of work. He intended to show that Greek drama was written to be performed upon the stage, not to be classroom texts for students, and he believed that it could be living theatre for his own generation. Not, of course, if the Greek were literally translated. Housman's parody of a strictly literal translation was often in his mind:

> *Chorus.* O suitably-attired-in-leather-boots
> Head of a traveller, wherefore seeking whom
> Whence by what way how purposed art thou come
> To this well-nightingaled vicinity?
> My object in inquiring is to know.

But, with his knowledge of a previous translation of Euripides which was not a parody, that by T.A. Buckley, Gilbert Murray was convinced that a good translator could not be literal. Buckley had made a prose translation of Euripides. One chorus in his version of the *Trojan Women* began:

> O Telamon, King of bee-nurturing Salamis, inhabiting the territory of a wave-encircled isle, lying close upon the sacred hills, where Minerva first showed forth the branch of dull-green ivy, a heavenly crown, the adornment of fertile Athens; thou camest to act gloriously in company with the bow-bearing son of Alcmena, to sack Troy, Troy, our city.

To Murray that was not theatre and certainly did not convey the spirit of Greek poetry. When he rendered the same chorus for performance on the stage it became:

> In Salamis, filled with the foaming
> Of billows and murmur of bees,
> Old Telamon stayed from his roaming,
> Long ago on a throne of the seas;
> Looking out on the hills olive-laden
> Enchanted, where first from the earth
> The grey-gleaming fruit of the Maiden
> Athena had birth;
> A soft grey crown for a city
> Beloved, a City of light
> Yet he rested not there, nor had pity
> But went forth in his might,
> Where Heracles wandered, the lonely
> Bow-bearer, and lent him his hands
> For the wrecking of one land only,
> Of Ilion, Ilion only,
> Most hated of lands!

Obviously Murray's version was longer — and much better theatre. It was also, in Murray's view, better translation. The Greek original was in metrical verse, so the end of a line was never in doubt in the Greek; hence his own use of rhyme to convey the same effect. In English there was no 'volume of sound' or 'sonority' to match the Greek, but the resources of the English language could be used to convey the effect by the emphases which classical Greek neither possessed nor needed.

With such a view of translation, coupled to a view about English poetic diction and measure, Gilbert Murray laid himself open to the criticisms of those who held a different view of both Greek and English poetry. Some actresses and actors might love his 'speakability', but dramatic and literary critics did not always love his readability. The most formidable and sustained attack was that of T. S. Eliot. He elaborated what had earlier been a joke in Oxford. Bowra told an admittedly apocryphal tale in his *Memories* that in one lecture Murray said to his students: 'I will read you my version, "Death and a cold white thing within the house".' And his hearers found in the Greek text e e â â. Eliot's attack on Murray's style of translation was fundamental. He disliked the poetic models Murray used. He objected to the anthropological approach of Murray's friends and colleagues. He denounced Murray's versions as 'masquerading as a vulgar debasement of the eminently personal idiom of Swinburne', as habitually using two words when the Greek required one and where the English language would provide one. Murray, said Eliot had stretched Greek brevity to fit 'the loose frame' of William Morris and blurred the Greek lyric to the 'fluid haze' of Swinburne. For example, in *Medea*, Murray wrote:

Hath sapped my soul, I dazzle where I stand,
The cup of all life shattered in my hand.

It was Professor Murray, wrote Eliot, not Euripides, who had 'sapped the soul and shattered the cup of all life'. Professor Murray habitually interposed 'between Euripides and ourselves a barrier more impenetrable than the Greek language'.

What Eliot recommended as the model for translation from the Greek of Euripides was the work of H.D. — Richard Aldington's wife — whose choruses were in his opinion much nearer to both Greek and English than those of Gilbert Murray. H.D. had translated occasional choruses from Euripides' plays for the Poets' Translation Series, but never a whole play to be acted upon the stage. The choruses in *Iphigeneia in Aulis*, she explained, could not be literally translated: that would be 'useless and supererogatory'. But a 'rhymed, languidly Swinburnian verse form is an insult and a barbarism'. Rhymeless, 'hard' rhythms 'would be most likely to keep the sharp edges and irregular cadence of the original'. H.D.

therefore omitted the 'useless, ornamental adjectives' of the original Greek itself which were a 'heavy strain on a translator's ingenuity'. In the result, her versions of a few choruses were what Bowra called 'dehydrated', 'lustreless'. They were also, unlike Murray's, neither playable upon the stage nor in fact intended to be. Such a verse as:

> Next, equal oared ships
> Were stayed from the port of Argos
> By one of the Mekistians.
> Sthenelos was with him.

appealed to an Eliot who was seeking a colloquial form, poetry as the language in which one was despairing about a life measured out in coffee spoons.

Murray specifically rejected 'ordinary' language for tragedy; he did not believe in 'too much fuss over single words and phrases: that was "the ruin of poetry"'. He knew that poetry was not dependent on so-called poetical subjects; it could be made out of blood, sweat and tears. What mattered was the spirit in which a theme was treated and, for a translator, that meant: 'I know I cannot reproduce the quality of the original, but I love it and hope that I can, to a certain extent, suggest it.' Chiefly, in Murray's view, suggest it by poetic diction and poetic form in metre and rhythm, in order to convey a message which was never a mere statement or a piece of information.

> It is an appeal from emotion to emotion . . . Every word and phrase has, besides what we call its 'meaning', a magnetic cloud of atmosphere or association hanging about it, and the nearer it is to poetry or to religion the deeper is that cloud and the more richly charged with memories and emotion.

That was Murray's considered judgement about what poetry was, what he aimed at in his own poetry, and what he thought poetry in translation should be.

As the sharp decline in the sales of his translations in the 1920s makes obvious, poetic fashion changed. When Murray established his poetic reputation in the early 1900s, his translations had the charm of novelty while at the same time carrying on the poetic tradition of the Pre-Raphaelites who had seemed so revolutionary in the 1860s. They owed something of their success, too, to the feeling Max Beerbohm so often pointed to: the feeling of pride in an audience that it could understand and enjoy the ancient classics, and an appropriate feeling of reverence for something which had religious affinities. Some contemporaries, however, always had reservations; they found the translations too sentimental, too 'lushly Swinburnian' or 'too decorative'. Such critics were reacting to the results of Murray's search for the 'stunning word' to render Greek adjectives into English. They were, however, a minority, for Murray first published his verse when contemporary taste acclaimed the Georgian poets with their pastoral themes of woods and streams and sea-shore, and his world of Euripides had obvious affinities: as the *Daily Telegraph's* critic said in 1911, he had 'brought out the affinity between the mind of Euripides and the mind of modern Europe'.

The years of leisure at Barford Court during which Murray thought that he might become a poet were nevertheless full of hard work. His Greek edition of Euripides texts was partly completed at Barford before he returned to Oxford. It may conveniently be discussed in the later context of Murray's scholarly work, but it filled months of his time in 1902 and 1903. In memory, however, it was overshadowed by his involvement in the literary world of London to which his plays and his poetry led him. Whatever the quality of Murray's poetry, Greek drama played upon the stage was a novelty. Murray enjoyed being part of the literary world, and residence at Churt gave him easy access to the capital and its literary society.

He spent weeks in Town each year, usually staying at the Carlisles' house in Palace Green, while his plays were in production and playing, regularly in the company of such playwrights as Barrie and, more particularly, Archer and Shaw. With the latter his intimacy was close enough for G.B.S. to delineate him in the character of Professor Cusins in *Major Barbara*, a play which its author indiscreetly called in conversation 'Murray's Mother-in-Law', for he drew on Lady Carlisle for the character of Lady Britomart, and on Lady Mary herself for that of Barbara. Those characterisations caused a breach between Mary and Shaw, but Gilbert continued his association. Shaw drew on Murray's classical knowledge when he needed it for plays such as *Caesar and Cleopatra* and *Major Barbara* and he acknowledged the debt, specifically in the prefatory note to the latter. When Harley Granville-Barker, in playing Cusins, dressed as did Murray, the caricature was recognisable among London theatre-goers. Murray, in short, was a figure in literary and theatrical society, a position recognised by other dramatists when he was included in the group which launched the movement for a National Theatre, and W.B. Yeats involved him in 1903 in the attempt to establish a Theatre of Beauty 'to produce only those works which convey a sentiment of beauty'. More significantly, Barrie, Galsworthy and Barker enlisted his help in the campaign against stage censorship, and when, in 1907, a deputation waited upon Prime Minister Asquith, the draft of the petition it took with it was Gilbert Murray's handiwork.

Murray's stature in this London world was not that of a professional dramatist, for he was never dependent upon the income from this work. When his name was mentioned, as it frequently was, by such a critic as Max Beerbohm it was usually accompanied by some other qualification; he was the 'scholar-poet' or 'poet-scholar'. In a world of professionals, he was always the amateur whose standing came from other things besides his literary and dramatic work. He was 'Professor' Murray, even after he had left Glasgow and before he had returned to Oxford. But he was also more than that. Even without the reminder of 'Murray's Mother-in-Law' upon the stage, in what was still London society he was known as a member by marriage of a great political family. The Barford years might in his memory become ones of involvement with the theatre and literary life. His Greek textual scholarship might pale in recollection. But another aspect of those years which faded in later memory was his involvement in politics.

When the Murrays went to live at Churt, the Liberal Party was in disarray, following Gladstone's retirement from the leadership and the factionalism which followed. To the internal party dissension — which involved the rift in the Howard family — was added in 1899 the external and public dissension of the South African War. Both of these claimed Murray's time and attention during his years of leisure. He could have had a political career, and the temptation to take an active part in public affairs was always there. While he still held the Glasgow chair, he had been invited to become a Liberal parliamentary candidate in 1891, 1897 and 1899. On each occasion he had declined without very much reflection. After he had resigned the chair, he considered the possibility more seriously. Lady Carlisle, after her differences with the Executive of the Liberal Women's Association in June and July 1898, still had more than sufficient influence to secure her son-in-law's adoption as a parliamentary candidate. Even before he left Glasgow she had taken pains in March 1899 to exert her influence at Leeds — not far from Castle Howard — to secure his adoption as a candidate when, in his own words, he was ready for it. He had always identified himself with the party. When Arthur Balfour, the Conservative candidate, beat Lord Aberdeen in the Rectorial contest he announced to his wife that, in the Duke of Wellington's words, 'we have had a damned good hiding', because Balfour had secured a majority in three of the four Nations. This identification with the Liberal Party, although it had led to those earlier invitations to stand as a candidate, became more complicated with Gladstone's retirement in 1895.

Gilbert Murray, like his mother-in-law Lady Carlisle and his wife, belonged to the radical wing. He had admired the German socialist Liebknecht. He did not admire Lord Rosebery who succeeded Gladstone as the Liberal Party leader, employing the factional label 'roseberyite' to describe the otherwise affable Haldane whom he met at dinner and with whom he argued about the Fashoda incident of 1896. Nor yet, as that argument shows, did he admire those other imperialists in the party during the South African War, Asquith and Grey: 'jingoes', he thought them, whose bloodthirsty talk depressed him. In 1896 he described Rosebery as weak, a man who cared only for himself; he would have much preferred John Morley, the intellectual in politics, to be leader, but 'if I can't have Morley, I want Sir William (Harcourt)'. He recognised that other party leaders, Acland, Campbell-Bannerman and Asquith, each had contempt and dislike for Harcourt and therefore, *faute de mieux*, there was nothing for it but Asquith himself.

That, however, was before the Boer War had actually broken out, the result of imperialism for which in part he blamed Asquith and Grey. Morley's stocks, in spite of the fact that he was weak on Women's Suffrage, therefore revived on the Murray exchange. In January 1899 he was 'greatly excited' by Morley's speech in Glasgow and decided to follow him in order to hear him speak again at Montrose. What had excited him was Morley's obvious opposition to the imperialists of the party. He agreed with his wife and his mother-in-law's secretary, Leif Jones, that Morley had put his case weakly, but this Murray excused as intentional, a desire to avoid an overt attack on Asquith and Grey. Morley had laid great stress on the fact that enthusiasm for foreign aggrandisement meant a loss for social reform at home, and in consequence, in Murray's opinion, he ought therefore to have proclaimed a progressive reform programme. But this Morley did not do and so, in Murray's judgement, he left himself open to a damaging counter from that ex-radical Joseph Chamberlain: 'Joe can say "I give attention to imperial expansion but still am more of a force for social reform." ' Murray was in fact disappointed with Morley even while excusing him: he could have been more definite on old age pensions which he had 'considered' for 15 years; but 'I shall still follow him more than any other leader'. Nevertheless, Murray thought that other Liberals would not, although he himself was 'profoundly grateful to him for raising his voice against the bloodthirsty talk of the last six months'.

With divisions of this sort within the Liberal Party exacerbated by the war, and with his doubts about the suitability of the intellectual Morley as a leader, the chance of a parliamentary candidacy at Leeds in 1899 was at first not altogether welcome to Murray. Lady Carlisle took the necessary steps to secure his adoption, but even in March her son-in-law had doubts. He thought, with a majority in the constituency of 1,100 against the Liberals at the previous election, that he probably could not turn it into a win whenever the next election came. Still, he was glad to be in the swim with Lady Carlisle and the politicians of the family — with her own two sons, her other son-in-law Charles Roberts, and her secretary Leif Jones — and he stifled his doubts. After a rest he was prepared to face the election.

In the meantime, living in the country close to London, he took an active interest in the political discussions and arguments within the party. In July, while staying at the Earl's house in Palace Green, he attended a meeting on the principles of Liberalism, at which Hilaire Belloc spoke brilliantly although Murray could not afterwards remember a word that he had said. He undertook to write articles for J.L. Hammond from whom he heard 'awful' news: Mrs Phillimore and Haldane wanted Grey to lead the Liberal Party in the Commons with Rosebery as Prime Minister in the Lords, on a programme to include: (1) Home Rule suspended; (2) houses for the poor; (3) an education bill for voluntary schools;

(4) temperance reform but not the local vote (in support of which Lady Carlisle had broken with her Liberal Women); (5) a Rosebery foreign policy. Gilbert Murray's advice, with which Hammond agreed, was 'oppose it like the devil'. In November, having learned that Massingham had resigned the editorship of the *Chronicle* after a disagreement with the proprietors on the South African question, Murray regarded it as serious that there should be no Liberal morning paper in London and actively attempted to raise money for a new radical paper, yet all the time wondering what on earth he was doing in this gallery.

The Boer War answered his question. By September 1899 public feeling about the Transvaal, the shouts of 'Rule Britannia' which interrupted one of the Countess's meetings at Manchester, had shocked and bewildered him. His feeling of bitterness began to grow that the 'jingoes' cared only for conquering and ruling until 'the crash comes and the world will tolerate it no more'. By December, recognising the popular strength of 'jingoism', doubting whether there was even a slim chance in the circumstances of war of reversing that anti-Liberal majority at Leeds and disturbed by the factions he had seen within the party, he was inclined to withdraw his parliamentary candidature. That he might be on the losing side in an election never in itself worried Murray, any more than it did in those St John's College debates in Oxford. He was always prepared himself to raise or to follow the voice of calm reason against emotion, especially war emotion against the Boers, in the belief that sooner or later reason would prevail. The reasons he offered for the withdrawal of his candidacy were primarily those of family. Lady Mary had always been against his standing for Parliament and now declined to give him any advice. More important — 'the real point' said Murray — was the children's health. Rosalind, believed to be tubercular, needed an establishment in Italy. The other part of his reasons for withdrawal were self-doubts. After his own illness in Glasgow and convalescence at Barford Court, he felt that he could stand the strain neither of a contested election nor of parliamentary life. More fundamentally, he doubted if he had a clear vocation for political life because he felt that what drove him to take any political action was not a clear consistent aim but rather 'just the spur of indignation', a generous impulse not unlike that of his father whose political career had ended in the neutrality of the Speakership in New South Wales.

The 'spur of indignation' nevertheless continued to goad him after his candidacy was withdrawn. He still regarded himself as a radical. He publicly opposed the war. In 1900 he told Lady Carlisle that he would not mind an Irish seat if he could sit as an extreme radical, but he would be 'worried to death as an English Liberal'. Or even as a Scottish one. For, when he was invited by the College division of Glasgow to stand in the Liberal interest in August 1903 he 'of course' declined. He had not, however, lost his interest in party politics, attending the Liberal conference in July 1901 where he 'liked the ring' of Campbell-Bannerman, as opposed to Asquith and Grey, and was 'content with him for the moment'. He urged the Countess of Carlisle, as a duty to the nation, to constitute a radical *salon*. He read with general agreement the proofs of J.A. Hobson's famous analysis in *Imperialism*: 'very good and practically our point of view'. He met the Boer generals, Botha, de Wet and de la Rey when they came to England after the South African settlement, the first disconcerting him, when he expressed his pride at meeting them, by replying 'on the contrary, it is I who am proud to meet you'. He became miserable over the Russo-Japanese War — otherwise a splendid victory over tyranny — because it left the Turks with a free hand in Bulgaria, while the Murrays welcomed the news of the Russian revolution of 1905 as 'glorious'.

This interest in politics, as distinct from an active life in politics, never left Murray; indeed, political compatibility and sympathy were the basis of his close personal and professional relationships. At this time of his life those relationships were all radical or progressive ones, for the Boer War had divided London society as the Spanish Civil War was to do in the next generation. Even the election of a Liberal government in 1905 did not remove the divisions within the party. Suspicions of the Liberal 'imperialists' remained.

If Murray, in these years when he had the opportunity to play an active role in national politics, held back, nevertheless it was his devotion to radical and progressive causes which held his other interests together. 'Ibscenity' was a progressive cause. Shaw was a Fabian. Euripides was a proto-radical. As will presently appear, Murray regarded his scholarly work, too, as radical.

Radical, in a slightly different sense, was one other interest which he began to develop in these years. He had long been struck by the prophetic quality of some of his dreams, and he noted examples as

early as November 1890. The usual type of incident was one which
he described to his wife in May 1897, when he woke up one
morning with the names of two friends in his mouth for no obvious
reason, and then found a letter from one of them upon coming
down to breakfast. Such incidents were common enough to arouse
his interest in the phenomenon. While staying in Dr Eccles's clinic
in April 1898 he read a psychical paper which caused him to think
he should follow up these things more, and when, in the process of
making his Euripides' text, he stayed with A.W. Verrall and his
wife in Cambridge, he had an opportunity. Mrs Verrall was a
member of the Society for Psychical Research and in the course of
his visit she introduced him to such things as planchette boards and
spirit writing. Murray's systematic interest in his apparent telepathic abilities came later, but the years of leisure saw his earlier
casual interest replaced by a more deliberate one.

Murray certainly had opportunity to look around during his six
years in the English countryside, but his use of his time was
Victorian. He worked hard. The sinews of the leisured life were
there: income, servants to deal with the mechanics of life, a wife to
protect him for the important work he had to do. What he achieved
was remarkable in its quantity and quality, and in its range. Yet
presently he began to be dissatisfied. Without the regular round of
formal duties he began to feel uneasy. The nervous strain of
successful work without a job was dissatisfying. At Naples in 1903,
when, he said, he felt the Greek scholar in him revive, his mind
turned towards a job: 'I wish they would make me a professor of
Greek at some nice place. But, of course, there is no place except
Oxford.' Friends — Fisher, for example — dropped remarks that
he ought to be professor of Greek at Oxford, which both flattered
and tantalised him. 'Oh, I wish I could get properly to work and be
among workers.' Not only that, of course. He wished he could, by
his own earnings, shake off the dependency upon Lady Carlisle's
generosity. This was unstinting, but it led Gilbert constantly to
apologise for its necessity. For a man who had cultivated
detachment from childhood, it was peculiarly hard to bear; any
position of dependency, as he had once said of an assistant in
Glasgow, was dreadfully destructive of frankness. In his own case,
it was a disappointment and a limitation that he fretted against,
whatever success he might achieve in these years of leisure. By
October 1904 he lacked the courage to speak to people and could

feel no interest in his work. He very much wanted a proper job for himself. He had maintained his Oxford connections by examining for the Schools. In April 1904, when simply to move house seemed a desirable change which might benefit Lady Mary's health, he thought of buying a residence on Boar's Hill, near Oxford, which he described as one of the most beautiful sites in England. He knew then that arrangements could be made for him to do a little lecturing at the university. Later in the year a definite proposal came: a teaching Fellowship at New College where he had originally been elected a Fellow in 1889.

Whatever Gilbert Murray felt in retrospect about the Barford years, when he had leisure and could involve himself with the theatre, by the end of 1904 he was dissatisfied with himself and his existence. His marriage had gone through a period of strain, and Lady Mary's health in itself was grounds for moving house. Murray felt that he had made her miserable and that he had lost confidence in himself, 'at least, not exactly in myself but in my power of seeing things in the same light as other people . . . no, not that either. Perhaps it is in Providence that I have lost confidence.' His own health had recovered, but he could not regard himself as a successful man of letters nor as an original playwright. His edition of Euripides was incomplete. He had indeed had a striking success with his staged translations of Euripides but it was a limited one. And his ambition to be a significant poet was unfulfilled. When the news of his election at New College came in January 1905 he passed judgement on these years when he told Fisher: 'it will be . . . a great satisfaction to be doing some honest work again, after so long languishing as a superfluous minor poet.'

6 RETURN TO OXFORD

'I have grave doubts about my competence as a tutor. I have done almost no really advanced teaching since I left Oxford.' Gilbert Murray returned to Oxford in that frame of mind. Barford Court was given up in May 1905. The Lady Mary arrived in Oxford in that month to supervise the redecoration of the large but not attractive Victorian house in North Oxford at 131 Banbury Road, bought for the Murrays by Lady Carlisle. Lady Mary liked neither the house nor Oxford society. She forbade her husband to help with unpacking, causing him to reflect upon his uselessness. Gilbert helped the family move by arranging the sale of some of their shares in London to meet expenses, but he was involved with rehearsals in London until June 1905. Then he came to Oxford, finding his first pupils 'delightful', his shyness 'dropping away'. In July he left on holiday with Ernest Barker for Constantinople and Greece, while his wife was invited by her mother to Castle Howard. Murray returned to England late in July to a hurtful family quarrel, after which he joined Lady Carlisle at Naworth while his wife took Rosalind to Switzerland. Not until November was the Murray household properly established in Oxford.

Murray's teaching duties at New College, where he took over Margoliouth's old rooms, were two hours a week in each of two terms, but his time was more taken up by the rehearsals in London, by completing his Greek edition of Euripides which he had begun at Glasgow and continued in Surrey, and from mid-1906 by the preparation of the Gardiner Lane Lectures for 1907 which he had been invited to deliver at Harvard University, in recognition of the reputation as the interpreter of Greek poetry which he had acquired in the United States, as well as in Britain, through his Euripides translations. Indeed, as early as October 1905, he was complaining of overwork, because he took his teaching and its preparation with great seriousness and devotion, while still completing the work in which he had steeped himself during his years of leisure. Trying out his Harvard lectures upon his pupils, he set before them what a colleague once called 'one of the richest offerings ever set before a roomful of undergraduates more than half-bored with their Greek'. Gilbert Murray, who had acquired a reputation as a teacher of undergraduates in Glasgow, began at once to establish one in Oxford by the pains he took with those first students in 1905. Yet his reputation also rested upon his scholarship, in a technical sense, as judged by his professional peers. No matter that he was applauded by undergraduates and by a wider public; as a don in Oxford, holding a formal position, he was judged by his academic colleagues, many of whom were suspicious of the public fame and reputation of a man of letters, and some of them jealous both of that reputation and of Murray's aristocratic connections and independent income, to which they added dislike of his radical politics.

In returning to Oxford, Murray went back to a society of college societies. It was the colleges and their tutors who taught undergraduates, rather than the university in which lectures were not compulsory. And in the classics that teaching was still largely of the kind which Murray had condemned in his Glasgow Inaugural: the translation and elucidation of set texts. In short, Greek, not Greece. Moreover, because the colleges emphasised teaching, it was not usual for their classical dons to emphasise research, even textual research. There were a few Oxford dons, not many, who themselves edited texts, but even fewer were outstanding textual scholars when Murray returned to Oxford; there was no equivalent, for example, to Jebb at Cambridge. This background is important, for it is the perspective against which Murray's scholarly achievement must be judged in the pre-First World War period after his return to Oxford, and its disregard has vitiated the judgements even of Murray's admirers. For they have tended to justify Murray's literary approach to Greek and Greece as against strict textual scholarship. For example Isobel Henderson, drawing her sympathetic picture of Murray in his *Unfinished Autobiography*, draws a contrast between scholarship and literature, by which the former shrinks into a specialist corner, there dwelling apart from *humanitas* and the love of literature, and seeing its duty as the training of professional editors of texts. Not many Oxford dons themselves then edited texts, still less trained others to do so. What they chiefly did was to train their pupils to translate from and into Greek, to scan and to construe set texts, very much as Sixth Form masters did in the public schools. Indeed, the interchange between college tutorships and public school masterships was common enough, and their work was substantially the same. The Oxford to which Murray returned in 1905 was not significantly different from that which he had left in 1889, which he had found disappointing.

Murray's textual work in Greek scholarship must be seen against this background. When he had accepted the invitation to edit the Greek text of the plays of Euripides for the Oxford Classical Texts series, he had committed himself to scholarship by which his professional peers would judge him, both then and later. Nevertheless, he differed from them even at the time in attempting an edition of *all* of the plays, not just of a single play; and the edition was intended for teaching purposes, not for other professional scholars whose editorial expertise, then and now, was concentrated upon a single play or two, rather than upon the whole body of Euripides' work. Murray determined to take as much pains over the edition as any other scholar, but none had edited the plays in whole since Paley's edition some 30 years earlier, and since that time German scholarship had transformed Greek scholarship. Murray was familiar with German classical scholarship through his correspondence with Ulrich von Wilamowitz-Moellendorf. When he was first elected to a prize Fellowship at New College in 1889, he had thought to go to Wilamowitz' seminar at Göttingen to obtain the training which was unavailable anywhere in England. He had never gone to Germany, but he tried to offset the lack of formal training by correspondence and consultation. Still, the edition finally depended upon Murray's own abilities as a scholar and his capacity to learn the skills and craft of an editor by experience as he went along.

What skills did he need? The obvious *sine qua non* was fluency in the language, wide reading in Greek and familiarity with Greek metre. This Murray had beyond question. Then an editor needed industry and patience; and Murray was capable of hard sustained work upon the text, whatever the personal circumstances of his life. Beyond those basic requirements, an imaginative understanding to correct doubtful readings, to decide between manuscript variants and to make informed guesses about missing readings. Murray certainly had imaginative power and he had his own clear image of the Greek world. Moreover he was a practising playwright who, in a circle of dramatic friends which included Archer, Shaw, Barrie and Galsworthy, knew more than most classical editors about practical stagecraft. But imagination of this order in editing a text was not always a help. Because he had always an image of the

Greek theatre and of acting, there was the temptation to conjecture about doubtful readings by its light, to imagine what must have been so on the Greek stage, partly at least from his experience of the modern. Just as his view of Greek history, as expounded in his book on Greek literature, was essentially a Whig attitude to the past, so his edition in a sense became a Whig view of Euripides' plays. Still, Murray was well-equipped to be a classical scholar in the strict textual sense; and Euripides, even if he became in Murray's eyes a proto-Whig, had captured his imagination.

The problem with Euripides, Murray told his publisher, was that 'you have to get the text out of so many manuscripts instead of one or two good ones'. The Euripides' manuscript tradition is corrupt, partly because the plays were unofficially copied in their own day, partly because the Greek actors had altered some lines and inserted others in performance, lines which were later included even in the official texts, partly because the *scholia*, the ancient commentaries, were sometimes also in transmission included in the text. And this is wholly apart from the more ordinary, mechanical sources of error and corruption, deriving from copyists and physical mutilation. At the time Murray made his edition, he could constitute a text from those already published, beginning with that of 'the arbitrary Nauck', with those of Kirchoff and Prinz-Wecklein, using the collations of Euripides' manuscripts made both by those editors and by such correspondents as Wilamowitz and Verrall. Indeed, with the first volume of plays, comprising *Cyclops, Alcestis, Medea, Heraclidae, Andromache* and *Hecuba*, Murray had little choice but to work from already published texts with help from his correspondents, because his publisher was anxious to get the edition out and Murray, because of his Glasgow duties and his poor health, had no opportunity to go abroad to Italy where the more important manuscripts were, nor to France where the *Bibliothèque Nationale* held two. So the first volume of the edition of the plays which he brought to completion at Barford was finished before Murray had himself been able to consult the chief manuscripts. Wilamowitz in 1894 had offered him any of his own material; he had, he said, fairly accurate collations of M, the Venice MS, and of C, V and P (all Vatican manuscripts) for some of the plays; he was in any case glad to read and correct the galley proofs. So too was Verrall. Oxford University Press sent Murray on request three sets of galley proofs so that these two scholars as well as the editor himself could correct them. Murray went to stay with Verrall in Cambridge while he was correcting the first volume, being offered by his host, he said, many subtle and attractive emendations about which he had doubts. The Press itself asked Ingram Bywater, then Regius Professor of Greek at Oxford, to read the proofs for them. Murray was troubled by the number of corrections all this proof-reading produced — corrections due, he claimed, largely to Wilamowitz — which went £20 over the limit the Press allowed to editors and authors. Still, in the result, he was able to be confident that no one could say he had not taken pains with the edition. He believed that a text approved by himself, by Wilamowitz and by Verrall was in a strong position. Jack Mackail corrected and passed the Latin of the preface.

Not every scholar accepted that Verrall's approval was really a blessing; Housman was to talk of his 'baleful' influence. But Ulrich von Wilamowitz-Moellendorf's approval was in a different class. Wilamowitz enjoyed an enormous reputation in a day when English scholars, in Greek as in history, revered German scholarship. Wilamowitz very quickly read the proofs of the first volume; he agreed to Murray's invitation to do so on 2 June 1901 and his corrections were back with the Press by 23 July. The volume was published in 1902. By that date Murray had finished a major part of the work for the second volume, consisting of another six plays. But before these went to the Press he was able, in the leisure time of Barford Court, to visit Italy in order to collate his text with the most important manuscripts in Florence, Rome and Naples. Murray had visited Florence in February 1903 to look at the Euripidean manuscripts in the Laurentiana, feeling 'rather shy' as he first entered the library. At first he found the work strenuous, but by early March he was beginning to be fascinated. Examining the 'L' manuscript, he discovered 'some very curious things . . . which Wilamowitz and Wecklein must know, but have not said anything about'. Physically he found manuscript work slow, trying to his eyes and much more of a strain than he had expected. He also felt his own limitations: 'I shall never exhaust it but I understand it better than I did.' In just over a week he had finished work upon the 'L' manuscript, and upon another less important one, G; then he moved on to two others, O and D. Within a fortnight he had looked at all of the Florence manuscripts, with the occasional help of the distinguished Italian scholar, Vitelli, who had noticed 'just the same points as I and had stuck at the same difficulties'. From Florence, Murray went by way of Perugia to Naples where he examined the 'Nap' manuscript which included the Hippolytus *scholia*, feeling as he said, 'the Greek scholar revive in me'. Thence to Rome where, in the Vatican library at the end of March, he concluded his manuscript work with V, 'very curious and a better MS than I expected'; having cleared his mind about it he then examined P. Basing his text upon that of Wecklein, or rather, as he said, upon Prinz who had actually done the Wecklein collation, he had found few mistakes and was in general struck by the Germans' thoroughness.

His trip to Italy, however, had not only revived his scholarly interests; it had 'thoroughly shaken him up', altered the course of his thoughts and refreshed his mind. After his return to England, early in April 1903, he quickly sent the texts of the six plays to the Press, receiving the first batch of proofs in September. He was worried that Wilamowitz, who had agreed to correct this second volume as he had done the first, would be unable to do so because of a proposed visit to Asia Minor. In the event Wilamowitz's father-in-law, the great historian Theodor Mommsen, died, the Asian visit was postponed and so the German scholar was again able to read Murray's text before publication. Wilamowitz had himself been at a conference in Rome but did not know of his correspondent's presence in Italy until it was too late to meet for what would have been their first encounter. Instead, after his return to Germany, he offered Murray advice upon the points in the Italian manuscripts of Euripides which had puzzled his English colleague. Wilamowitz, with the help of a colleague, read the proofs of the second volume in January 1904. He doubted Murray's chronological order of the plays, putting *Iphigeneia in Tauris* before *Electra*, a view Murray did not accept. He also thought Murray had been a bit unfair to such English scholars as Porson, Elmsley and Dobrée, and that some of his arguments for his readings needed a more careful defence: 'one easily says something which captivates for the moment, but which gets embarrassing in the long run'; he himself wished to 'extinguish the follies of my youth' in the *Herakles* edition.

Nevertheless, in the midst of all his work, Wilamowitz had taken great pleasure in Murray's proofs and his remarks, he said, were

only for the purpose of reconsidering the passages and then finding a decision: I expect you neither to answer nor to accept them. If I did, my help would be tedious rather than useful.

Surely the only right way is to start off again and again from the MSS, leaving out at the beginning even the commonly received emendations — indeed you have freed me from many commonly accepted readings. Porson's school, and especially he himself, knew the language and the usage of the tragedians so well (for they read the poems essentially only to make such observation) that their clear sense with its sobriety was incomparably accurate.

Wilamowitz treated Gilbert Murray seriously as an equal in scholarship and as a fellow expert on Euripides. Wecklein he described as 'such a poor fellow, his edition so lacking in judgement, that one must find it difficult to treat him like a gentleman, which he is not. The mere fact that he feels your edition will push him out causes him to write his polemic.' With such *furor Teutonicus* aimed at his German critics, Murray was reassured of the merits of his own second volume which, when Wilamowitz wished to prepare a new edition of his own German translation of Euripides, he described as 'the best recommendable text': *den empfehlens-wertesten Text*. The second volume was published in 1904, but it was not until 1908 that Murray had almost finished the third volume of what by then he called his 'disgusting task'. A fourth volume, intended to contain the fragments of Euripides' plays and for which Murray had particularly asked when he undertook the edition, never appeared. Murray never really found editing a congenial task, although he recognised it as a duty and he believed he had taken pains with it. He was always nervous about the reception of his edition, hence his anxiety for Wilamowitz' approval. 'I don't think it can be said that I have not taken proper pains over the book, but of course one may always find some important thing omitted. I leave it with the gods.'

Learned books and editions are also left with professional scholars, with the judgement of one's peers. The Oxford Classical Texts series was designed to provide standard texts for the student, both in school and university. So those teachers who used these editions of the whole of an author's plays, rather than the single edition of a particular play, had to be convinced of their quality. Murray's first two volumes of Euripides appeared very early in the Oxford series, side by side with John Burnet's edition of Plato's works, S.H. Butcher's edition of Demosthenes and Ingram Bywater's of

Aristotle's *Ethica Nicomachea*. This was good company to keep; and it set a standard of editing by which contemporaries could judge and compare.

Gilbert Murray expected that the friends and admirers of Wilamowitz-Moellendorf would praise his editions, those of Wecklein revile. He was right. In Germany there were two very unfavourable judgements upon his text by Wecklein himself and by Mekler, while Dr Schelis of Bremen asked the Press in 1910 for a review copy so that he could write a long critique in answer to these criticisms which did not, in his view, in the least do justice to an edition which made 'a good step forward in the production of a conservative text'. 'Conservative' was not, however, Murray's own opinion of his work. He believed that he would have to write an article, although he had a 'physical abhorrence for writing in periodicals', to explain the new readings and interpretations and the originality of his edition. A.E. Housman, after the first volume appeared, had warned him that radicalism in textual criticism was just as bad as conservatism, but the former was not then so rampant as the latter which 'wants rebuking'. This was what Murray thought he had done, but when the second volume appeared Housman detected the 'baleful influence' of Verrall of whose radicalism he did not at all approve: in the *Supplices* he noted 'a perfectly impossible reading. Why didn't Porson make the conjecture?' In fact, Housman continued, Attic tragedy had been studied for so long and so minutely by such great men that all corrections which consisted in iteration of syllables or separation of letters must almost necessarily have been made already; at this date any conjecture of this sort ought to be made 'with one's hair standing on end and one's knees giving way beneath one; because the odds are that it is a hundred to one that it is a conjecture which our betters were withheld from making by their superior tact'. Still, although Housman suggested one or two emendations, he largely agreed with Murray's readings and his criticism was mild, far from the savagery he vented upon other editors. He called the edition 'much the pleasantest' and the apparatus the clearest to use. Walter Headlam of King's College, Cambridge, whom Murray had con- sulted about metre, privately suggested some corrections. C.B. Heberden, who was making a school edition of one play, *Hecuba*, largely accepted Murray's text. Such private reactions, although they did not hail Murray as a brilliant editor, nevertheless reinforced his confidence in his text in the face of the German criticism.

English public criticism was longer delayed. Not until 1912 did A.C. Pearson review the edition for the *Classical Review*. Pearson, himself later indifferently to produce the text of Sophocles' plays for the same series, was critical, especially of the apparatus, but not offensively so. Murray, with the self-control Housman had earlier admired in his translations, wrote to thank Pearson for the 'most practically useful review' he had ever read. He was

> shocked at the number of inaccuracies of which I appear to be guilty. I can probably clear myself of some when I get back to my notes. A number of my variations from Wecklein came from manuscript corrections sent by Wilamowitz-Moellendorf but I admit I never worked out that side of the subject — I mean I never took much trouble to find out who had really propounded a particular conjecture first. As to manuscript readings, I may sometimes be right as against Wecklein. I have examined all the Italian manuscripts, except M, the Paris and the manuscript of the Rhesus independently. I am only too conscious that great press of work during volume 3 and which prevented volume 4 may have led me into many bad slips.

Not, however, only the press of work. In asking his publisher to read this letter before he passed it on to Pearson, Murray explained not that he was simply too busy, nor that he had had to shorten the apparatus for the Press, nor that he was too original, but that he was 'devilish inaccurate by nature'. He had, he wrote, recently been revising an essay on the Olympians, written mostly without his books, and he had found nearly every quotation somehow wrong. 'It is only natural I suppose when one trusts to memory rather than written notes.'

Any scholar can, of course, make mistakes for the reasons Murray explained, but such mistakes are meat and drink to reviewers whose own abilities and achievements may be far less than their victim's. Murray was perhaps unduly modest in the face of them; other contemporary scholars took a more favourable view of his edition, as did one later one who credited Murray with establishing the 'canon' of the Euripides manuscripts which, coming at the beginning of the Oxford Classical Texts series, set a respectable standard of editing in the eyes of Wilamowitz and his pupils. Still, for a man like Murray who had been accustomed to brilliant success and to praise in his classical career, anything less than enthusiastic approval of his major textual work reinforced his nervousness about and his revulsion from the details of editing texts. He had all the equipment for it — except the temperament. He worked on a large scale; the edition was of the whole of Euripides' plays. Such an edition, by reason of time and of publisher's space, precluded the detailed scholarly attention which can be given to an edition of a single play. Those scholars who edited such single texts could always, therefore, be critical of Murray's selection of readings for a particular play. A recent editor of *Hippolytus*, for example, can criticise Murray's text for its collation of the B manuscript in the *Bibliothèque Nationale* because it 'has many gaps and errors'. But the same modern editor notes that Kirchoff, Prinz-Wecklein and Meridier gave only selected readings in their complete editions, as did Wilamowitz himself when he edited the single text of the play. Still, in its day, Murray's edition of all the plays, by the light of the resources of textual criticism then available to him, was a considerable achievement. That later scholars have corrected some of his readings of the Greek and have considered with more sophisticated methods the manuscript tradition of Euripides is not a criticism of Murray by the standards of his own day. One later scholar, indeed, ascribes to him 'the best selection of Euripidean ms . . . which established the present vulgate', while detecting flaws in his analysis of the manuscripts themselves. Another, while describing him as 'an ingenious and subtle (sometimes over-subtle)' textual critic, prefaced his own edition of the *Bacchae* in which he used Murray's text with the tribute that he owed to Murray 'my first real understanding of the play's greatness . . . All of this book is ultimately his: a part of it he made; the rest grew from seed he planted thirty years ago.'

E.R. Dodds, in that acknowledgement of Gilbert Murray's work, was talking of more than his textual scholarship. In the Greek edition of Euripides, Murray stood in a tradition of Victorian scholarship, the scholarship which, in history, so quickly produced the Rolls Series texts of medieval chronicles from the hands of men deeply involved in public affairs and in teaching, men such as William Stubbs, the Regius Professor of Modern History at Oxford who has commonly been regarded as the 'Father' of the Oxford School of History. In detail, the achievement might be faulted. In whole, it represented an extensive foundation upon which future scholars could build. Like Stubbs, Murray acknowledged an obligation to undertake the labour of exacting textual work which demanded every scrap of his brain. Like Stubbs, too, he believed that he had an obligation to interpret the past revealed by his texts to his generation. Like Stubbs, he accepted demanding public duties, the work for Humanity and Progress which his wife and mother-in-law believed to be fit for a gentleman of great talents. Greek poetry was after all 'a force and the embodiment of a force making for the progress of the human race'.

Gilbert Murray had largely completed his Greek edition of Euripides by 1908; the third volume was published in 1910, and republished in 1913, by which date the second volume was in its third edition. The completion of his 'disgusting task' was subordinated to a press of work, especially by the obligation to make Greece meaningful to his own generation. In December 1906 he was preparing at Alassio the lectures he was to deliver in the United States at Harvard in 1907. He did so 'almost without books of reference', in an attempt to 'puzzle out a little more of the meaning of a certain remote age of the world, whose beauty and whose power of inspiration seem to shine the more wonderful, the more resolutely we set ourselves to understand it'. The lectures made up half of *The Rise of the Greek Epic* which Clarendon Press first published in 1907 and reissued in a slightly revised form four years later; two further editions, the third a good deal revised, appeared in 1924 and 1934.

This book, in order to demonstrate the thesis that Greek poetry was a force making for the progress of the human race, set out to study its growth out of savagery to the Hellenism which 'is a collective name for the very forces which . . . strove for his [Pagan Man's] regeneration'. To illustrate this thesis, Gilbert Murray drew the anthropological analogy with primitive peoples on the west coast of Africa and in the Pacific islands (in one of which, Papua, his brother Hubert was governor). As Greek civilisation 'rose from the swampy level' of the neighbouring peoples, it could not 'shake itself clean all at once'; remnants of savagery — totemism, canni-balism, human sacrifice — lingered in obscure parts of Greek life, to puzzle the Greeks themselves, although this savagery was expur-gated and made 'comparatively innocent'. Murray believed that these remnants were the reverberation of an extinct barbarity, not the actual barbarity itself, although he characterised Greek society as a handful of men holding an outpost, a barrier against barbarism still near at hand and against some sudden blind resurgence of the savage. He dismissed as 'mock' the ritual slaying of the *pharmakos*, the scapegoat, at Ephesus and as based on 'weak' evidence the story of Themistocles, just before the battle of Salamis, sacrificing three prisoners; but that such stories could be told, Murray explained, put them within the bounds of action men thought possible. Lesser horrors, which even shining Athens could not conquer — slavery, the subjection of women and unchastity in the relations of the sexes — he regarded as the reverse of what was characteristically Greek; they were the remnants of 'primaeval slime'. With such a view of progress firmly in his mind, Murray argued that its inspiration was particularly strong in Greek poetry. Not, indeed, in the final stages of Homer, nor in Pindar nor Sophocles (nor, in parenthesis, in Chaucer and Shakespeare). But in Aeschylus, Euripides and Plato, as in Shelley and Tolstoy, human progress was the source of poetic inspiration, the 'very breath of life'.

This argument of the book was an expansion of that which Murray had advanced in his *History of Ancient Greek Literature*. What he did at Harvard was to expand the argument, using recent scholarship to trace this evolution in Greek epic poetry and especially in the *Iliad* of Homer. This poem he regarded as a 'traditional' book. To explain how the poem was created and handed on, he first of all described the people and the society in which the transmission occurred. Murray drew a picture of an Heroic Age, the age of the Trojan War, of Agamemnon and Priam, of Achilles and Odysseus, of Hector and Paris, whose cities, founded on seaborne commerce, were destroyed by successive waves of migration or invasion from the north. There followed a Dark Age, a chaos in which tribal customs and religion were exposed to change or destruction in the attendant anarchy but in which the 'seed of regeneration' was left. That seed was nurtured by literature, by the story-tellers, the bards who were *grammatikoi*, men who could decipher the scratches on a precious roll, who passed this knowledge on to disciples. The *grammatikos*, the man of letters with his book written on expensive, valuable skins, added to or even changed his book so that over generations new elements came in and expurgations occurred, by analogy, argued Murray, with the Biblical book of Deuteronomy. It was the expurgations that revealed the moral progress which was the force of Greek poetry. This was the central theme of *The Rise of the Greek Epic*. Murray proceeded to illustrate moral and ethical advances by examining the elimination of sexual aberrations, of human sacrifice and of barbarous torture from this story of Achilles which had, by the fifth century, assumed a central place in the education of Greek children.

Such a moral development in a traditional story of the wrath of Achilles involved Murray in, although he did not deliberately discuss, the Homeric question. Perceiving the *Iliad* and, to a much less extent the *Odyssey*, as a gradual working over and rehandling of traditional poems, and reinforcing the evidence of moral progress by anachronistic details of armour — iron in the *Iliad* when it should have been bronze — he made the case for the existence of anachronisms in the epic which proved it to contain material of much later date than the Heroic Age. His conclusion was that 'the *Iliad* is not an independent work of fiction but a Traditional Book, dependent on a living saga or tradition. It was meant to be history, or what then stood for history.' It was one of a great number of such traditions, and it incorporated 'foreign' elements from the others. But there was no 'primaeval and all-wise' poet, Homer. His name might conceivably once have been borne by a living person, but if so, 'we know nothing of him, except indeed that he did not, in any complete sense, write the *Iliad* and the *Odyssey*'. *Homeros* was more safely to be regarded as the name of an imaginary ancestor worshipped by a school of bards called *Homeridae*. Yet the theory of authorship was of little importance to the greatness of the poem which was clearly the work of many ages. Greatness in poetry depended upon intensity of imagination. Does it transport us to a new world? How interesting or beautiful is that world when we get there? This imaginative intensity is nowadays associated with an individual artist, but artists had not always wished for individual ascription. These Greek artists did not: they gave themselves up to the tradition and each added to its greatness and beauty all that was in him.

The lectures which made up the core of *The Rise of the Greek Epic* greatly widened Gilbert Murray's reputation. They attracted large audiences at Harvard (T.S. Eliot, in later years a severe critic, ironically enough was one who heard him) and the President of the university was so astonished by the queues before the hall that he asked what they were for; a colleague replied, 'I think they are a revival of learning, Mr. President.' The American visit was also the foundation of a number of firm friendships: with Felix Frankfurter, with Grace McCurdy and with the Lamonts. It established a connection — strengthened by the subsequent performance of Greek plays in his versions — with the United States that Murray never allowed to wither. When the lectures were published, President Theodore Roosevelt was added to the American circle of admirers and friends. The author himself sent copies to over three dozen friends and colleagues in the United States, Great Britain and Europe, including some who, like Andrew Lang and T.W. Allen in Oxford, strongly disagreed with Murray over the Homeric question. Jane Ellen Harrison had read the lectures in manuscript, for it was upon her work on Greek religion that the lecturer drew most heavily for his account of the Greeks. J.W. Mackail read the proofs.

The book was a 'popular' one, originating as it did in lectures delivered to an educated audience, although not necessarily one composed of those who read Greek. The lectures were heard, and the book read, by many who, knowing no Greek, yet were interested in poetry and literary criticism. Hence the reviews, when it appeared, came in as wide a range of newspapers and periodicals as the later notices of Max Reinhardt's production of *Oedipus*. The *Morning Post* said that 'few books on ancient literature are more suggestive or more delightful than this'. The *Yorkshire Post* employed a series of adjectives: imaginative, charming, vivid, vivacious, learned, bold, acute, convincing. The *Outlook* remarked that 'instead of confusion and fog of argument . . . he gives us a clear picture of dawning civilization'. The *Primitive Methodist Quarterly Review*, after describing Gilbert Murray as 'distinguished' and 'brilliant', went on: 'one quality . . . is Dr Murray's passionate belief in progress and enthusiasm for it. This is one of the things that makes him so sympathetic with the Greeks. He sees in that tiny people a white-hot centre of light . . . set in a world of horrible savagery.' Some had reservations. Margoliouth could not put the book down when he started to read it, but he offered no praise. The *Manchester Guardian*, although a Liberal paper, thought the lectures disjointed and unbalanced, and believed in more unity in Homer than did its author; but it liked the contrast of shining Hellenism with pitch-black circumjacent savagery, and also the idea of expurgations from a traditional book as moral progress occurred. The *Westminster Gazette* was more whole-heartedly unitarian: 'sorry, G.M., but you can't fool us — we know that the ancient Athenians were sexually immoral, in every conceivable way. Further, we know that the Iliad and the Odyssey were written by Homer, so away with your "schools of poets".'

This last criticism fastened upon two characteristics of the book. The first was that Murray explained away or ignored evidence about Greek society that he did not wish to accept: he abhorred, as Bowra later said, physical frankness. The second was that, although he had tried 'never to think about making a debating case . . . but always to set out honestly and what with much reflection really seems to me to be most like the truth', he had, as he acknowledged in his preface to the second edition, entertained the vain hope that he could walk in Homeric territory 'without arousing the old lions that lie wakeful behind most of the larger stones'. It is easier now, when political ideologies and religious faiths and the polarisation of politics engender so much heat, to understand that Greek scholars of Murray's day could be equally heated over the unitarian, the single-poet theory of Homer and over what the author in his second edition called the 'advanced' theory of textual criticism of the poems. The bitter argument among classical scholars was the counterpart of an even more bitter argument, also reflected by Murray himself in the Harvard lectures in *obiter dicta* on the *Pentateuch*, over the 'higher criticism' of the Bible. In both controversies the *odium theologicum* was immense. Murray heard the echoes of the classical bitterness. T.W. Allen, his Oxford colleague and rival, owned up to the review in *The Times Literary Supplement* where the editor had 'toned down' his criticisms. Andrew Lang directly told Murray that it 'beat' him how he could be on the one side and Butcher and himself on the other:

> Well, I don't think you have found bottom yet: and indeed I do not understand what your theory *is* . . . Lectures (I presume mainly to ladies) are a poor form: a man can't do his ideas justice . . . I don't see how, or where, I can have a shot at you: but I pine to criticize your totems and taboos, exogamy and female descent.

Many of the details of Murray's book — especially the historical account — have been overtaken by later scholarship, but that is the normal and proper course of scholarly argument. At the time it was published, it was a lucid and elegant description of much more technical discussions of a topic which had received a great deal of attention in the preceding half century. Murray was not partisan; he stated his conclusions and reflections reasonably and with moderation; his disagreements were courteous and restrained. The lions behind the Homeric rocks did not roar too fiercely. But even the subdued roars confirmed his belief that he was an original and controversial scholar, and by 1908 this had become something of great importance to him.

In June 1908, while on holiday at Kynance Cove, he heard the news that Ingram Bywater was to resign the Regius Chair of Greek in Oxford, and those who mentioned it to Gilbert thought that he was the obvious successor. His recent book on the Epic had made a great impact; the two volumes in the Oxford Classical Texts series had, despite some German criticism, established a respectable scholarly reputation; his translations, both on the stage and published, had established him as the foremost interpreter of Greece to his generation in England. His fame as a lecturer had spread from Glasgow, via the United States, while his recent classes at New College in Oxford had put him, as Housman put it, well on his way to taking that place in the public eye which used to be occupied by Benjamin Jowett at Balliol and then by Richard Jebb at Cambridge. He had gained a reputation as a man of affairs. But he was also identified with the particular radical section of the Liberal Party which was not that of the Liberal Prime Minister Asquith in whose gift the appointment lay.

Gilbert Murray thought himself the obvious choice for the Regius Chair and, although he had doubts of himself, he early decided that, if offered, he would accept it. At the beginning of June 1908 he believed that acceptance of the chair would mean a loss of freedom but a great opportunity for helping the study of Greek 'on good lines'. Since he was regarded as a 'heretic', the appointment would also mark the acceptance of his authority. When he listed the disadvantages he placed the Lady Mary's dislike of Oxford at their head, but he also felt his learning was not adequate; he read slowly and had no bibliography. His scholarship was as 'good as any-one's, but I had no notebooks' and knew none of the duties. He was too much in the habit of relying on his imagination and artistic faculties 'such as they are'. Nor was he competent, he thought, to guide other scholars. Still, he discovered his egotism was 'as sensitive as that plant generally is'; it did not like 'to suffer what has the appearance of a defeat by men whom I easily surpassed

twenty years ago'. On 21 June, L.R. Farnell called upon the Lady
Mary in Banbury Road. He explained that he had called upon a
'delicate personal matter' and went on to ask if her husband would
like the Regius Chair. T.W. Allen had asked him for a testimonial,
but Farnell had replied that an 'intimate friend' of his was in the
running and therefore he would not express an opinion. Lady
Mary, feeble and nervous as she was, formed the view that Farnell
thought himself of standing for the chair, but he told her that
Bywater had said Murray, J. Burnet of St Andrews and T.W. Allen
were possible successors. Farnell said 'we would all welcome your
husband's appointment', but, when Asquith came to the Gaudy
and consulted Balliol College, he thought that Balliol would 'go
strong for Burnet', and that the Prime Minister would lean to a
Balliol man. Lady Mary concluded that Allen was not really in it;
he was rude and lazy and hadn't 'come off'. For Burnet there
would be some backing as a good teacher who had conducted a
good seminar at St Andrews University, and as an excellent
organiser; but he was not a brilliant man and even Balliol would
not solidly back him. Gilbert Murray himself described Burnet as
'quite good, very good', and could have co-operated with him had
he been appointed to the Regius Chair: 'I could make Burnet a
chariot.' T.W. Allen would have been difficult: 'I do not respect
him enough.' In the watches of the night, Gilbert believed that he
himself was not fit for the Greek chair; he was neither learned nor
industrious enough, too diverse in his interests, but he saw no one
better. Although he believed he had no solid achievement, nothing
'which would entitle a man to be called a great scholar, I am not
ashamed; because I think in a way I have [been] faithful to
something — to some sort of Hellenism, some task of
interpretation and keeping alive'. Asquith thought so too. In
October 1908, after Gilbert's nerves and desires had gone up and
down, he offered the Regius Chair: 'I am certain your acceptance
of the post would be hailed with particular satisfaction by all those,
in Oxford and elsewhere, who value at its proper estimate the great
service which you have rendered to scholarship and humane
learning.'

Well [wrote Murray] it is a great post . . . and I must try to fill it
properly. That element of the artist in me which has helped my
work has also damaged it. I feel greatly how I lack Bywater's
solid control of the whole subject. And I have rather lost the

power of working at things that do not interest me.

The appointment to the Regius Chair at Oxford was welcomed not only by Murray's family and friends but also by those who had reservations. John Burnet wrote a handsome note saying that he was in many ways rather glad that the Prime Minister's choice had not fallen upon him and was in any case extremely glad that it had fallen upon one whom he could honestly and sincerely congratulate. The Conservative John Buchan said that the Liberal government had one act to its credit for which a bigoted Tory would always forgive them. Ingram Bywater wrote that it was a real satisfaction that Greek studies would be in stronger hands than his. Housman wrote warmly, comparing Murray with Jowett and Jebb and anticipating one of his own later witticisms: 'as you are a much better scholar than the one and a much better man of letters than the other, the public will be the gainer without knowing it and good judges (by which I mean myself) will be less at variance with the public'. Verrall and Jane Ellen Harrison, Cambridge friends and collaborators with Murray in his approach to the study of Greece, were naturally delighted; to have such a sympathiser and supporter in the Regius Chair in Oxford was of the first importance. Agnes Murray began her letter to her father: 'Joy, joy, joy. I am so glad . . . I used to think it was the Eggregious Professorship . . . I was pleasedest.' Lady Carlisle took her own line. The news came as no surprise for she had heard that Mr Asquith's mind was made up to honour and recognise the scholarship deemed too original by some, but she thought her son-in-law's fame lay in other directions:

> I hope the toilsome work as Professor will not take you from your real sphere. There are many learned Greek professors, there are few poets . . . But you wanted it so I do. Your needs are my needs, your ambitions are mine.

There were, however, reservations about the appointment in inconvenient quarters. Some Oxford colleagues were doubtful about Murray's originality and about his scholarship: they applied the adjective 'brilliant' — but not as a compliment; they meant 'unsound'. One of the immediate inconveniences was the location of the Regius Chair in Christ Church, the Oxford college which was also the Oxford cathedral. Dean Strong, the head of the foundation, wrote expressing the hope that Gilbert Murray would wish to become a Student (the equivalent of Fellow) of the college upon his election. The new professor was agreeable, although he was much attached to New College and was now to become a member of a foundation deeply ecclesiastical in its history, associations and fellowship. One of his new classics colleagues in Christ Church, S.G. Owen, achieved a marked degree of pettiness in his attitude to the new Regius Professor, raising difficulties over his rooms and available lecture rooms in the college which he justified by severe judgements upon Murray's scholarship. Still, Gilbert was not in fact a good college man. His interests were wider than college walls. As a teetotaller and vegetarian, he took no pleasure in dining at High Table nor in sitting over wine, drunk by other men but not by him, in the Senior Common Room, nor in ecclesiastical or conservative company. As Regius Professor he had no college tutorial links with Christ Church. His friendships with sympathetic colleagues such as Margoliouth and Fisher lay in New College where he had formed the habit of taking lunch and which made him an Honorary Fellow. Presently he made some friends in Christ Church — Dundas, Harrod, Masterman, for example — but, although he did his formal duty by attending college meetings, he did not do much more than that. When he thanked 'The House' for electing him to an Honorary Studentship upon his retirement from the chair in December 1936, he confessed that it was always an anxiety and a self-reproach to him that he had seen so little of members of the House during his Studentship, while the Dean felt it necessary to explain that, although there were contrary votes and voices at his election to an Honorary Studentship because of this apparent lack of interest, once there was a majority its view became the view of all the college. The matter was carried off gracefully, but the fact was that Gilbert Murray never limited his interests to the view from a college. His 'real sphere' was much wider and more diverse than that.

Election to the Regius Chair of Greek at Oxford, at the age of 42, with a tenure of almost 30 years before him, gave him a public position and an authority which previously he had not had. The post precluded tutorial teaching, except for the difficult circumstances of the war and its aftermath when Bowra, for example, had Murray as a tutor. It meant that his teaching was by way of the lecture, at which he excelled, through the seminar or advanced class, and through, after the First World War, postgraduate supervision. The post gave him the opportunity to reach a wider undergraduate audience and to impress upon small groups of the more advanced of them his own approach to Greek studies. For his Inaugural Lecture, prepared while he was staying at the Villa Splendide, Alassio, in December 1908 and delivered on 27 January 1909, he chose to speak on *The Interpretation of Ancient Greek Literature*.

Remedying the unfortunate omission from his Glasgow Inaugural almost 20 years earlier, Murray paid tribute to Jebb as well as to Ingram Bywater, his predecessor at Oxford, and then went on to define the duty of a Greek scholar. Research, he said, was a necessity to discover new things, but the main duty was not discoveries or new methods but to master and re-order existing knowledge. He detected a certain lack of guidance of young graduates which he planned to remedy by a seminar collectively to study and eventually to edit some small and interesting pieces of Greek literature; for example, Sallustius. To maintain the unity of the subject, he proposed seven or eight lectures with a wider scope in each Summer Term for those who had just taken Moderations, to be delivered by specialists on a particular theme. The range of Greek to be understood was much wider and vastly greater than it had been in Porson's day, but so were the new aids to knowledge: for example, E.B. Tylor's *Primitive Culture* and James Frazer's *Pausanias*. Greek religion was now a special subject; the days were gone when, as Housman said of Porson, once a passage of Greek would scan and construe, no further questions were asked of it. Of course one must not lose a grip on the *minutiae* of language and knowledge of books: that was the real foundation. The paleographer and the grammarian must help us to get the words right, but their meaning depended upon all kinds of other questions to be asked. We must strip the past naked of all false sentiment, admit the failure of Hellenic civilisation and the infection of primitive savagery. Greece was one of the highest moments of history. Greek scholars must see that it did not die, must show the higher evolution to progressive and eternal things, must make the effort to think as Plato thought. He quoted — incorrectly — the words of Wilamowitz before the same university which he had himself translated in 1908: 'we all know that ghosts will not speak until they have drunk blood, and we must give them the blood of our hearts.' That was the great sacrifice and privilege of a scholar's life. 'We stand between the living and the dead.'

In an Oxford where the serious classical scholars were then chiefly textual critics, this was a manifesto of a new direction, 'an excessively literary tinge' as Housman put it to Murray. It was a breath of fresh air that inspired many of the young, such as Arnold Toynbee who was present as a young undergraduate. From Jane Ellen Harrison it produced an ecstatic letter. When she received a copy of the text two days after it was delivered, she exclaimed: 'How *could* you say it was dull? . . . how the roomful of old Dryasdusts must have stirred and heaved . . . I am glad I was *not* there — I should have just given one long rapturous howl, and vanished.' Miss Harrison had discerned, in that Inaugural Lecture, that Gilbert Murray's interests were turning towards the study of religion. Shortly before he delivered the lecture he had privately written: 'As I grow old, I get to feel that I care for almost nothing except Liberalism or Christianity or something — the sort of religion you get in Tolstoy and, in a sense, in Ruskin.' Not, naturally, an interest in dogmatic Christian religion, but certainly an interest in the growth of the 'sense of God'.

Gilbert Murray had been an undergraduate at Oxford when anthropology seemed to be making astonishing revelations of primitive origins. E.B. Tylor was appointed to a newly created Readership in Anthropology in 1884, the year Gilbert went up to St John's, and Tylor, who exercised great influence over Andrew Lang and R.R. Marett, had shifted the emphasis in anthropological studies from primitive institutions to primitive religion, in part by his attack upon the work of Max Muller, hitherto the dominant figure in the study of philology which was one of Murray's special interests as an undergraduate. Tylor was preoccupied with survivals from primitive societies on the path of social evolution. This anthropological interest was already reflected in the preface to Murray's first book; he fully accepted the relevance of anthropology to classical studies, a necessary background to the classics as Andrew Lang had held. Because Tylor's emphasis, followed by Frazer, was upon primitive religion, Murray's interest in the relevance of anthropology necessarily meant that Greek religion was particularly significant to him, especially the origins and development of that religion.

What gave additional impetus to that interest was his acquaintance with Jane Ellen Harrison whom he first met at the Verralls when he was staying in Cambridge in March 1902. She explained to him the plan of her book *Prolegomena to the Study of Greek*

Religion which he thought 'very original and important'; he was honoured when she asked him to read part of it in typescript. When Murray went to Italy in 1903, Miss Harrison joined him at the Berensons' villa, *I Tatti*, near Florence, bringing with her the text for her companion to read in that 'over-brilliant' society which he found unpleasant because of its pagan ethos and malicious gossip, and which reduced Miss Harrison to tears through its impious treatment of Tennyson's poetry. Reading the proofs, he thought she was a remarkable writer, but her views often struck him as foolish, 'like Aunt Fanny trying to be naughty', although 'in many ways she is so clever'. Always setting a high value on originality, Murray was impressed by Miss Harrison's approach to primitive Greek society and contributed to her book an appendix on the Orphic tablets, the inscribed prayers, some of which they examined together in Naples in March 1903, in order to illustrate her thesis.

Jane Ellen Harrison was a classical archeologist. In her *Prolegomena* in 1903 she began by explaining that the habit of viewing Greek religion through Greek literature had produced a fundamental error, because the poems of Homer were not primitive; he was a culmination, not a beginning. The origins of religion, reappearing in poets later than Homer, especially in Aeschylus, were to be found in rituals which existed long before the Olympian gods. These rites of primitive society, she explained, existed to promote fertility by the purgation or purification of evil, by averting the malevolence of demons which in such societies were made in the image of man's own savage and irrational passions. To this primitive stratum in Greece was added the religion of an immigrant god, Dionysus; on to the worship of an old god of vegetation was grafted the worship of a spirit of intoxication and a belief that first through wine and later through spiritual ecstasy a human man could become divine. This cult might have retained its primitive savagery but for another religious impulse associated with the name Orpheus, another immigrant god from Crete, and perhaps ultimately from Egypt, who brought a religion of spiritual association. Orphism added the doctrine of the possibility of complete union with the divine so that man could become immortal. This doctrine was expressed in the Orphic tablets. When what she called the 'puppet show of the Olympians', the gods of Homer, was played out, the two gods of the Orphics, Dionysus and Eros, remained potent in the Dionysian rituals. To these gods the playwright

Euripides in particular paid respect, while he attacked the Olympians; and to Euripides' *Bacchae*, in Murray's translation, the authoress paid the tribute that, in trying to understand the religion of Dionysus, it was to that play she owed most.

Miss Harrison's view of the development of Greek religion had close affinities with Murray's own general view: it looked for origins and survivals; it assumed an evolution and moral progress; it suggested the connection between Greek drama and religion. She acknowledged her travelling companion's help, although it is impossible now to know exactly how great that was. Certainly she later explained that if you gave anything to Murray to read he would say: 'Yes, very good. I like that,' and then re-write it. But in 1903 there was scarcely time in Italy for any such major revision by Murray; at most he may have offered suggestions to remove or improve those things he regarded as foolish. Miss Harrison's influence upon Murray's work on Greek religion is clear. To one who was primarily concerned with the literature, as illuminated by the light of anthropology, she supplied an archeological dimension and an early acquaintance with the work of Durkheim and Bergson under whose influence she herself avowedly wrote. Murray applied her findings to Greek tragedy. In *The Rise of the Greek Epic* the debt, as he wrote, was visible, and it continued to grow.

Jane Ellen Harrison had neither the mind nor the temperament to let her views stagnate; on the contrary, in so enthusiastic a spirit, her beliefs grew and developed. What she had first suggested as a connection between ritual and drama in 1903 had by 1907, in her second edition, become a conviction, for she had by then found confirmation not only from Émile Durkheim's work but also from Henri Bergson's. She then saw that Dionysus was an instinctive attempt to express 'that life which is one, indivisible and yet ceaselessly changing', whereas the Olympians were merely literary inventions. The discovery of the *Hymn of the Kouretes* tablet showed her that a group-emotion towards life must underlie all primitive religious representation. The *Hymn*, sung by the Kouretes, invoked a *daimon*, a spirit, the greatest *Kouros*, and was accompanied by a magical dance to commemorate or anticipate a New Birth. The Dithyramb which was concerned with the New Birth was the origin of drama, for this ritual of spring, the renewal of the year, produced both the athletic contests and the drama contest which were such prominent features of Greek civilisation. The victor in the greatest of these, the Olympic Games, became the *daimon* of the year. From this conception Miss Harrison coined the name which became famous, or perhaps infamous, among classical scholars: the *Eniautos-Daimon*, the Year Spirit who was the victor incarnate as the *daimon* of the group and the 'luck' of the year. She did not like the translation 'Year Spirit', but of its existence in Greek religion she had no doubt. From the rituals of the 'Year Spirit' she derived Greek tragedy, as opposed to the origin propounded by her old Cambridge teacher, Sir William Ridgeway, who found it in the funeral ceremonies held at the grave of some hero or chieftain.

The ensuing controversy was bitter. It divided classical scholars. Murray, accepting the *Eniautos-Daimon*, ranged himself with the 'ritualists'. Indeed, he did more. He contributed an *excursus* in *Themis*, the book published by Miss Harrison in 1912, on 'The Ritual Forms Preserved in Greek Tragedy'. In this he assumed — an advance on his theory in 1897 that tragedy derived from the goat-song — that tragedy was in origin a ritual dance, in origin that of Dionysus, performed at his feast, in his theatre, under the presidency of his priest, by performers who were called *Dionuson technitai*. Dionysus in this connection was an *Eniautos-Daimon*, a vegetation god who represents the cyclical death and re-birth of the earth and the world, i.e. for practical purposes the tribe's own lands and the tribe itself. Comedy and tragedy he now traced to different stages in the life of this Year Spirit: comedy led to his marriage feast, tragedy to his death. And he supported this acceptance of Jane Ellen Harrison's belief by reference to the work of another of her friends and supporters, Francis Cornford, who had written the *Origin of Attic Comedy*. Together these three scholars and another Cambridge don, A.B. Cook, made up the group which has been labelled the 'Cambridge ritualists'.

Yet, Murray was never completely a follower of Miss Harrison's whole-hearted beliefs. He still recognised the non-Dionysiac elements in tragedy; it was influenced by the epic, by hero cults and by other non-Dionysiac ceremonies. Still, he believed a pattern was common to all vegetation rituals of primitive people: an *Agon* — the year's contest against its enemy, summer against winter; a *Pathos*, the sacrificial death or tearing to pieces; a Messenger who comes to announce the death; a *Threnos* or lamentation; an *Anagnorisis*, a discovery or recognition of the slain; a *Theophany*, the resurrection of the slain in glory. He discerned this pattern in the plays of Euripides. He also naturally discerned it in the central event of the Christian religion (as an argument against an actual historical event of a Resurrection) and, more remarkably, in *Hamlet* which was the subject of his Shakespeare Lecture to the British Academy in 1914. Nevertheless, between Jane Ellen Harrison and Gilbert Murray there was one important difference. She was interested in ritual, rather than in religion. He was fascinated by these 'beastly devices of the heathen', but each one was 'somehow touched with beauty and transformed by some spirit of upward striving'. So, when he followed his Inaugural precept of seeking to re-order and re-interpret existing knowledge rather than to pursue new knowledge for himself, he concentrated upon Greek religion, not rituals, in the lectures he prepared to deliver at Columbia University in 1912, upon his second visit to the United States.

Those lectures were the basis of *Four Stages of Greek Religion* published in 1912. Murray believed that the great literary works of Greek imagination were habitually penetrated by religious conceptions and postulates not obvious to the reader until such work as Jane Ellen Harrison's had been done. Nevertheless, he thought that she had made the title 'Olympian' a term of reproach, a challenge to the canonical gods of Homer and of Greece. He proposed 'to explain their historical origin and plead for their religious value'. Murray accepted that there was a first stage, an Age of Ignorance or *Urdummheit*, which evolved to the second, Olympian, stage which was, after all, Hellenism: the antithesis of savagery and barbarism, the victory of man over beast which was a moral expurgation of the old rites, an attempt to bring order into chaos, an adaptation to the new social needs of the city as opposed to the countryside. The Olympian stage failed to achieve moral expurgation, or an order which would have led to monotheism, or to provide a universal religion for the cities. But it was a vital force, 'a type to the world of beauty and freedom and high endeavour'. The failure of the Olympic gods, improvement as they were on rustic barbarism, to become the religion of the cities led to the Greek 'failure of nerve', a phrase Murray had borrowed long ago in Glasgow from J.P. Bury to account for the decline of Greek civilisation. Now Murray used it to describe a rise of asceticism, of mysticism, of pessimism: a loss of self-confidence in normal human effort, a cry for infallible revelation. This was the stage he regarded as a preparation for Christianity in which stage people believed that they possessed supernatural knowledge. This was followed by his fourth stage in which there was a 'last Protest', the pagan reaction of the fourth century A.D. as epitomised by Sallustius' treatise, *About God and The World*, in which Julian the Apostate believed one great truth: the presence and glory of the gods who, no doubt ultimately one, manifested themselves under conditions of form, time and personality. A religious system like that was built of 'much noble life and strenuous thought and a steady passion for the knowledge of God'.

Murray believed that, in publishing his Columbia lectures, he had written a book on the Greek sense of god, tracing an evolution from primitive savagery to the classical pagan ideal described in Sallustius' treatise which he included in full, in translation, in the published book. By 'god' he did not mean the God of Christian theology whom he thought to be narrow, authoritarian and cruel, but rather the 'faith at the back' of all the myths, 'the great region in which you must be agnostic, but nevertheless you must have something like conviction'. This was a far cry from the *Eniautos -Daimon* which preoccupied Miss Harrison, however much Murray accepted her interpretation of the earliest Greek rituals. He was fascinated, in the climate of anthropological discoveries, by origins and survivals. That approach was, until B. Malinowski and A.R. Radcliffe-Brown published their anthropological field researches in 1922, the great theme of anthropology. Gilbert Murray, nevertheless, had a harder-edged intellect than Miss Harrison. Accepting her work, he looked at it from the wider perspective of his own mastery of the Greek literary sources and from the still wider perspective of his belief in moral evolution — hence his use of the characteristic word 'stages' — and progress. That was why, in 1925, he discovered yet a fifth stage in Greek religion between the Olympians and the 'failure of nerve': the stage of decline from the fourth century. What Miss Harrison's work on primitive Greek religion offered him was the intellectual excitement of new confirmatory evidence of the unity of his scholarly, political and moral beliefs. What he offered it was his unrivalled skill as the interpreter of Greece to a far wider audience than that which read Jane Harrison's books. It was Gilbert Murray who launched the *Eniautos-Daimon* on the Greekless world. And paid a penalty.

Mackail, having read *Four Stages*, was not convinced that there was such a thing as Greek religion, whether indeed one could rationally speak of Greek religion at all. 'Of course it is a convenient phrase and avoids circumlocution: yet I am not sure

that the convenience is not bought too dear.' The real penalty for
Murray was not that. Rather was it the method: the application of
anthropological studies to classical. For, whatever the intellectual
excitement created by the 'new' science in the last quarter of the
nineteenth and the first decade of the twentieth centuries, the comparative method was, in the 1920s, abandoned and despised by a
new generation of anthropologists. Falling into professional
disrepute, especially under the 'functional' influence of
Malinowski who rejected 'survivals' and condemned the historical
approach in social anthropology, the application of 'dated' anthropological theories to Greek studies also brought the latter into
disrepute. One or two of Murray's contemporaries had always had
reservations. Wilamowitz and Verrall never cared for the
approach. The young John Shepperd, reviewing *Four Stages* for
the *Classical Review*, took Miss Harrison's work as a serious
scholarly attempt to analyse Greek religion but had doubts about
Murray's more literary account which he believed to pile hypothesis
upon hypothesis. Gilbert Murray's brother, Hubert, went further.
As a governor interested in the practical application of anthropology in colonial administration, he welcomed his brother's
interests in the 'beastly devices of the heathen', but he described
anthropology as 'a most fascinating study, though . . . purely
fantastic; the alleged facts being unsupported by evidence and the
inferences forced'. He detested the Year-Daimon. This fraternal
judgement upon the social anthropology of classicists like Frazer
and Tylor is misleading. Hubert Murray, from his career in Papua,
was familiar with the anthropology of those natural scientists, such
as C.G. Seligman and A.C. Haddon, who had moved away from
emphasis on origins and survivals to the actual examination in the
field of existing primitive societies, not as stages along the path of
social evolution but as contemporary societies, as valid a social
organisation in their own place and circumstances as European
ones.

Such a comparative judgement of societies had little appeal to
Gilbert Murray. Convinced of evolutionary social and moral
progress, he made absolute judgements. Barbarism was always
horrible, never excusable, never to be tolerated or accepted by
civilised men and women. The clinging remnants of the primaeval
swamp might be interesting, but only as a measure of progress. The
Year-Daimon was one such measure which he never doubted until
the very end of his life. In 1915 he defended the 'ritualists', with

whom he identified himself, against the attack by Ridgeway whom he privately thought to be so polemical, 'never to be seeking for truth, but only to slay his opponents' that 'he cannot ever be right'. In particular, he said that when Ridgeway asserted that the Year or Vegetation Spirit was an abstraction and that abstractions were not worshipped by simple folk, he was 'beating the air'. Of course the term was an abstraction 'invented by us to describe the object of certain classes of worship', but so was any invocation by peasants in charms for wheat or fruit growing; whatever the name they called upon, they were invoking a Vegetation Spirit; whatever the historical or unhistorical person thus called upon, he was acting as a Vegetation Spirit. To this belief Murray remained, against all attacks, committed until the end of his life. In 1956, when asked to revise his article on the origins of Greek drama for the latest edition of the *Encyclopaedia Britannica*, he wondered whether his view needed restatement, whether he might not have been carried away by his enthusiasm for 'the A.B. Cook/Frazer/Jane Harrison discoveries'. But for most of his scholarly life he had no such doubts. Shining Hellenism had grown out of pitch-black savagery. Progress was a fact.

By 1912, when *Four Stages of Greek Religion* was published, Gilbert Murray had established a great reputation with an educated audience in Great Britain and the United States. The coincidence of his scholarly views with his social and political faith, the assurance this lent to his message, carried conviction with an audience as diverse as Lord Bryce and Harold Laski, Theodore Roosevelt and Oliver Wendell Holmes. Still, this was a select audience of those who knew Greek or something of Greece, and Murray aimed beyond that. He wished also to reach an audience which knew no Greek and was still seeking its education. Hence his involvement in 1910 with the Home University Library series of little books to be published by Williams and Norgate. Murray became one of three general editors, the other two being H.A.L. Fisher and J. Arthur Thomson of Aberdeen. The initiative came from Williams who, describing the project as one of epoch-making importance, invited Murray to become a general editor of the proposed series of 100 volumes designed to answer Sir George Reed's question: 'when will a literature be established to satisfy the legitimate intellectual curiosity of Young England?' Williams explained to Murray that the idea was a low-priced series of studies of the great periods of history, literature and art, the latest phases and conceptions of science, philosophy and religion, and the best information on economics and practical affairs. He wanted Murray's name as a guarantee of the high spirit of this enterprise, in publishing for the first time a comprehensive series of original books for the under-privileged reader. It was an appeal Murray could not resist. The editorial fee was fixed at 350 guineas, for which he undertook to read all the volumes but to deal editorially only with those within his special field.

The first ten volumes appeared in the spring of 1911, the second ten in the following June. Among them were those written by Murray's friends: John Masefield on Shakespeare, Hobhouse on Liberalism, Margoliouth on Mohammedanism, Hobson on the Science of Wealth. The series was warmly welcomed by *The Times Literary Supplement*. Having praised the idea of an attractive series, the reviewer remarked that 'not one falls below a high standard of interest'. By October 1913, the first group of ten volumes had sold almost a quarter of a million copies, and all of the early groups of books were well over the hundred thousand mark. Of the individual volumes, Hilaire Belloc's sold over 37,000 and Ramsay MacDonald's over 28,000.

The undoubted success of the Home University Library series meant more work for a general editor than he had bargained for. In April 1911 he was being asked to read the proofs of a volume on *Crime and Insanity* and to send his comments to the author. He was actively engaged in the search for new authors (for example in trying to induce G.M. Trevelyan to contribute), and in correspon-dence with Edwyn Bevan who wrote one of the most distinguished volumes of the series on Christianity. Above all, he was engaged in writing his own volume upon Euripides. The publishers had doubts about this particular topic when it was first suggested in 1913 — it gave them a slight tremor — but they felt it so important immediately to have a book from Gilbert Murray that, if he wanted to write it, then he ought to, although they insisted the title should not simply be Euripides. When the book appeared as *Euripides and His Age*, it sold ten thousand copies within the year. It said, brilliantly and concisely, what he had earlier written on Greek drama, religion and the playwright himself; and in that particular series it reached the young and the Greekless, to fire the interest even of those who later came to disagree with Murray's image of Euripides and of Athens.

Nevertheless, to the burden of editorial work connected with the series, there came to be added financial worries. In spite of the large sales, Williams and Norgate needed the capital the series took for other parts of their business in May 1914. Gilbert had thought in October 1912 of resigning his editorship after the first 100 volumes were out because of the pressure of the work, but with the financial threat he stayed on to help set up the Home University Library Company. Some of his friends took debentures in the enterprise; Sir Edward Grey took up 400 in February 1914; Walter Leaf subscribed £500, as did Murray himself. With the war, however, the finances remained shaky and the future doubtful. Even when sales boomed again in 1924, Williams and Norgate were unable to continue and in November 1928 the series was taken over by Thornton Butterworth. The general editors agreed to remain on an annual retainer of £50 until the series was back on a paying basis. It never achieved that, but Gilbert Murray remained as a general editor when the books passed to Oxford University Press in 1941 and their salesmen began to do very well with the books in the schools. This was precisely the audience Murray had initially hoped for, the intention of the series. 'Fisher and I hope to make it the vulgarest and most successful thing ever seen in the publishing trade.' It was the readership he himself obtained for *Euripides and His Age*.

That book was an extension of Murray's writing. It was a frankly popular exposition, without footnotes or critical apparatus, for an audience neither classically educated nor necessarily educated at all. His earlier books, although elegant surveys of major themes rather than detailed works intended for fellow classicists, yet supposed some acquaintance with Greek or at least Greek civilisation. None of these books helped Murray's reputation with some of his fellow scholars in Oxford. Those who, like S.G. Owen, doubted the Regius Professor's 'soundness', did not recommend their pupils to attend his lectures. Others, with more justification, shared his own view that he did not get his pupils very good classes in their examinations. Yet others regarded him as a 'snake in the grass' because in 1910, when the debate raged in Oxford about the abolition of compulsory Greek at entrance, the Regius Professor was at first against compulsion. Only when schoolmasters told him that abolition would result in schools teaching Greek only to specialists did he change his opposition. He believed that young men who had been stuffed with classics at school came to hate the subject at university. He and the Professor of Astronomy proposed a compromise by which Greek at entrance should be required only of those who, apart from Moderations and Greats, were to read History, English or Modern Languages for their degree. His support of abolition displeased some of his colleagues in the faculty; in their view he betrayed the classics when it came to the vote in Congregation which could alter the university statutes. His support of compromise displeased the abolitionists who wanted even Greats without Greek. Compulsory entrance Greek was finally abolished in Oxford, with Murray's support, in 1920, but by that time he had established his position as the foremost Hellenist in England.

Whatever the Oxford critics might say of his scholarship, he was a good teacher to the young. When, during the war and its aftermath, because of the shortage of teachers, he was allowed to tutor undergraduates, he was remarkable. He firmly corrected their Greek prose and verse with such comments as 'I like that' or 'I prefer mine here', then reading his own version in lucid Attic, and only occasionally resorting to gentle irony with a student who produced wooden hexameters: 'have you been reading Quintus Smyrnaeus lately?' Not everyone responded, but the best students profited. In his seminar class he stimulated interest, although, as Eric Dodds recalled, he might pursue a point with an old pupil like Janet Spens to the mystification of the others present. In his lectures in the pre-war years he transformed a dull grind into an exciting experience, although not necessarily one very relevant to examinations. As a teacher, Murray made Greek live for under-graduates of the pre-First World War generation, and he had a lasting effect through his pupils: through Dodds who succeeded him in the Regius Chair in 1936, through Dundas whose election as a Student he secured at Christ Church, through Bowra whose election to a Fellowship he influenced at Wadham. Gilbert Murray's return to Oxford set a direction in Greek studies there, and stimulated an interest in Greece and Greek studies well beyond the university. As prophesied by Housman, he had indeed come to take the place in the public eye occupied by Benjamin Jowett and Richard Jebb in the two previous generations.

ORDEAL OF A GENERATION

If Gilbert Murray's tenure of the Regius Chair at Oxford had given him public recognition as the foremost Hellenist in Britain, his standing in public life was never dependent upon that post. There have been Regius Professors whose reputations have never extended beyond their professional colleagues. But Murray was independently a man of letters and of the theatre. Moreover, his radical Liberal principles and his marriage into a great political family necessarily involved him in public affairs. His academic standing was recognised by his Fellowship of the British Academy in 1910, a Trusteeship of the British Museum in succession to Sir William Anson in 1914, and appointment to the Council of the British School in Rome in the following year. These last two appointments were in the Prime Minister's gift, and, while they honoured Murray's formal position, they too recognised an eminence other than that of his professorship. Asquith, indeed, offered greater political recognition. In the parliamentary crisis over the House of Lord's rejection of the Budget in 1910/11, Murray's name was on the Prime Minister's list of peers to be created had it become necessary to 'swamp' the Lords, although Lady Mary, with an old aristocrat's dislike of new titles, threatened to leave him if he accepted. In 1912, when the Prime Minister offered a knighthood in the Birthday Honours List, Murray declined, with his wife's strong approval; neither of them would have welcomed a title and they both disliked Asquith's brand of Liberalism.

What this combination of academic status and public eminence, together with Murray's strong sense of duty to Humanity and Progress might have led to, is an interesting, if hypothetical question. It is unlikely that Murray would have followed the example of Herbert Fisher into a vice-chancellorship, for in Oxford he displayed little interest in faculty, university, or college administration. His strong concept of public duty rather took the form of public persuasion, of influencing public opinion and public taste, of public education in the broadest sense of the word. He might, in short, have remained the eminent man of letters. That he became an eminent man of public affairs was the result of what he called the 'ordeal of this generation'.

In retrospect, the First World War has come to seem to western Europeans an ever more savage scar across modern history: at worst the ruin of civilised Europe; at best the origin of a predicament from which there has been no escape. Obviously that war decisively changed many lives. Obviously, too, the shock of the war was peculiarly great for a sensitive, civilised man of letters who hated physical cruelty, whose nerves could be shattered by the sight of cruelty to animals, and who believed so deeply that Progress was a fact. But, shock though the actual coming of war was, unthinkable as it had seemed in civilised European society, the horror of what was happening was perceived only gradually as the war went on, and the profound consequences of the war later still.

In June 1914 Gilbert Murray was on holiday at Beckhythe Manor, Overstrand, a country house in Norfolk which the Murrays had acquired in the previous year in order to establish a household for their youngest son, Stephen, whose health was believed to be weak. In that summer of 1914, Gilbert was flying kites with his son, playing tennis with guests like 'Sandy' Lindsay who came to stay, preparing the text of his Shakespeare Lecture to the British Academy on 'Hamlet and Orestes' for the press, translating *Alcestis*, and complaining that the actor Martin Harvey had so delayed the American production of *Oedipus* that the contract had been broken and Harvey was now trying to get reduced terms from him. Only on 23 July did he describe the crisis as 'rather more puzzling, but not, I think, quite so bad as it seemed at first'. He added: 'I think it is all old Asquith's doing, not that of a cabal in the palace forcing Asquith's hand.' Two days later he met Mrs Winston Churchill and Lady Gwendolyn who, in the same unapprehensive spirit, had secured orders to view all the houses to let in the neighbourhood and were going over them just for fun. A day or two later still, he was asked to sign a declaration in favour of British neutrality in the case of a war between the Powers, and as a Radical he did so without hesitation. For he did not believe that there would or could be a war. His confidence was shaken only in the following week, but he still had reservations about British policy in the hands of such imperialists as Asquith and Grey. The actual outbreak of the war came as a dreadful shock, but his doubts about British policy were not resolved until, sitting in the Distinguished Strangers' Gallery at the House of Commons on 3 August, he heard Sir Edward Grey's famous speech. The calm reason and moderation of the Foreign Secretary commanded his intellectual and temperamental assent, and at that point he parted company with his radical friends.

Some of those radical friends, notably his wife's cousin Bertrand Russell and his old student Noel Brailsford, were shocked by Murray's strong support for the war; but they should not have been surprised. Gilbert Murray was never a pacifist, and he always regretted the association of radical causes with pacificism because the latter damaged the former in public opinion. After 3 August 1914 he was absolutely clear that the war was justified; and with that intellectual conviction, as always with Murray, came action. He had been a member of the Oxford Volunteers as an undergraduate; now he became, in his own words, an aged Lance Corporal in 'Godley's own' Oxford militia unit. Rupert Brooke, a friend of his daughter Rosalind, had the pleasing fancy of Gilbert Murray and his English professorial colleague, Walter Raleigh, practising dawn rushes across the fields and hedgerows of Oxfordshire, but the Lady Mary and Gilbert's doctor put a stop to this in 1915. Gilbert's real war effort — in spite of gaining a 'first class' in rapid fire — lay in other directions. As the war went into September 1914 he told his wife that as a sensitive man of letters, he became

> utterly abased and crushed by the misery of the war, feeling that the death and maiming and starving of Germans and Austrians is just as horrible a thing as the same suffering in Englishmen. But mostly I do feel strung up and exalted by a feeling of the tremendous issue and the absolute duty that lies upon us to save Europe and humanity. We did not know, until the war revealed it, what this German system meant. Once it is revealed, I do feel that we must strike it down or die.

He, like his brother Hubert far away in Papua, wished he was younger and could be 'in it', and as he became angry, his nerves on edge with the daily bad news of the initial German advance through Belgium and its accompanying policy of frightfulness, and the apparent failure of the Allies to hit back, he began to wish that trouble-makers could be dealt with: 'why doesn't K of K put Carson in irons?' But it was Bertrand Russell who, in the event, went to prison: Murray's friend and relation by marriage, whom Gilbert came to regard in 1914 as 'such a sophist'. His initial war effort was to combat such men in print.

In August 1914, Murray contributed an article to the *Hibbert Journal*: 'How can war ever be right?' His answer was that a war could be just. 'Of course we have our faults, but we are not creating Blood and Iron into a system.' In an Oxford Pamphlet published in 1914, he explained that he hated war, not simply for its cruelty and its folly, but as the enemy of all the causes he had championed. He did not, however, believe that he had changed any of his opinions in holding that the war against Germany was right; to the contrary, he believed that to have remained neutral would have been, in his own words, 'a failure in public duty'. Germany — or some party in Germany — had plotted the war beforehand. To the counter-argument that to do almost infinite evil for a doubtful chance of attaining something which half the people think good but the other half think bad was neither good morals nor good sense, he replied that war was not such a profit-and-loss account: 'in some causes it is better to fight and be broken than to yield peacefully . . . the mere act of resisting to the death is in itself a victory.' Honour and dishonour were real things, and the honour of one's country went to the root of the whole concept of citizenship. Belgium and the British obligation to it was the point of national honour with which national interest, defined by Murray as the 'observation of public law and the rights of nations', coincided.

After hearing Grey on 3 August, Murray returned to the Woodstock Road house in Oxford. He found that the town was to have a big base hospital, and was in the middle of preparations for the enormous casualties which the fighting in Belgium indicated. Soon he was writing to the Director General of the Army Medical Department, offering the Overstrand house as a convalescent centre, but chiefly he began to work upon a pamphlet on the origins of war. He read the Russian Yellow Book which 'exactly bears out our White Paper'. He read the documents published by the other governments. At the beginning of September he attended a meeting of eminent writers who might counter the organised German press and lecture campaign in neutral countries, and he signed the ensuing manifesto. By the end of September, he had reached the end of the writing of his pamphlet on *The Foreign Policy of Sir Edward Grey*. It was published by the Clarendon Press in mid-1915, and it promptly involved Murray in a family as well as a public quarrel with earlier friends. In his introduction, he particularly singled out for critical comment two pamphlets published by E.D. Morel's Union of Democratic Control, written by Bertrand

Russell and by Noel Brailsford. These high-minded and very clever men, who believed that German actions were understandable and excusable and that the responsibility for the war lay with other governments than the German, but especially with the British, and that the true British interest was to stand aside, were, in Murray's words, 'not at present in a state of mind which enables them to see or even to seek the truth'. In the hundred pages which followed, Murray set out to lay the truth before his readers.

He began with a *resumé* of the events of the twelve days preceding the outbreak of war, from which he passed to an examination of the criticism of Grey and of British policy for its vacillation, especially on the question of British neutrality over Belgium and over its course of action if France, not Belgium, were attacked by Germany. In dealing with British relations with France, Murray examined the accusation that Grey had concluded a secret alliance with the latter, a charge which he dismissed as a 'romantic hypothesis', completely disproved by Grey's offer of 31 July that, if Germany would get from Austria 'any reasonable proposal', the Foreign Secretary would press its acceptance at St Petersburg and at Paris and, if Russia and France did not accept it, then the British would have nothing to do with the consequences of their rejection. Such a letter, concluded Murray, 'could not possibly have been written by one who was "unconditionally bound" to France'. Although he acknowledged that staff talks had occurred which accounted for the present dispositions of the British and French fleets, these did not constitute a 'secret' engagement. He could see the case against the whole policy of such *ententes* but, if the policy was good, then the staff conversations were also good policy. In his next section, on the eight years preceding the war, he set out to show that for any Liberal there was always a problem in foreign policy: suspicion of intrigue, of the assertion of 'interests', of dangerous familiarity with force or fraud, of silken phrases as a cover for brutal facts. Foreign politics, by contrast with home politics in which you worked with friends for ideals, looked like the relations between so many bands of outlaws. Nevertheless, the principles laid down by Grey — no extension of British territories, the removal of frictions and the establishment of cordial relations with neighbours — these were such that any Liberal could accept. Murray even defended 'secret' treaties, although the Moroccan one of 1904, the object of so much attack by those who suspected British diplomacy, had indeed been concluded by Grey's

Conservative predecessor, Lord Lansdowne. That treaty, Murray explained, was different from other secret treaties, because when 'civilised Powers are dealing with a Power which is uncivilised, misgoverned, torn by disorder and rebellion and very nearly bankrupt, all history shows that it may be impossible, even with the best will in the world, to preserve the independence of that Power'. You could not, said Murray, make a public treaty because the clear expression of what you would do would tend in itself to bring about the circumstances in which you would have to do it. To make no treaty at all would cause friction, not remove it. Therefore, *faute de mieux*, a secret treaty was necessary. To the objection that the people of Morocco had not been consulted, Murray replied that there was always a tragedy in relations between civilised and uncivilised nations, but that 'civilised man, at his best, can do great things for uncivilised man'. When, in 1911, there was the further Moroccan crisis between France and Germany, during which a warning was given by the British Liberal Chancellor of the Exchequer, Lloyd George, in his Mansion House speech, Murray found the sentiments unexceptionable and the language polite. More important, the speech had the desired effect: the crisis blew over. Along the same lines of clear, firm speaking in foreign policy, Murray similarly found the 1907 Treaty by which Britain settled its disputes with Russia to be a reasonable and honest agreement which put an end to constant friction, suspicion and intrigue, and set limits to the freedom to interfere with another decaying empire, that of Persia. In all of these years preceding the war, he found that, from the standpoint of common sense and of international idealism, Sir Edward Grey's principles were 'triumphantly right'. What was wrong was German *Weltpolitik*: the bid for power in Europe as a means to *Weltmacht*, power in the world. On this policy, believed Murray, basing himself upon the actual words of German military theorists, Pan-Germans and moderate and responsible Germans alike were all agreed. A policy of reasonable and pacific common sense, such as was actually followed by Grey, could achieve little in the face of what the Germans wanted; and what they wanted could eventually and rightly only be resisted by war. 'There is an extreme degree of proved iniquity in a government which would justify other nations in declaring war on it, even if their own interests were not affected.'

Gilbert Murray's pamphlet can be regarded as the orthodox defence of Grey and British policy, but it would be truer to say that, other than Grey's own in the House of Commons, it was the first systematic defence of British policy after war had broken out, and that, whatever similar defences later followed, it was the first published justification based upon a careful reading of the different coloured books published by a number of governments. Murray had not been an admirer of Sir Edward Grey nor of the policies which he and the other Liberal 'imperialists', Asquith and Haldane, had in the past proclaimed. Nor had he simply adopted the official Foreign Office view. Although he sent the draft of the book to the Office, through his friend William Archer who had gone to work there during the war, to seek corrections or additions, he in fact received none until the book was already published. When he sent it to Grey himself on 8 July 1915, he assumed that it would seem inadequate and superficial to one who knew much more of the events than he did, but he had made a careful study of the available material and he believed that Grey's critics — that 'grumbling old ass', E.D. Morel, and those 'sophists', 'Bertie and Co' — had not. He did not expect the critics to like it. He assumed that Bertie and Brailsford would forge their thunderbolts in reply; and Russell did indeed publish an attack on the book which completely prejudiced his relations with Lady Mary who publicly upbraided him on a railway station. But the basis of Russell's reply was not at root an argument about the interpretation of the available documents; rather was it an argument against foreign policy as such: an argument not about historical detail but about principles. What Russell attacked was Murray's pragmatic choice between greater and lesser evils. Privately he wrote to Murray that he felt 'our friendship still lives in the eternal world, whatever may happen to it here and now. And I too can say God bless you.'

The origins of the First World War have been a continuing historical controversy down to the present day and scholars have, of course, had access to far more material than Murray had in 1914. In particular, German *Weltpolitik* has largely figured in the Fritz Fischer controversy, while the significance of the Anglo-French staff talks and the extent to which Grey kept his cabinet colleagues informed of them have also been a matter of argument. Nevertheless, given the speed of its writing and the occasion of its publication, it is fair to say that Murray's main argument would still receive some respectable scholarly support, while his principles of foreign policy would also receive some assent. What is also remarkable about his little book, given the strong feelings he undoubtedly had, is the care he took to state the objections to British policy before he answered them, and the care he took, as with Russell, to preserve friendships despite the differences he had with radical friends. Morley, for example, who resigned from the government when Britain entered the war, and who had earlier been the Liberal leader Murray most preferred, could not stomach the British commitment through France to Russia in 1914. Nevertheless, Murray wrote sympathetically to Morley who responded that, in spite of their differences of opinion, Gilbert's letter had given him little but pleasure: 'The tone of it marks affectionate friendship.' Murray was very firm in his opinion that the war must be fought to a successful conclusion, and strong in his public support of a government about which he had had doubts and hesitations as a radical, but he never failed in sympathy and understanding for those whom he opposed. The war was the clearest indication of his capacity to hold firm opinions and yet deal fairly with opponents.

Murray's position on the war itself was one of the few occasions in which he was on the clear majority side, an unusual situation for him. While he never wavered in his view of the need to win, agreeing with Grey that the essential thing was to upset Prussian Junkerdom, he nevertheless still found himself in minority positions about particular policies during the war, particularly after the fall of Asquith's wartime government and the formation of the coalition government in December 1916. Until the Liberal government fell Murray could give it whole-hearted support, to the point of humorously describing himself to his wife as a 'party hack', although in the Convocation at Oxford he was still one of the minority which voted against the Decrees which allowed people who had been at war to take their degrees by payment of a fee and without further examination. In 1915, while he worked on his Grey book, he spent the Easter vacation at Overstrand (which did not in the event become an Army hospital) and the terms in Oxford where he carried a heavier load of academic duties, including tutorials not normally a part of professorial work. A not unusual day for him was to drill with his platoon in the morning, to correct college essays and to attend, for example, a Somerville college council meeting; apart from his own duties as Regius Professor and a Student of Christ Church, he had been on the council of Somerville College since 1908 and took his duties in cause of women very seriously. His health began to suffer. He felt 'so tired'. In April he was laid up with a boil on his heel. Another tooth broke, and early in 1916 all of his teeth were taken out. The end of the war began to seem dreadfully far away and the news of the Dardanelles and the battle of Neuve Chapelle made him realise how long it would take. Nevertheless, his own weariness did not prevent him from undertaking still further duties.

Towards the end of 1915 the Foreign Office suggested that he might go to neutral Sweden on a cultural, not a political, mission to do something to counteract the pro-German feeling in that country. On 8 January 1916 he had a meeting with Robert Vansittart of the Foreign Office (whom he liked), his old friend William Archer and a Swedish representative. The details of the trip were arranged for February. The Lady Mary was to accompany him and they sailed in the Norwegian ship *Jupiter* from Newcastle to Bergen. Gilbert proposed to be very moderate and scrupulously honest in his speeches and lectures, although he supposed that in the face of pro-German sentiments his combative instincts would be aroused. Before he left, he had for the first time a long talk with Grey. Archer went with them to introduce Murray in Norway where Archer was well known as the translator of Ibsen for the English stage. In Sweden, Murray, through his classical talks, put forward his views about the civilised nature of fifth-century Greece which, by implication, stood in contrast to what Europe had now become because of German policy. He sensed the pro-German sentiment sharply enough, but the only direct expression of it which he encountered was the attempt on one occasion to embarrass him by moving the vote-of-thanks in Latin. With an apology, he replied to it in Greek. The fierceness of the Swedes in their drinking habits, of which his brother Hubert warned him, presented no risks for Gilbert and Lady Mary.

Such a cultural mission, in Murray's opinion, was a form of propaganda not altogether to his taste, but it was a service he could render and therefore a duty. He undertook a similar mission to the United States later in the year, after another long conversation with Grey in June 1916. He was well known in America from his Harvard Lectures of 1907 and his Columbia ones of 1912 and had many American friends who were glad to entertain and help him. But in the United States, as in Sweden, there was an active German lobby and, more important, there was a strong Irish sentiment which was very hostile to Britain after the Easter Rising in Dublin and much more so after the execution of Sir Roger Casement. Grey told him that he and Asquith had been opposed to that execution, but the military had pressed for its carrying out because of Casement's attempt to suborn British prisoners of war in Germany. This conversation with Grey was not the only preparation Gilbert had for his American visit. In May 1916 he had been invited to France as the guest of British General Headquarters and spent 5 May chiefly at the Front. The courage, magnanimity, cheerfulness and discipline amazed him: it was 'wonderful and perfectly indescribable', and his direct experience of it was in his mind when he travelled, again with Lady Mary, to the United States in June 1916.

Something else was also in his mind. During his interview with Grey, the Foreign Secretary asked him particularly to notice what feeling there was in America about a League of Nations after the war. 'After the War', even when in 1915 it had seemed to be dreadfully far away, had already begun to occupy Murray's mind. When his version of Euripides' *Trojan Women* was widely on tour in the United States in 1915, sponsored by the Women's Peace Party, he had written a Translator's Note:

> To 'crush' Germany is fortunately a sheer impossibility, deliberately to 'hate Germany' is a sin against civilisation. But I believe that in order to secure the rule of Peace and Public Right in Europe certain safeguards must be obtained and certain reparations must be made. And therefore, as I believe it was the duty of my country to declare war on August 4, 1914, so I believe that it will be her duty, both to herself and to humanity, to scrutinize earnestly, though I hope generously, the proposed terms of Peace.

That was the message he took, as a cultural emissary, to the United States in 1916. It was a presidential election year in which the incumbent Woodrow Wilson's supporters campaigned with, amongst other slogans, 'He kept Us Out of War'. After Murray's return to England in August, Lord Bryce, former British Ambassador to the United States, told him that he entertained no fears that Hughes, the Republican candidate, as president would be 'any less well-disposed to us than Wilson. I used to know him well and have great faith in his uprightness.'

The re-election of Woodrow Wilson later came to have great importance for Murray, but the idea of a just peace had already come to preoccupy his mind. Even before he went to America, he had begun to be anxious about the survival of the Liberal government in England. When John Simon resigned in January 1916 on the issue of conscription, Murray recorded that he felt as Simon did, but nevertheless had to support the government because he wanted 'every possible unit of liberal force on the government bench with a view to the [peace] settlement'. The danger to such a settlement was that a Tory, a 'Jingo', government might get in. He did not anticipate what in fact happened, even though he sensed the weakening of Asquith's government. The downfall of Asquith and the formation of a coalition government in December 1916 under Lloyd George left him as embittered as it left many other Liberals, in a party which had already shed many of its prominent radical figures because of the war. Immediately after the publication of a letter which he wrote to the *Westminster Gazette*, putting his 'expurgated and printable' views about the government's fall, he was invited to stay with the Asquiths at Walmer Castle (seat of the Lord Warden of the Cinque Ports, an office Asquith retained), where for the first time he talked at length with the ex-Prime Minister, with Margot Asquith, McKenna, the Bonham-Carters and Howard Cust, a Tory, one of 'The Souls', who was disgusted with Lloyd George. It was perhaps symbolical that Gilbert Murray found himself taken into a circle of those out-of-power; it represented his usual position with the principled minority, although he had doubts about the company he was keeping. Margot Asquith inflamed his radical passions, because she and her set seemed so permeated by the atmosphere described by the Independent Labour Party: 'a game of skill between two groups of rich and smart people'.

The replacement of Asquith's government by a coalition which included 'untrue' Liberals as well as Tories presented a problem to Gilbert Murray. Whilst a government which he could wholeheartedly support was in power, he could conscientiously and scrupulously undertake cultural missions to neutral countries, in the belief that his reasoned, rational exposition of the situation of the Hellenic world had a 'spin-off' benefit by analogy for the cause of civilisation which his country represented. With a government under a 'treacherous' man, which excluded men of principle and included men he deeply suspected of lack of principle or worse, what was he to do?

He had to face the dilemma at once. H.A.L. Fisher, his old

Oxford friend and colleague, now Vice-Chancellor of Birmingham University, accepted office in the Lloyd George government as President of the Board of Education. Early in January 1917 he invited Gilbert to come to the Office to take the place of the official who had dealt with universities, and incidentally to advise on education policy. Murray thought that it was 'useful' work, but he was not really interested in the organisation of education and he might be 'muzzled' in his public views of the government and its policies for 'after the war'. Nevertheless, he wanted to help the war effort, and this kind of work was 'less political' than any other which he might now get. He asked his mother-in-law's opinion. Lady Carlisle was, as usual, forthright. She told him that it was a pity he had asked her opinion, but since he had, she could not say what she did not think. 'You evidently wish to do some public work and a temptation comes your way, but surely the straight course is to take no work *in* or *for* this government.' Gilbert's answer was that, to his surprise, it was 'practically impossible not to help'. The Reviewing Committee, earlier established by Haldane, was just completing its job of reviewing various schemes of educational reform so as to recommend a definite policy. It was dealing with provincial universities and with Gilbert's own special concern: the provision of classical language and history teaching in secondary schools. He had promised Haldane before the war that he would help. The work had been done inside the Office and Lloyd George knew nothing about it; Fisher, indeed, had not been able to see him since he took office. Gilbert explained to his mother-in-law that there was no question of working for the government, only for the civil service; and that her son, Geoffrey Howard, a Liberal Whip, agreed that he could properly take such a post. Lawrence Hammond, an old friend and fellow radical, was anxious to have Gilbert in the Board of Education to support him as a member of the Reconstruction Committee. The Countess did not press her objections. By 20 January 1917, Gilbert had agreed to work for three days a week and to be responsible for two sections: 'U', universities; and 'DIR', Director of Inquiries and Reports. Formally, he was appointed Principal Assistant Secretary of the Universities Branch at £600 p.a. Lady Carlisle asked him to stay in her house in Palace Green for the two nights per week he had to spend in London, for she and her son-in-law, the new civil servant, did not disagree politically about the government; Gilbert came to dislike Lloyd George's administration more as it went on. He came to put his trust for the peace in President Woodrow Wilson.

Meanwhile, he did his duty as a civil servant. When he first went to the Office on 31 January 1917, he discovered that his main work was to be dealing with two or three large and newly arising problems which were not 'matters of precedent', including relations with foreign universities. It took a while to feel at home in the civil service ethos. He discovered within his first week that the work would be mixed, in the sense that any official has to deal with a number of different topics at once. On 7 February, for example, his afternoon included the differentiation of old and new universities, Workers' Educational Association questions and proposed courses for prisoners of war. He also concluded that it was proper to wear a stiff shirt and keep a change of dress in his office. Throughout February he sat through a series of conferences upon university matters, but by March he was also chairman of a committee to frame a scheme of visits by lecturers to troops in France. He became Chairman of the Committee on the Supply of Teachers for Day Continuation Schools; he was Oxford University's representative on the State Scholarships Committee; and a member of a committee under the Higher Education of Ex-Service Officers and Men Scheme which administered an extension of the scheme to permit study at foreign universities. But Murray's main achievement, as head of the universities branch, was to ensure that the series of conferences of the heads of British universities resulted in a regular meeting of the vice-chancellors of British universities, and in machinery for permanent contact between them and the government.

Murray conscientiously did his half-time civil service work and, as always, his original reaction that it was not at all his kind of thing changed into active involvement. Nevertheless his heart was not really in it. He recognised the importance of the issues, but he recognised still more important ones: the peace and what came after the war. His work at the Board of Education entailed his residence in London for at least half of each week. (It was at this time that he began regularly to use the Athenaeum to which he was elected, on the nomination of Lord Bryce and the Archbishop of Canterbury, in 1917). And London was, after all, the focus of political power. Murray never made the mistake of ignoring or underestimating the importance of influence in the centres of power, and London was therefore as important to him as was Oxford.

While he was at the Board of Education, he was also beginning to be deeply involved with those who were also concerned with what happened after victory. In June 1917 he met an American committee which sought the prosecution of a vigorous war leading to a just international settlement, a settlement which would involve the German evacuation of Belgium, Serbia, Rumania and 'perhaps more', with all else to be settled by an international conference including Germany. He was not enthusiastic, however, about the Lansdowne Letter and the German peace proposals in late 1917. On 29 November he met Lansdowne at lunch with Asquith and, while congratulating him upon his courage in writing the letter, shared Asquith's own reservations, since the German proposals which, as Murray heard them, were to evacuate Belgium and France and to make an arrangement over Alsace-Lorraine in return for German colonies, contained not a word about Eastern Europe. Asquith, for that reason, vetoed any public resolution by the Liberal ex-cabinet ministers in support of Lansdowne, although the latter believed — wrongly as it turned out — that Arthur Balfour as Foreign Secretary supported him. Such a peace offered too little of what Murray thought just. His feelings were then 'knotted up into bundles. I feel as if Greek and Peace and Liberalism and idealism in general were all one, and all being threatened by the same enemy.' His interest in the idea of a League of Nations came from its linking, in one cause, most of his deepest concerns and from his conviction that a national government such as that of Lloyd George was evil. By late 1917 it seemed that

> the whole horizon is now ghastly. Death is everywhere and it no longer seems as if our men were fighting for the same causes as we followed at the beginning of the war. I still trust Wilson . . . I still keep a hope that the heart of the nation is still more or less sound, however evil our governing forces are.

The League seemed to be the only answer.

Murray's active involvement in the cause of a League began after his American visit in 1916, but while he remained a civil servant he could not engage in any activity which was overtly political. By mid-1918, when he heard that the government itself was 'plunging' for the League of Nations, any support he could give became an easier matter, although in his opinion the cabinet wished to make it an anti-German League which would defeat what in Murray's view was the whole object of such a League. In particular, he became aware that Lord Robert Cecil, Minister at the Foreign Office, was a keen League man, and was very willing to discuss the matter. But if Cecil was sympathetic, other members of the government were not, or at least not sympathetic to certain of Gilbert Murray's views. He had first met Balfour, the former Prime Minister, now Foreign Secretary, at lunch in November 1917, and he found him to be 'very clever and agreeable, never indiscreet, never speaking ill of colleagues' although, he added to his wife, he voted 'for the Drink Trade and the Church'. Balfour had, early in 1917, been glad to entertain the idea that Murray might work for the Foreign Office in the United States, although the possibility was overtaken by work at the Board of Education.

In January 1918 another possibility came up. An unofficial body — the League to Enforce the Peace — proposed to meet in Chicago. Because it was unofficial, the British government would send no official representative, but it was happy with the idea that Gilbert Murray should be there, and it was willing to provide a letter of commendation. On 6 March, however, the *New York Times* quoted Murray as saying that 'if the world desired a clean, democratic and durable peace, it would follow Trotsky's international policy in preference to that of President Wilson and Mr Lloyd George'. Balfour thereupon asked for the return of his letter of commendation because he could not have it construed that he approved or shared those views. Murray returned the letter, commenting that his message to the *New York Times* epitomised views he had already expressed in England, and that they were the views of the ordinary 'average-minded' Liberal. He also informed the American Ambassador of the return of the letter, adding that the affair was the result of a newspaper attack by the *Globe*, quoting the *New York Times*, on his supposed pacificism or even Bolshevism. The storm had blown up after the Bolshevik government of Russia signed the Treaty of Brest Litovsk with the German government, taking Russia out of the war, and then published the 'secret' treaties between the former Russian government and its allies. The Imperial German aims, in the Treaty of Brest Litovsk, were clearly annexationist. Trotsky was obliged to accept the German annexations, but then proceeded to reveal what his former allies had proposed in dividing enemy territory between themselves. What Gilbert said was indeed what he had been saying since 1916: a just peace, no annexations. But in March 1918 this seemed to denounce allied policy and to agree with Trotsky. To

Balfour he wrote that he did not quarrel with the 'secret' treaties, nor did he ignore the fact that the present government included Balfour and Cecil, and even Curzon and Milner, who were 'thoroughly able and honest men', but he could not entirely trust the Prime Minister, and the Northcliffe and Beaverbrook newspaper groups were 'amongst the worst influences in the country'. Balfour declined controversy over these views, while professing not to understand the distinction between the government's war aims and those of the average-minded Liberal. The secret treaties, he pointed out, were the work of Asquith and Grey — he did not criticise them for that because he believed they had no choice — but this was no justification for the charges of annexationism and imperialism which Murray had brought against the present government. Murray, in the event, did not go to America, and the incident, although he could describe it as a storm in a tea cup, pointed up the dilemma for him of work in the civil service under the government of a Prime Minister whom he distrusted and despised. He refused two honours consecutively offered in 1917 for his work during the war. The work, he felt, had been mostly propaganda and, when a government could be so cynical as to appoint Northcliffe to office, he believed that Lloyd George did not think it mattered whether a statement was false or true: all that mattered to the Prime Minister was the effect produced.

Such radical Liberal bitterness towards Lloyd George, in coalition with the Tories, was not peculiar to Gilbert Murray, although its intensity was the more remarkable in one who was not a professional politician. He knew the gossip among his Liberal politician friends that Lloyd George had been called by Northcliffe 'a treacherous little hound' and, when the Northcliffe press began to attack the government in April 1918, he told Lady Mary that he had always said that the time would come when he would have to support Lloyd George against something worse. But two weeks later he was drafting a statement of Liberal policy for those who had not followed Lloyd George, even though his brother-in-law, Geoffrey Howard, who had been the Deputy Whip under Asquith, convinced him that the party prospects were bad: although it might not be captured by Lloyd George, it might well be destroyed. Gilbert Murray's views about the government led him to leave the Board of Education immediately after the war ended, but he had already become involved in the non-party aspects of the League of Nations' activity in England. When he went to the Board of

Education in 1917, Geoffrey Howard had suggested that this official work should be temporary until a suitable moment came for him to throw up his Oxford chair and stand for Parliament as an Asquith-Grey Liberal. Gilbert had had doubts; he did not wish to give up his permanent work and his salary unless he could be of real use. Eleven days after Armistice Day, however, he told the Oxford University Liberals that if they wanted him he would stand for the university constituency, where the question of his retaining his professorship would not be an issue, and where parliamentary life would be a great deal easier than in an ordinary seat. Nevertheless, the omens seemed to him bad: by the end of the war the Liberal Party seemed to have little hope as a political force; the League would probably fail.

The unfolding effects of the war upon European civilisation were an ordeal for a man like Murray, because they represented everything he most hated, but the ordeal had its more personal costs. In part this was a professional one. In 1915, he wrote to Wilamowitz-Moellendorf in Germany and he received a saddening letter in reply. Wilamowitz, acknowledging an attempt to preserve some bridges across national enmities, believed that they would never meet again in their lifetimes, and that the international life of scholarship they had both taken for granted would seem to a younger generation like memories of a lost paradise. His eldest son had been killed. His second, like Murray's own son Denis, was a pilot: 'May they both stay alive.' Wilamowitz was unsure whether his greetings would still be welcome to Oxford friends. The letter greatly saddened Murray, for it brought home the damage the war was doing to what he had cared for most. The sadness became the greater as the brilliant young classical scholars, like Wilamowitz's son who left behind an unfinished book on Sophocles, were killed. New College, always closer to Gilbert's heart as a society than Christ Church, suffered particularly heavily. Arthur Heath and Leslie Hunter, both young promising Fellows, were killed. Their photographs and those of other pupils began to fill the Murray house, arranged on the wall, as a visitor once observed, like a crucifixion. He, like Herbert Fisher, became increasingly concerned about the damage which was being done to society by the appalling loss of talent through the deaths of the next Oxford generation, while the personal losses of friends were a moral and an intellectual laceration to one who had been so confident in Progress and Humanity, and still believed that the war was being fought in that cause.

The death-rate in the younger generation was in itself a heartbreak, and one made the more bitter for Gilbert Murray by the fate of other young men who were not prepared actually to fight in the war. Strongly supporting the war itself, opposed to Brailsford, Russell and Morel as he was, and himself subject to attack by those who, like Ramsay MacDonald, professed to reject violence in any form, Murray nevertheless upheld the rights of individual conscience. He sympathised with John Simon who resigned from the government on the issue of compulsory military service, but he still supported the government because in 1916 he was 'inclined to think' that conscription was then necessary. The Conscription Act of March 1916 he thought to be a generous measure, worthy of the tradition of English tolerance, because it allowed complete exemption to those who, on conscientious grounds, however mistakenly refused to take part in slaying their fellow-men. The operation and administration of the Act, however, caused him anguish. In May 1916, he recalled for G.M. Trevelyan in 1920, he had just returned to England from his visit to the Front and he found a telegram awaiting him from the parents of a conscientious objector, stating that 34 conscientious objectors had been sentenced to death, after being taken to France under military authority, for refusing orders. Murray went at once in a 'very untidy' state to the House of Commons where he saw his brother-in-law, Geoffrey Howard, who advised him to see Lord Derby, Minister for War in the Asquith coalition government. He saw Derby in the Lobby, who simply said that the men were condemned, would be shot, 'and quite right too'. Murray went back to Howard who got him five minutes with the Prime Minister. Murray briefly stated the situation to Asquith who read the telegram, muttered the word 'abominable', asked one or two questions and then rapidly wrote a letter to the Commander-in-Chief to the effect that no death sentences on conscientious objectors were to be carried out unless with the consent of the cabinet. Gilbert Murray, as a supporter of the war and of the government, was shocked by such harsh treatment of conscientious objectors, and horrified by the attitude of men like Derby, for 'it is quite easy for a large engine like the War Office to crush any one man's body, to destroy his reason by perpetual solitude, or put an end to his life'; but it was not the action of a civilised government.

On this occasion, Murray's intervention was on behalf of a group of conscientious objectors whom he did not know and who did not know him. He intervened on a principle which he believed any civilised society should accept. More heartrending was the involvement in the individual cases he took up, of which there were a number. He wrote on Clive Bell's behalf to a Tribunal hearing conscientious objection cases. He contributed to Bertrand Russell's defence fund. He helped a friend of his daughter's who had had a nervous breakdown and who was allowed to serve under the Society of Friends; and he helped Palme Dutt who was released from prison. But the case which touched him above all was that of Stephen Hobhouse.

The young man was the son of rich parents, educated at Eton and Balliol. While still an undergraduate at Oxford he had resigned from the Volunteers and in 1909 had become a Quaker. Under the Conscription Act, a Tribunal disallowed his conscientious objection, and sent him to serve with the Friends' Ambulance Unit. But Stephen, unlike some other Quakers, did not accept this form of service either, partly because the Unit was auxiliary to the Army, partly because the order made him in effect a conscript. He refused to obey a military order and was imprisoned for a term, after which, refusing to obey another order, he was again imprisoned for two years at hard labour. After Asquith's intervention he was not sentenced to death, for, as Gilbert Murray privately knew in May 1916, the cabinet had decided to hand conscientious objectors not to the military but to the civil authorities, but his treatment was harsh. Murray, indeed, was certain that the Tribunal was wrong, unjust and uncomprehending. He publicised the case in 1917 in a public lecture, printed in the Hibbert Journal in 1918, and in the preface he wrote in 'I Appeal Unto Caesar', although, as Hobhouse pointed out, with 'small inaccuracies' and drawing a veil of romance over his life which had inconsistencies and a lack of faith. Still, Murray had got the main issue right as Hobhouse thankfully acknowledged, and had stood up for someone with whose principles he disagreed. In doing so, Gilbert Murray did not endear himself to the government and he was little thanked by the conscientious objectors. On principle he believed that a nation which could not live at peace with its saints — and that was how he regarded Stephen Hobhouse — was not a 'very healthy or high-minded nation'. And it was his nation — at war, he was convinced, for the survival of civilisation — which persecuted such saints. 'A

Wise ruler', he wrote, 'would be very circumspect, a conscientious ruler will be very tender, before challenging the lowliest of souls to battle on the soul's own ground.'

The war was an ordeal for Murray because it outraged the principles of Humanity and Progress, but when the suffering was that of his own family, the war and its effects became a more personal ordeal. For, of his five children, the lives of three were tragically affected directly or indirectly by the war. His eldest son, Denis, whose pre-war aeroplane engineering business had failed, became a pilot, passing his sea-plane test in September 1914 and then being posted to France. After his aeroplane failed to return from a mission, he was interned in Holland early in 1915. When his mother visited the prison camp in 1916, she was shocked by the folly and aimlessness of the lives of the young prisoners: so foolish, so wild, so ungovernable, their careers ruined and, in Denis's case, so bitter and so angry. This war-time imprisonment had the bad effects Lady Mary foresaw. After the war Denis was unable to settle down, the drinking which had seemed a way to bear the boredom and frustration of the camp became chronic and, in spite of the care devoted to him in the country by his aunt Cecilia and her husband Charles Roberts, he never recovered. In March 1930 he died, as much a casualty of the war in his parents' belief as those who had been killed in the fighting.

The second tragedy was that of Agnes. For her the war was a liberation. After taking her Third in Classical Moderations in 1915 she began the Greats course, but discontinued her studies in spite of her father's help with tuition and his advice to take her degree before she did anything else. Agnes wanted passionately to be at the centre of things, a feeling her father could understand: 'when something big is going on one is drawn nearer and nearer to the heart of it, perhaps like a moth to a fire, perhaps a quite natural and healthy wish.' Murray used his influence to find Agnes a job in France — after she had nursed in England, and had in 1916 become engaged to Saumarez Main who was serving in France — but such war-work, while it appealed to a vivid and imaginative girl, entailed risks. Her parents worried about the young men who were attracted to Agnes and still more about Agnes's pursuit of them. When her father thought of more permanent jobs for her, such as the diplomatic service, he had to remind his daughter that any such position made correct behaviour imperative. As it was, Agnes found the wartime freedom of women exhilarating, with removal of inhibitions on smoking, drinking and dress. When she had dinner with her father at the beginning of 1918 she was 'painted so as to be visible a mile off. I could not bear to look at her.' With the end of the war, Agnes went first to work in Vienna with the Friends' Relief Committee, where she was 'busy and beloved' but had 'many admirers' about whom her parents also worried, and then in the office of the League of Nations Union. The wildness of her behaviour was that of the generation of the early 1920s which had survived the war, and in Agnes's case it led her to leave her work and, in the company of a friend, to stay at an inn in France where she died of misdiagnosed peritonitis in August 1922.

The third tragedy was also a generational one. Her younger brother Basil was in his teens at school during the war, affected as all schoolboys were by the possibility of going to the fighting when they left school. In 1916 his father was complaining about his 'scatter-brained quality' in spite of his cleverness, and also that 'instinctively he goes off with more amusing friends', even though his father wished to see as much as he could of him. This restless quality of wartime schooldays, as adolescent boys neared military age, carried over into Basil's undergraduate career at Oxford. He might, his father believed, get a 'rather good second' in Classical Moderations, but in fact he got a Third. At Oxford, he had even more amusing friends and things to do, and he earned the epithet 'satanic' from his contemporary Evelyn Waugh, who used him as a model for Basil Seal and perhaps, in part, for Lord Sebastian Flyte in *Brideshead Revisited*. Roy Harrod defended Basil against his mother's severer criticism, but nothing could explain away the debts he continued to run up after he had gone down from the university. He failed to make a success in any career, as he also failed in his three marriages. He was a model for Basil Seal, a Waugh casualty in a lost generation of young men who might have, but who did not, die at the war. In Basil's case, death finally came in Spain in 1937 during the Civil War.

Such were the tragic deaths of the children which came after the war was over. 'The death of a child seems to tear one's heart', wrote Murray of Agnes's death in 1922. But the ordeal for him was not so much the deaths themselves as the behaviour of his children under the effects of war. Death tore the heart because it was, in Agnes's case, as in the case of that decimated Oxford generation of young men, the extinction of brilliant promise. But the Murrays could never be sure that it was simply the war which caused the ordeal with their children. When Lady Mary looked at Basil's university results in 1922 she was miserable for her husband:

> it is too hard on you. I know it was hard enough Denis not being able to pass examinations and Stephen too delicate, but Basil is perfectly clever and able and strong, and ought to have been your pride and delight . . . You poor dear thing you ought to have had such a good, clever family. Do you remember saying it was my brothers coming out in them? Of course I was hurt — I don't think it's so much my brothers as me, and too much money and insufficient discipline.

Lady Mary came close to heartbreak over her children's behaviour, for like her mother before her she would not countenance any frivolity which detracted from the serious purposes of life. She told her husband 'between us you and I haven't dowered our children well . . . but self-blame would be fruitless, such little things may have overset the character'. Whatever the explanation, however, the Murrays carried the knowledge that Denis was alienated from them, perhaps hated them, that Basil preferred the companionship of others, and that the youngest boy, Stephen, grew up away from them; in early 1917 Gilbert told Mary: 'I am so glad that you have been able to show real affection to him . . . it may save him from hating us.' In 1923, his father resolved to see more of Stephen whom he took on holiday to Switzerland, but he, like his wife, believed that all of their children had an anti-virtue complex which made their behaviour unacceptable: 'one of the greatest faults in the education of the present generation is that they are not brought up to the common-place duties of family life — good temper, serenity, yielding to others and generally refraining from self asser- tion;' the children seemed to feel that there was a duty to rebel. With Stephen, whom he never pressed to do anything he did not like, he found that sudden severity produced an improvement in behaviour which consisted too often in 'grousing and rebelling'.

The Murrays found all of their sons an ordeal when they reached adolescence and young manhood. During schooldays they had seen relatively little of them, separated as they were by boarding schools in term time, and by servants and separate establishments in the vacations. This was not in itself an unusual pattern of upbringing; it was common enough in English society. What was unusual was that, having so little direct contact with the boys, the Murrays nevertheless expected them to observe the same strict code of behaviour as they themselves upheld, and were deeply disappointed when they did not. Even with Rosalind, married to Arnold Toynbee in 1913 before the war came, there were worries. Lady Mary was anxious over the birth of the first child in 1914, not simply because Rosalind's health had always worried her but because she judged Toynbee to be highly-strung and, with the war, living on his nerves. A second baby in 1915, after earlier adverse medical opinion, and then a miscarriage in 1919 caused her still more worry, for she knew that the Toynbees were depressed and anxious about Arnold's post-war academic jobs and temporary unemployment.

Rosalind, nevertheless, had the care of a husband to occupy her and, while her attitude to life had never been the same radical, progressive philosophy of her parents, it was at least serious and not frivolous as was the case with Agnes. Even at the age of 22, Agnes was still addressed by her mother as 'dearest childie', a girl to be protected from the temptations of a gay life and from dangerous admirers. Gilbert Murray, too, recognised and worried about these dangers, about what he called her 'escapades and naughtiness', but for him Agnes, unlike his other children, was redeemed by her great love and enjoyment of life. Unlike Lady Mary, he could bear his other children's troubles with equanimity, but with Agnes he felt far more. After she had taken 'Mods', he began to treat her as a companion with whom he could discuss politics and people, and whose views he began to seek as worth having. He retailed political gossip to her. He thought of her as a possible sub-secretary if he were to go to Washington as ambassador. Her death affected him more than any other tragedy, except one, that of Rosalind's conversion to Catholicism, which afflicted his family. Murray was sick with anxiety when she was reported ill in mid-July 1922, and after her death he wrote to Arnold Toynbee the saddest letter he ever wrote in his life.

We buried her yesterday in the little cemetery at Chambon. A beautiful old place with a little Romanesque chapel and some very old grey tombstones as well as some tawdry modern ones; it is up above the road and has a wonderful view up the valley. She was uninterruptedly loving and unselfish to the end, trying to smile when she could not speak and wagging her finger to me as a greeting . . . She had amid all her escapades and naughtiness a wonderfully loving and generous nature and she lit up our lives for us . . . Mary is holding out wonderfully . . . The death of a child seems to tear one's heart. There seems to be a sort of physical basis on which are built all the more reflective feelings . . . the loss of a companion and friend and the extinction of such brilliant promise. It leaves me frightened of life — for the time. My dear love to the Creature, the only Creature left.

The grief came acutely back to him from time to time in the next two years. In March 1923 he wrote to his wife: 'I lie awake sometimes . . . simply aching about the child,' and on the anniversary of her death: 'I find Agnes always with me: I have never had any experience at all like it with others who have died.' A year later still he felt 'her quite often as a gay and encouraging presence: as I told you she told me to drive the car and always urges me to enjoy myself and not to mope. (I put it as if I believed it, which is far too much to say.)' By the end of 1924 he could think of Agnes without unhappiness, but the other family deaths could always bring back a sharp pang. In April 1937, when his second son died, he told Lady Mary: 'I just sit and think of dear Basil and beloved Agnes or you and incidentally of Isobel and other young people threatened with death. One wants to weep and weep.'

But Murray did not easily weep, and his grief for his favourite child was caught up in a more impersonal concern for others in general. His grief and pain were at the waste and loss of a bright spirit, and this loss could be made up by other than his own children. His moving letter about Agnes was sent to his son-in-law, Arnold Toynbee, whom he greatly admired and found deeply sympathetic to the causes he held so dear. Toynbee was the son he never had; 'he makes up for so much'. The flashes of memory of Agnes he also confided to two young women whose bright spirits, imaginative intelligences and initiative struck a deeply sympathetic chord: Audrey Richards and Isobel Henderson. These young graduates of great promise in academic life took the place of Agnes. The former became 'Dear Child', 'you dear clever and brave creature, I hope you will be happy and your work always good'; the latter, away from Oxford 'ought to come with the spring and the azaleas and the shining spring dawn', and in her absence in Spain in September 1930, when Murray had been depressed and made 'frantic inside' by the sight of reapers killing animals in the corn, he had upon waking, sought peace by thinking about her.

Suddenly a sort of veil began to lift and I saw, low down on the left, a landscape opening out, full of sun and with an extraordinary atmosphere of peace and happiness. It was not like Spain particularly. It lasted a few minutes, getting clearer and more delightful, then was gone.

Gilbert Murray's ordeal with his children was real enough, but it was the ordeal of a cultivated stoic mind rather than a deep emotional harrowing. What he valued in his children was represented by Agnes, but it could be more than replaced by younger and sympathetic colleagues and friends, in the same way that, in his younger days, he had found a communion of spirit with Janie Malloch, Margaret Mackail and Penelope Wheeler which was missing inside his family.

Lady Mary was no happier about her husband's outside friendships when they were both in their sixties than she had been 20 years earlier. In 1929 she spoke of 'my usual damnable jealousy of the various young women', but this was at a time when she was at a low ebb and feeling 'so morose'. For she had borne the family troubles more deeply than her husband. In 1916, when she visited Denis in internment, her heart was 'all wrought up for these young men. Half the day I spend in regret and vexation for the folly and aimlessness — no work, few interests, extravagant drinking at all hours.' By 1918 she saw in Basil 'carelessness' and 'unpopularity' and told her husband that he must have a serious talk with him. Rosalind terribly upset her mother by saying that Gilbert wished her to be with him in London, while other friends were worried at the way Lady Mary rushed around, with its implication that it was all due to nervous restlessness. 'My activities', she said, 'are much more tiring than professional work, but they have been an attempt to make up for the lack of steady work, by doing house-keeping properly with indifferent maids and keeping up connections (you not having the time) with relations and neighbours.' Lady Mary never doubted the importance of whatever work her husband was doing, and she knew very clearly what her duty was, but she resented any criticism of the way in which she did it, especially from her daughter. By 1922, however, the burdens she had assumed, the criticisms to which she felt subjected, together with, in her opinion, possible physical causes such as microbes, led to a 'black form of depression'. In hospital in March of that year, she wondered

whether you realized how sorry I am for this debacle, for getting things into a mess and allowing our differences of opinion to result in hard words and then breaking down like this and having to leave everything and cost money and pains for weeks and weeks. If you do not, please do realize it. I am a bit old to begin afresh and to learn the lessons of humility and contrition. I've not had quite an easy life. Your work is so important and so hard that you haven't had time to share in the ordinary cares and responsibilities of family and friends and my own nature isn't, as you know too well, an easy one. But if I am restored to any measure of strength and serenity I will indeed start afresh and try to keep order and to please you and make you happy.

Lady Mary's collapse in early 1922 followed the death of her mother in the previous year and the extended family responsibilities that she then had to shoulder, as joint Executor with her husband of Lady Carlisle's Will:

All the grief and pain I have gone through . . . made a complex from which I am not yet freed. We were so happy in our sunshiny childhood there but then came such gloomy times . . . my not very happy grown up girlhood, the troubles and quarrels, the wild border I used to love and don't. I've always scorned to give way to such feelings, but it does seem my past life and repressions are punishing me.

The extended family troubles haunted Lady Mary in early 1922, but her own family tragedy with Agnes may actually have helped her to recover. In May 1922 she was in hospital. By August she was taking charge of Agnes at the Villa du Lac, Chambon. In April she told her husband that if anything could help her it would be thinking that he missed her and cared whether she was well and at home. Gilbert reassured her about his feelings, but in the summer Agnes actually and demonstrably needed her and then, as her husband put it, she bore up wonderfully. But by 1925 she was again worrying over family criticisms of her management of the practical affairs of life which by then included the inheritance from her mother. She felt that she had worked so hard at the accounts, at administering them 'so wisely and thriftily for you and your children and then it's always implied I'm extravagant to the point of lack of balance'. She described herself as 'rather a crock, tired and low in the world'; and she turned to the Quakers. During her mother's illness and in her own depression she came to have no doubt of the effect of prayer; it might, she said, be autosuggestion, a low explanation of undoubted phenomena, but it was very tenable. In the face of Denis's tragedy, she relied on the plan the Quakers pressed on her: ceasing to struggle and putting the matter on to God. But by July 1929 she again thought herself 'a proper crock', after 'a mixture of spiritual, intellectual and physical *accablement* caused by a variety of things'. One of them was jealousy of various young women; another was lack of a holiday; but the first cause she mentioned was a reaction from worry over her youngest son Stephen, while her concern over Denis's health and Basil's debts was always in the background.

To the ordeal of war and of family, Gilbert and Mary Murray reacted differently. The differences were a major factor in Lady Mary's dejected and weakened state in 1922, 1925 and 1929; they were a lesser one in Gilbert's own state of mind. In 1925 the illnesses and deaths of family and friends haunted him a good deal: Agnes, his wife (the 'Beloved Puss') and his old family friend William Archer weighed on his spirits. When the invitation came to him in 1925 to occupy in the following year the Charles Eliot Norton Chair of Poetry at Harvard as its first holder, he urged his wife to come with him;

> If you came, being both away together, we can come closer to each other again. If you stay behind, the separation that there now is will be the greater. We shall both be more unhappy and we shall neither of us do our work as we should. Do agree to this. I cannot bear being separated from you.

Gilbert tried to help Lady Mary by recognising the crosses, her own and others, that she had to bear, while telling her that she used them to ennoble life; and by his reassurances that she *was* of help to him where she thought she was not. Away in London in July 1926 he exclaimed: 'I hate going away from you and I will really try to be nicer to you and let the love that is below come above the small irritations of the surface.' Lady Mary did accompany him to

Harvard in 1926, but in her illness in 1929 her husband was still trying to bring them closer together again: 'my own dear pussy, you never come to nice places where you ought to be.'

If it was the ordeal of what she saw as her own and Gilbert's failure with their children that was a principal cause of Lady Mary's suffering, it was nevertheless not the only cause. During and after the war she turned both to Quakerism and to the Labour Party, neither of them causes in which her husband could follow her. The Quaker religion did not of course commit her to the dogmatic theology which her husband so disliked in organised religion, nor in 1925 did she suppose that she had any more 'real belief' than he did, but she was determined to act on Quaker guidance, to think and act 'on the hypothesis' of God, and that, she said, 'makes a considerable difference'. She quoted Pascal: 'thou woulds't not now be seeking me, if thou hads't not me already in thy heart.' Murray himself did not reject the idea of a 'sense of God', but he told his wife that he thought it

extremely improbable that any one of the religious systems known to history is true. On the other hand it is equally improbable that all are based on nothing at all. I take them to be attempts to conceive and put into words things that are beyond human thought and still more beyond human speech. In other words they are, as Plato says, 'images' or 'metaphors' . . . so the Christian myth is not a fact but a shot at suggesting what the nature of the unknown universe is like.

The Lady Mary might think her religion to be a barrier between herself and her husband, but he could accept Quakerism more readily than he could tolerate dogmatic religion. He could accept his wife's religious views — which did not, for example, include a belief in the divinity of Christ — where he could not accept, indeed was deeply hurt by, his daughter Rosalind's conversion to Catholicism in August 1933. Like his other children, he believed that she was rebelling against the things her parents admired, but when he had himself detected the signs of increased religiousness in his daughter in March 1929 while on holiday at Lerici he hopefully thought that it was more Quaker than Catholic. When Rosalind actually converted, Arnold Toynbee was very worried about the effect upon her father. Rosalind had told Gilbert that it was 'not possible to delay indefinitely so vital a step from any considerations of affection and sympathy'. Murray could not bring himself to talk to Lady Mary about it; he went off alone on the glacier at Eggishorn. His wife told Arnold Toynbee that 'he has minded this like a Liberal all along', but she could not think that it would 'really separate them speculatively much more than has been the case for some time'. Lady Mary herself believed that Catholicism put the mind in blinkers. Gilbert believed it to be a cruel and superstitious myth in which he could not really bring himself to believe that his daughter had any real belief: it was really opposition to Bloomsbury and what it stood for: 'she was always more influenced by her dislikes than her desires.' The Murrays took comfort from the fact that Arnold Toynbee professed himself more undogmatic as time went by and from his explanation that 'in my generation some go morally anarchic . . . and others like Rosalind go back to institutions from which, after all, we all came out of'.

His wife's Quakerism aroused no such pain in Murray, but he still reacted against any supernatural religion. When, in July 1928, he learned of his wife's seance with a medium, during which Agnes's dead fiancé Saumarez was said to be watching over Denis, he described it as 'regular twaddle . . . I would be rather sad if you got thoroughly into that atmosphere'. The Lady Mary had told him of the experience she had had in 1922 during Agnes's funeral service in the little church at Chambon, where she had experienced a feeling of liberation from almost unbearable pain. He had himself had the sensation of Agnes as a friendly presence, but he did not regard these as any manifestation of the supernatural. The deaths of loved ones during the First World War, the sense of sudden bereavement and loss, had led in Britain to an upsurge in spiritualism, but this was not the kind of comfort Murray could ever seek. Indeed, spirit communication seemed to him irrational, unworthy of modern man and pathetic, when not comic or trivial in its results. His friend, the Irish poet, W.B. Yeats, for example, had appealed for his help in 1917 over a young psychic researcher who had made a machine to bring messages from the other world and had been reckless enough to publish one of its messages in German. The police seized the machine as a wireless transmitter and detained its inventor for communication with the enemy. Yeats might assure him that the machine was important, but Murray's help came despite his belief that nothing supernatural had occurred or could occur.

Murray's rational humanism rejected the supernatural, although his own telepathic abilities caused a good deal of interest among those who investigated psychical phenomena. He had met Mrs A.W. Verrall when he visited her husband in Cambridge while preparing the Euripides' text, and that lady was a prominent figure in the Psychical Research Society. She was interested in Murray's telepathic ability, and, together with another very prominent member of the Society, Mrs Salter, reported upon his thought-transference experiments which thus became known to a wide audience of those interested in psychic phenomena. Many of the phenomena the Society investigated were and are popularly identified with spiritualism, mediums, ghosts, poltergeists, seances and other dramatic manifestations. Gilbert Murray's were less spectacular. In his dreams he had sometimes experienced instances of what can be called clairvoyance, although such phenomena in which such a future event is foreseen and happens are significant only when compared with those on which an event is foreseen but does not happen. Significance, in short, is a matter of statistics. So, too, were the telepathic phenomena with which Murray was chiefly concerned. These were not clairvoyant dreams, but experiments conducted with family and friends. As Murray and others who were involved describe them, Murray would leave the room, one of those remaining would select an incident, either from life or fiction, which was communicated to the others, usually by voice, sometimes in writing. Then Murray would return and, sometimes taking the hand of the person who was selected as 'agent' (who was usually *not* the person who had selected the incident), attempt to identify the topic. From the notes kept of those occasions, it is clear that he was able to arrive at an identification far more often than statistical probability would allow. The records of these identifications have not been challenged, but their significance has.

Part of this challenge comes from the uncontrolled nature of the 'experiments'. The surviving notes of them simply record the subject chosen, Murray's remarks or questions upon returning to the room, and his success or failure in identifying the topic. What is not recorded is the place to which he withdrew, its distance from the group, whether the topic was discussed aloud at any length: in other words, the precise circumstances of the 'experiment'. Nor is it always recorded who selected the topic, whether or with whom Murray held hands while trying to identify the incident. The absence of such details does not necessarily invalidate the results, but it leaves them open to challenge as evidence of telepathy. Most obviously, it has been suggested that hyperacuity of hearing can explain Murray's successes; and some of the results, as Murray himself recognised, can plausibly be accounted for in this way.

It is a different thing, of course, to conclude that Murray was himself aware of his incredible hearing facility which produced his successes and chose to pretend otherwise. In fact it is beyond doubt that Murray was tone-deaf; musical sounds meant nothing to him. All the evidence suggests that, if hyperacuity of hearing is the explanation of some or even most of Murray's identifications, then he was not himself aware of it; there was no conscious deception on these occasions. But, even if that were the explanation of some of the results, it by no means follows that it is the explanation of *all* of his success above statistical probability. Indeed, a careful analysis of published and unpublished records of Murray's experiments seems quite clearly to show that hyperacuity of hearing is not a sufficient explanation of the results.

Whatever the explanation may be — and there is no agreement among those who have been concerned with telepathy, although there is a tendency to concentrate upon states of consciousness — Murray himself was quite clear that it was not supernatural, nor even, to use a word preferred by the Psychical Research Society, paranormal. When he accepted the Presidency of the Society and delivered his presidential address in 1916, he quoted one of his predecessors in that office, Henri Bergson, in support of his own view that his facility was not abnormal. He looked upon it as an ability which many people might possess and exercise if the circumstances were suitable. He stressed that such results might come from a number of factors which could be grouped under the term hyperaesthesia, and which were well within the natural order of physical existence. He probably had in mind the abilities which the aborigines of his own country, Australia, were then commonly believed to possess and which may have had analogies in Greek religion. The echoes of the primitive were something Murray always detected beneath the surface of civilisation; but they were survivals of a human past, not of the supernatural.

Such a positive rejection of supernatural revelation scarcely came into conflict with his wife's religious views, for she too rejected the claims of revealed religion, whether these were Catholic or those of Dr Buchman and the Oxford Group. In 1930, she could be accused by her youngest son of putting teetotalism before Christianity. Apart from family disagreements, the more important difference of opinion with her husband was not religious but political. Political disagreements, as she well knew, had bitterly split her own Howard family. She had shared her sister Cecilia's bitterness about 'the horrid trickery and the bribery' of the coalition government under Lloyd George. She did not share her husband's and her mother's belief in the Liberal Party under Asquith. In 1918 she had wanted to hear the Bolshevik side of the story from Russia, and she had come to believe that the Labour Party, whose leader she knew because she had helped to care for his children after Ramsey MacDonald's wife's death, was the hope for the country. She had no confidence in her husband's hero, Edward Grey, and none in the League of Nations societies and their personnel: 'if you can't devise a scheme to get the old and the new League people to amalgamate, how can you expect nations to work together?' She was never prepared to follow an independent Conservative such as Lord Robert Cecil, for it was the social divisions which he outlined in his manifesto which drove her to the Labour Party. In these views she was opposed to what her husband came to believe in the last year of the war and the immediate post-war years was his most important work, and her adherence to the Labour Party came at a time when that party was opposed to co-operation with any other progressive political group. She could see the importance of the League of Nations, where many in the Labour Party could not, although her view of it was never the same as her husband's. In June 1918 she had indeed told him: 'what I long for most is that you should carry out your inspiration of throwing other work over and doing League of Nations ... incomparably the most important and constructive thing you can do and the branch of politics in which your genius is most wholly beneficent'; but, as the League of Nations Union rather than the League of Nations itself came to occupy her husband's attention, she reverted to her opinion that the first work he could do was his own as a man of letters: 'couldn't you do for the League of Nations what he [Cobden] did for the cause of Trade? Only he was a politician to his fingertips and nothing will ever take you away from being a literary man to your fingertips.' As Gilbert Murray became more deeply involved in the work of and for the Union, his wife's opinion strengthened. Asquith, she told him, had once said that for him to be in politics was like taking a razor to cut a block. I feel this bears out what I know i.e. that you are *very* great as a writer, very able and wise in guiding people, adequate (but not so great) at organisation of offices and the like, and so, at 59½ I want you to take breath and write. There!

Murray's deepening involvement with the League of Nations Union was a serious difference of opinion about the work he should be doing, about the work he was best fitted to do. He found the separation an ordeal which was hard to bear, knowing that his wife disapproved in the same outspoken manner that her mother had done within her own unhappy family.

The root of the disagreement was deep. The Lady Mary saw the main political issue as domestic: the need for the Labour Party to reconstruct the country, to lead 'the nameless people who matter, who make a great movement and fight the great moral fights — all except for a few great leaders like you and Wilberforce and Mazzini'. To Gilbert Murray the main political issue was international: the avoidance of war. While he did not fail to recognise the need to mobilise public opinion, to create an influential movement, while he might have blushed at the comparison with Wilberforce and Mazzini, he nevertheless saw leadership as the key issue: Grey or Cecil in the 1920s, Lytton or Samuel in the 1930s, were the men whom he believed mattered. Their differences of opinion were profound, but the marriage withstood it. For, however much Lady Mary might disapprove of her husband's actions, she never doubted his greatness, and he, whatever the ordeals through which he had passed, never failed in courtesy and reassurance of his wife: 'You reproach yourself far too much. All that is wrong with Puss is a sort of irritable generosity which always makes me proud of her and glad I did not marry anyone else;' 'I don't see how we could get on without each other.'

8 FROM LIBERALISM TO LIBERALITY

When the end of the war came, Gilbert Murray was almost 53 years old. To his reputation as the foremost Hellenist in the English-speaking world and his fame as a man of letters, he had added that of a man of public affairs in the service of a country at war. This reputation, however, still bore a party label; for Murray identified the welfare of his country with Asquith's Liberal Party. With the ending of the war and the immorality, as he saw it, of Lloyd George's coalition government, he was prepared to enter the political battle. He ran in successive parliamentary elections. In 1919 he was the Liberal candidate in the election for Rector of Glasgow University, standing against the Conservative Party leader, Bonar Law. In the following year he stood against Lloyd George himself in the Rectorial contest at Edinburgh University. He never came close to winning in any of these contests, often to his own relief. For his knowledge of party politics caused him to share Asquith's opinion that he was unsuited to parliamentary politics.

Who, too deep for his hearers, still went on refining.
And thought of convincing, while they thought of dining.

Nevertheless, the war had led Murray to wish to be actively involved in public affairs, and, given the causes he held dear, that involvement immediately after the war was distinctively Liberal in a factional party sense. He was the more inclined to this active participation because he also felt, in his post-war lectures at Oxford, that the young were ceasing to be interested in Greek literature as he understood it, but cared only for excavations. A new arena of activity, of seeing through Greek literature into life, was called for. He did not abandon his work as a university professor. Nor did he cease to be a man of letters, although his writings and lectures began to apply his knowledge of Greece more directly to the cause of Civilisation and Peace. Rather did he add the work in which he was now interested to what he had always done.

The new direction in Murray's life was associated with a change in its style. Murray's outside interests had always to some extent detached him from the inward-looking society of most Oxford dons and their wives. Lady Mary had never felt at home in Oxford. The war had brought home the burden of the large, unattractive house in the Woodstock Road, No 82, to which they had moved in 1912. In mid-1919 the Murrays moved out of Oxford to Boar's Hill, a rural setting a few miles away which Gilbert had described in 1905 as 'one of the most beautiful sites in England'; one, too, where the air was cleaner and fresher than in the town, and which had a congenial community of distinguished literary figures: Robert Bridges, John Masefield and the Blundens. The Murrays' house was 'Yatscombe', not a beautiful one in itself but standing in a magnificent garden which sloped steeply away from Oxford to the south, towards the Berkshire Downs, overlooking Bagley Wood. The garden became famous for its display of azaleas which a notice on the gate invited passers-by to come in and enjoy. After Agnes's death, the Murrays built a memorial cottage beside the gate which, in later years, housed refugees from European persecutions. The establishment on Boar's Hill, with which so many people's memories associate Gilbert and Lady Mary, was the setting for the remaining 38 years of their lives, close to but detached from Oxford, and with not-too-difficult connections to London which was increasingly the centre of Murray's activity. To Yatscombe came a stream of house guests and visitors: family, friends, eminent figures, refugees and others in need. The house at Overstrand they put out at long lease, for with Murray's new work the English seaside holidays were replaced by holidays on the Continent: in Switzerland, after Murray had attended his meetings in Geneva, or occasionally in France when he had to meet in Paris.

Yatscombe and Murray's work entailed a new life-style. There had to be more servants, with a cook and a gardener in the house or cottage. Murray's increased work required a secretary; and a succession of women graduates — Audrey Richards, Lucy Mair, Jacqueline Fulton to name some who went on to noteworthy careers. The Murrays' own personal tastes remained ascetic; there was, in the early years at Yatscombe, to be nothing that Lady Mary considered to be luxury. Nevertheless the Murrays became rich upon the death of Lady Carlisle in 1921. They had never, of course, been poor, for, apart from Murray's salary and the not inconsiderable royalties from his published work, amounting in all to an income of over £2,000 a year, Lady Mary had always had an allowance from her mother (about £800 p.a. in 1921) with occasional capital gifts as well. They had both, but Lady Mary in particular, given away a great deal to anyone in need. Under the Countess's Will, however, of which they were Executors, they inherited a major part of the Howard estate which Lady Carlisle had left away from the title of Earl of Carlisle. Some of this inheritance, such as Castle Howard itself, they passed on. They could not, Murray told his wife, refuse to act as Executors; that would be disrespectful to her mother; but where they thought the Will did not represent her real wishes, they should try to get agreement among the children to correct it, but not to re-establish primogeniture. The property which the Murrays themselves inherited, in land, farms and advowsons, was worth about £5,000 p.a. although almost a fifth of that went back into the land. Even so, the Murrays were, by the standards of the day, rich and, other than the causes they supported, they could make handsome allowances to their children, grandchildren and more distant relations, apart from any outright gifts of property, such as Ganthorpe Manor to the Toynbees in 1925. They could settle Basil's considerable debts. They did not alter their own style of life, but in 1921 Gilbert told Mary 'I should dearly like to see you — and myself — living a little more comfortably'. Never much more comfortably, however, for Lady Mary still worried over staying at luxurious or expensive hotels. They were still notably generous to anyone in need. When the Depression came in 1931 they thought seriously about selling Yatscombe, moving back to Oxford and doing without Edgington, the gardener, the car and Murray's secretary. By 1932 their generosity had resulted in a considerable overdraft, and their obligations again caused them to think of selling Yatscombe or at least shutting up half of it, but while they remained there a car was a necessity, although Edgington might be asked to accept a reduction and a secretary dispensed with. With Murray's retirement from his Oxford chair only three years away, his own view was that if they sold the house they should move to London, not Oxford. In the event they stayed on at Yatscombe so long as they lived, for as Leif Jones (later Lord Rhayader), Lady Carlisle's former secretary and friend who had helped them with her Will, pointed out, they could scarcely spend their capital before they died, even if they did live at luxury hotels. Yatscombe, in short, was a secure and, as it seemed to visitors, serene base from which Murray could undertake his post-war work while Lady Mary pursued her own more radical causes. For some it became almost a place of pilgrimage, the home of a humanist saint.

The Murrays' move to Boar's Hill coincided with the Paris Peace Conference which ended the First World War and set up the League of Nations. Murray had hoped — indeed had been prepared — to play a major part as head of the League of Nations group within the British delegation after he left the Board of Education on 30 November 1918, but his hopes were dashed when Lord Robert Cecil resigned from the government in which he was a Foreign Office minister and himself became available to head the group. Cecil was, Murray wrote, much better fitted for the position to which he was appointed than himself, but it was still a disappointment not to be intimately involved with what he had come to believe was more important than anything else: a League to prevent war, war being the ruin of civilisation. His interest in a League had been stimulated by Grey before his American visit of 1916. In the United States, he came to know the League to Enforce the Peace. When he returned to Britain, he had joined the League of Nations Society which had been established in 1915.

In the spring of 1918 he had had a caller at the Board of Education. This was David Davies, formerly a secretary of Lloyd George. Davies was involved in another society which had just been founded: the League of Free Nations Association. His justification for the existence of the second society struck a chord in Murray: the older society was too much identified with pacificism and with the left wing in politics. It was, in any case, too inefficient. Murray himself was clear by July 1918 that the League must not be left to pacifists like Leonard Woolf, Noel Brailsford and Lowes Dickinson 'or it must fail because it will have no majority behind it'. By that date he was also aware that Lord Robert Cecil was keen on the idea of a League, for he had invited him to call at the Foreign Office to discuss it at any time. He had heard too that Lord Milner had been converted to it. His worry was that Lloyd George's government would spoil the idea by making it an anti-German League, and that the League supporters outside the government, with people like H.G. Wells involved, would also spoil the idea by aiming at the too-ambitious project of a world federation. What was needed, said Murray was 'a practical scheme for an immediate need'. He took part in the committee which led to the amalgamation of the two League societies, although he declined Davies's suggestion of July 1918 that he leave the Board of Education and join the League of Free Nations Association as Director.

In January 1919 he accepted Cecil's invitation to join a Foreign Office Advisory Committee under Lord Phillimore to supply criticisms and suggestions on the subject of the League Covenant which Lord Robert would be dealing with at the Paris conference. He also served on the Management Committee of the amalgamated League societies which, as the League of Nations Union, aimed to secure 'the whole hearted acceptance by the British people of the League of Nations as the guardian of international right, the organ of international co-operation, and the final arbiter in international differences'. These objectives were not much less ambitious than a world federation. So, the League might quite likely fail, said Murray to his wife, but it was worth trying. Having, after November 1918, no position of official authority, the League of Nations Union was the best opportunity to help, but there was an immediate difficulty. It was hard to keep the League societies non-party: the 'good people' were all Liberals or Socialists. Murray's immediate concern was therefore with domestic policies.

The war had seen the ruin of the Asquithian Liberals; they were out of office and, in the professional opinion of his brother-in-law, Geoffrey Howard, not likely to regain it in any foreseeable future. The coalition government under Lloyd George might indeed 'plunge' for the League, but what they understood by that was a League which excluded the late enemy, Germany. To Murray a government which made such an exclusion was ruining a League, in which some of the government ministers in any case had doubtful faith. The immediate concern must therefore be to secure a government which *was* dedicated to the League and therefore to a peace which would end all wars. Until the war actually ended, however, it was a matter of duty to Murray to support even a government under Lloyd George, even though he was a treacherous and faithless Liberal who had displaced Asquith. But as soon as the war was over and Murray had left his Board of Education post, then it became a matter of duty to try to turn out a government which, although it had a minister like Robert Cecil until his resignation at the end of 1918, was dominated by reactionary militarists who could not possibly make a satisfactory peace. The irony, although it did not strike Murray, was that the men whom he believed to be needed at the head of affairs to make such a peace were the very Liberal imperialists, Asquith and Grey, whom he regarded with hostility before the war began, and whom his wife still refused to follow. They were now the leaders around whom Murray became involved in party politics.

In February 1918, while still a civil servant, Murray had been approached by a group of younger Oxford dons to stand for one of the university seats, either as a Labour Party candidate or as an Independent or as a Workers Educational Association candidate, on a platform of socialistic reform. He promptly declined. He was, however, prepared to take an active role inside the Liberal Party itself. In June 1920 he was elected to a seat on the executive of the National Liberal Federation, but in fact since 1919 he had been active in the attempt to revive Liberal fortunes.

When Asquith lost office in December 1916, Murray found himself invited into the Asquith circle. He had reservations about Asquith's leadership, for the latter took the view that it was a matter for the sound judgement of the country whether they liked Lloyd George's government and he himself should remain quiet; if the country did not like the government, they would come to him or to someone with whom he could act. Such restraint — others called it lethargy — was understandable during the war; it was a matter of public duty which Asquith himself said was not due to any lack of fighting spirit. Nevertheless, it seemed to Murray, as to others, not what was needed when the war was over. Asquith lost his seat in the Khaki election and was out of parliament until his triumphant return at Paisley early in 1920, so that the question of leadership in the Liberal Party seemed to Murray to be urgent.

In early December 1919 he received a letter from a prominent Liberal, Walter Runciman, asking if he knew where Lord Robert Cecil stood in relation to 'those of us who are free from entanglements and are Liberal'? This interest in Cecil ran through Liberal discussions at the time, and the question was addressed to Murray because of his 1919 connection with Lord Robert. Murray's acquaintance with Lord Robert was in fact relatively recent, for a Conservative high-churchman was not to be found in Murray's circle of friends until common devotion to a League brought them together. But he shared Runciman's interest in Cecil: they were concerned to find progressive leadership. Much as Murray admired Asquith, it was clear that he was not providing the leadership the Liberal Party needed, at a time when the question of clear British support for the League made the matter urgent.

In January 1918 Margot Asquith told Gilbert that her husband was urging Grey to come back into active politics and take a hand. This attempt to enlist the support of one who was generally believed to command respect across party politics also became the objective of Murray and Liberals who thought like him. Grey himself was most reluctant; he was not prepared to be President of a League of Nations committee in mid-1918, although he consented to be a member of the research committee of the League of Free Nations Association. This was far from being the active involvement in public affairs that Murray wanted. Runciman, in January 1920, told him that Lord Robert had proved 'shy as a red deer' at any political approach, but it was clear that he would support Grey, if Asquith would step aside as Leader of the Liberal Party, because he loathed Lloyd George and despised Bonar Law, the Leader of his own Conservative Party. For Cecil, having just resigned from his government office on the issue of Welsh Church Disestablishment, might as an independent Conservative play an important role in the construction of a progressive, pro-League government when the coalition fell apart as it was expected to do. The leadership of the Liberal Party was thus a critical issue, but beyond that was the possibility of a progressive party combining groups from all three political parties. Who was to lead such a grouping?

The first step in the persuasion of Grey was a letter, signed by a group of public figures, appealing to him to re-enter political life. Murray drafted this appeal and sent it to Cecil who, having made one slight alteration, was prepared to sign and to ask his Conservative colleagues, Lord Salisbury (his brother) and Lord Selborne, to do the same, and also prepared to sound out prominent members of the Labour Party such as Clynes and Henderson. The two Conservatives were not willing to sign a published letter but were willing privately to write to Grey making the appeal. Clynes was prepared to sign with a group which included Asquith. Grey's response, in a private reply to Salisbury of which Cecil told Murray, was encouraging, and in August 1920 Murray was Grey's fellow house guest in Scotland. The statesman he found to be in good spirits, but there was no definite conclusion to their discussion. Grey told Murray that if the independent Liberals were crushed he would vote Labour, but that the immediate danger was Lloyd George's personality which paralysed government by its irregularity and by his saying different things to different people. Grey was very reluctant to move, but he consented 'if he finds that he has in mind a definite policy, apart from his negative criticism of the government' to meet the signatories of the appeal to him, as a group with a view to common action in Parliament.

Parliamentary action: that was the problem, as Cecil at least had recognised, for he believed that Grey would have a fit if regular attendance at the House of Lords were suggested to him. The signatories, as Murray acknowledged, were not themselves a parliamentary group, and the formation of one depended not upon himself and the other non-parliamentarians, but upon Cecil, Buckmaster and Clynes. Without this parliamentary support Murray did not think that much more could be expected of Grey, for the latter's last words to him as he left had been to the effect that perhaps the group would do well, and then it would have quite enough people to support it without him. The practical politicians saw the difficulties Grey's reluctance posed. The official Labour Party was against any combination with any other political groups and Cecil could not carry many of the Conservatives with him. Grey was the leader, they could agree, who might be followed by some Labour people and by some Conservatives, but Grey was not leader of the Liberals. That post was still held by Asquith, and Asquith was the stumbling block.

When Murray looked at the Labour Party he saw two different aspects. On the one hand there was the party represented by Clynes, Thomas and Haldane, a former Liberal; on the other there were the Webbs, Laski and Cole. Sidney Webb he knew as the man who, when warned that lack of co-operation with the Liberals in progressive causes might mean the ruin of Europe, said with a snigger: 'that would not be too high a price to pay' for the ruin of Liberalism. Grey, he thought, did not see these two faces of the Labour Party. In these political circumstances, the attitude of Asquith was crucial, for, while some members of other parties could agree to follow Grey, very few were willing to follow Asquith. Cecil believed that Margot and the Asquith family were determined that he should come back as Prime Minister, that they treated their eviction from Downing Street as a personal affront and that they would never let the head of the family abdicate in favour of Grey. Cecil was prepared to accept Grey as his leader but his acceptance of Asquith's leadership would, he said, be political suicide: Asquith was a 'hopeless old man'.

In the face of the practical politicians, Gilbert Murray tried

again. In April 1921 he talked to Asquith himself. The best solution
to the domestic political situation, he explained to him, since it was
impossible to get another purely Liberal government under
Asquith, would be to have three groups: the Liberals under
Asquith, the independent Conservatives under Lord Robert, and
Labour under Clynes and Henderson. The question, said Murray
to Asquith, was then to find a national leader under whom all could
unite, and the only possible answer was Grey. Asquith, in Murray's
account to Herbert Gladstone, agreed step by step with all this.
They then discussed Grey's reluctance and his disqualifications
because of his health and failing eyesight, but, when Murray asked
if there were anyone else, Asquith replied unhesitatingly that there
was not. Murray then mentioned that Grey was reluctant to seem to
be a rival, a fact which Asquith recognised, but he said that he
would write to Grey. He was, said Murray, 'faultlessly generous
and public spirited from first to last'. When, however, Asquith
actually met Grey in June 1921, he did not mention national leadership, but pressed Grey to commit himself to avowed and open co-
operation, if his health permitted it. When Grey himself mentioned
his eyesight which would prevent him from reading office papers,
Asquith replied that he could be a non-departmental minister as
Lord President of the Council and Leader in the House of Lords, a
very different position from that of Prime Minister of a national
government which was what Murray had in mind for Grey. The
Liberal Party itself would not accept that its leader should thus be
displaced, even had Grey been willing to lead instead of Asquith.
Lord Robert Cecil made it clear that he would never serve under
Asquith nor join any government which was the Liberal Party in
disguise, although he also declared to Murray that he himself had
no ambition to become Prime Minister and that he was warmly in
favour of Grey.

Grey was indeed Murray's 'beloved leader', but in 1921 he was a
leader who refused to lead. Moreover, Murray was aware that some
whose opinions he respected had considerable reservations about
Grey. Lady Carlisle herself regarded Grey as moody and therefore
suspect. Lady Mary told her husband that she could not forgive
Grey's laziness over the League and that in any case there was considerable feeling against him because of the war; it was not so much
the 14 days which led up to British involvement in the conflict as
the Liberal imperialism which had led up to the 14 days which

prevented her and many others from having confidence in Grey, whose indecision and preference for a fishing life in Scotland in any case exasperated her. Her advice to her husband in May 1922, when a general election was expected in the near future, was to go to the country with Asquith, although she herself was attracted to the Labour Party.

Asquith invited Murray to lunch on 19 March 1922 to discuss the political situation. He seemed to Murray free from any personal animus, but it became clear that he intended to remain Leader of the Liberal Party while attempting to broaden the basis of his parliamentary support. In doing this he would, he told Murray, sooner keep Lord Robert than gain Lloyd George by any arrangement with the Prime Minister to re-unite the divided Liberals when the coalition government broke up. Indeed, he emphasised to Murray the unreliability of the coalition Liberals, including Herbert Fisher, because they had been so deeply committed by the policy of reprisals against Germany. It was a well-chosen argument to use with Murray who, in his deep concern for the success of the League, set the admission of Germany as one of the essentials. Nevertheless, it was clear to Murray by the spring of 1922 that his efforts over the leadership of the Party and then the leadership of a combined progressive political group devoted to honesty and principle and the League of Nations had been unsuccessful. At the beginning of April Cecil underlined the point: 'we now have neither leader nor policy.' Nevertheless, Cecil had himself drafted a national manifesto which he had shown to 30 of his party colleagues. They were non-committal, although they agreed that they would rather follow him than any other Conservative. Cecil was severe on Asquith's failure to lead, or even to attend at the House, but his own manifesto was in Murray's opinion too abstract to be itself a rallying call, although he nevertheless suggested some alterations and was prepared to ask his friends to back it up by letters in the press.

Cecil's manifesto declared that the old division of Conservative and Liberal had been overtaken by events. There were now two schools of thought which divided people: those who wanted a return to pre-war conditions and the balance of power in Europe and who also rejected economic change at home; and those who wanted to destroy existing institutions and incidentally regarded the League of Nations as a final capitalist plot to maintain a hold on the world. The great mass of the population lay between these two extremes. What was wanted was a middle course: progress with stability. We should apply the principles of the Covenant of the League to both foreign and domestic questions, so that man might be governed by spiritual and not by material forces. Murray hailed this in *The Times* as a Liberal document, although he accepted that Lord Robert should not call himself a Liberal because that Party had been rejected by the electorate in 1918, notwithstanding that its policy was right, so that suspicion was now attached to its policies. Britain, wrote Murray, needed conservatism, a return to habits of consistent and correct negotiation. He would, he said, publicly accept Lord Robert as one of his leaders. In private, he believed that there was a landslide away from the coalition government, although it did not know where to slide and plainly had belief neither in Asquith nor in the Labour Party but rather wanted someone free from war responsibility and war profits, with an honest belief in spiritual forces; 'Lord Robert' he said, 'may be the man, otherwise I feel despairing.' Asquith, however, told him that Lord Robert would have difficulties even in his own constituency, holding such views; but Asquith's own interest in politics was at a low ebb and he believed that the best result in the coming election would still leave a Conservative majority.

Murray still hoped that Cecil would join the Liberals and, after the manifesto, was not sure that he would not actually prefer him to Grey as Prime Minister. Yet, he had also become aware that most Tories were hostile to Cecil, regarding the manifesto as a string of platitudes and the man himself as too cantankerous and difficult to work with; but he still had some hopes. Cecil himself thought that nothing should be done until the coalition drifted apart; to attack it might hold it together. What was really wanted, in his view, was a public statement from Asquith that he would serve under Grey. Then, both Cecil and Murray agreed, there would be a united progressive party.

When the general election came in October, however, there emerged no such united progressive grouping. Cecil himself in his election address proclaimed that he was an independent Conservative who believed in ordered progress and in the League of Nations as the best guarantee of peace, in the reduction of expenditure in order to lighten taxes, in the improvement of education, health and housing facilities, and in a partnership between employers and employed in a League of Classes. To achieve this, Cecil told his constituents in Hitchin, he would support Bonar Law's Conservative government so long as it was guided by these principles.

The 1922 general election ruined the old Liberal Party. In the House it was divided almost equally between Asquithians and Georgites, but even in combination it had fewer seats than the Labour Party. It ceased to be the official Opposition. Cecil and Murray despaired of the Liberals' folly. Lord Robert believed that, if the party had taken their advice about Grey, it would have swept the country with an alternative Prime Minister. As it was, the Liberal chances seemed to have vanished. Gilbert Murray involved himself no further in party politics of the kind he had engaged in since the war, while Cecil said that he would rather see a pro-League Labour government in power than an anti-League Conservative one.

Both Cecil and Murray thus moved away from party politics. In Gilbert Murray's case, where he had in early 1919 wondered if the League ought not to be a definitely Liberal society, by late 1922 the failure of the Liberal Party and the obvious League commitment of some Conservatives like Cecil and of some members of the Labour Party like Henderson took him out of domestic party politics. Like Mr Gladstone, whom he later quoted in his Hibbert Lectures, he began to look not at the Liberal Party label but to ask: 'is he a man of real Liberality?' In the last year of the war Gilbert Murray had come to know Conservatives whom he could regard as men of the highest principles and goodwill. He put Arthur Balfour and Lord Robert Cecil into that category, and even Milner and Curzon. After the *contretemps* with Balfour over Murray's American visit in 1918, when they met after dinner at Lady Wemyss's in July Balfour had nevertheless been very friendly, while of both him and Cecil, Grey had earlier written to Murray that they were both good colleagues who put party politics on one side and dealt with issues on their merits. While both Balfour and Cecil were at the Foreign Office — as they were from 1917 until the latter's resignation at the end of 1918 — Grey said that you could rely on an upright policy. In the early 1920s they were men of principle with whom Gilbert Murray could co-operate when party politics seemed to offer no hope for the future, and the Liberal men of principle, reluctant leaders as they were, could achieve little. Lord Robert Cecil, in particular, although he would not become a Liberal and despite his High Church principles, was a man with whom Murray could gladly co-operate.

In June 1921 Murray received a 'most friendly letter' from Cecil, saying that it would be a 'great delight' to take him to Geneva, and that he would see what arrangements could be made. Cecil, having ceased to be a British minister, was going to Geneva to the second meeting of the League of Nations Assembly, as one of the South African delegation of three. Smuts, the South African Prime Minister, an acquaintance of Murray and his family during the war, and knowing of his stand during the Boer War, was happy also to include him, together with Cecil and the South African Agent General in London. Balfour went as head of the British delegation, with H.A.L. Fisher as a co-delegate, both of them anxious to see co-operation with the delegations from other parts of the Empire. In Geneva, therefore, Gilbert Murray had the chance to become better acquainted with the men of high principle from other political parties, and in particular with Lord Robert Cecil whom he came to admire even more than he admired Grey.

The relationship with Cecil was important. For the second time in his life — the first had been with Charles Gore — Gilbert Murray came into close and congenial contact with a man whose political and religious principles had nothing in common with his own. When Cecil resigned from the coalition government in 1918 it became clear to Murray that he was indeed a man of principle, and he became increasingly aware that, as Grey had told him, Lord Robert was an upright, honest man. In the party manoeuverings of the early 1920s Murray was even more impressed. And so, with increasingly close association in the cause of the League, Murray began to lose his politically partisan feelings. To him, as to Cecil, the difference between Liberal and Conservative seemed to lose its force, and, in supporting Cecil's manifesto of 1922, Murray actually came to acknowledge the need for conservatism. When they began to work together in Geneva the party labels began to seem still less important in the face of foreigners. For, what Murray had been accustomed to regard as conservative began to seem liberal when looked at through the eyes of his foreign colleagues.

Cecil, after his resignation from the government, had nevertheless gone to the Paris Peace Conference in 1919 as head of the League of Nations section of the British delegation. Murray had been involved in the organisation to support the League in Britain, but until 1921 he had no direct part to play in the League itself at Geneva. Because of his American connections and public reputation, he was a possible ambassador to the United States after

Spring-Rice retired in early 1918, although he thought himself unsuitable for the post and Lady Mary thought he could in fact expect nothing at the hands of Lloyd George's government. Nevertheless, that he entertained the idea at all reflected his anxiety to do some public work which would help the cause of peace. The British government was not prepared to include him in the British delegation to the first meetings of the League in Geneva for much the same reason as he was never a serious candidate for ambassador: a representative of the government was appointed to convey the government's view and policies, not to take an individual or a critical line of his own. From Gilbert Murray's point of view, Lloyd George's government was one about which he had considerable reservations, so any official British position was difficult, but membership of the South African delegation appointed by Smuts got round the difficulty.

His first impressions of the League in Geneva were unfavourable. On 4 September he was writing to his wife that the French and the Poles were making everything impossible inside the League, while the Americans outside it seemed to intend to wreck all that the French and Poles let through. He and Lord Robert, he said, were concocting various radical plots but at best they would come to nothing but a protest. The following day he went to a meeting in Arthur Balfour's rooms which assembled all of the British Empire delegations. Balfour spoke to them about the impending election of the first President of the Assembly and was anxious to have an Empire view. The President, thought Balfour, must be neither a representative of one of the Great Powers nor a member of the Council of the League. Some members of the League wanted a South American. The French wanted a Swiss. The final result was a Dutchman, Karnebeeck, a former Foreign Minister of the Netherlands who had, wrote Murray, neither voice nor presence but who was elected in the face of French attempts to secure the election of a Brazilian. This first experience of the politics of an international gathering was disappointing. Murray detected 'nationalism' which he regarded as the real obstacle to peace, although it is clear that he saw this nationalism as something which foreigners exhibited but not the British and the Empire delegations. From his acquaintance with Balfour and Cecil he took it for granted that, as men of the highest principle, who enjoyed, as he could see, immense respect among the other delegations, they were impartial. They were trying to make the League work, not to obstruct it by national interests as were the French and the Poles. He had some doubts about Balfour on the questions of disarmament and the mandates for the former German colonies, but he accepted that Balfour's influence in that League meeting was on balance 'so very good' that it would be a tragedy if his age — over 70 — obliged him to retire, for he and his fellow British delegate Herbert Fisher were the only League pillars inside the coalition government since Cecil had resigned.

Murray recognised that the first meetings of any large body entailed some confusion, such as luggage being sent to the wrong hotel. The preliminaries of any organisation involved difficulties until things settled down. Nevertheless it was not so much the absence of established routine which struck Murray at his first Assembly meeting as the characteristics of foreigners. He often used to say that he had not a drop of English blood in his veins — his father's family was Irish, his mother's Welsh — but at the League he began to feel 'John Bullish'. As he reported to Smuts in a private letter of 8 October, he 'was conscious of many weaknesses in the Assembly: some intrigue, some loquacity, a rather large proportion of small dark Latin nations and so on'. This initial impression remained with him as he became more absorbed into Assembly work. He was placed upon two of the Commissions through which the League Assembly handled its business. In 1921 he became a member of the Commission which dealt with Amendments to the Covenant and of the one which dealt with Humanitarianism. Neither, he was aware, was among the most interesting, but he liked them well enough.

At his first Commission meeting on the Covenant he made his first speech — badly, he thought, for he was nervous and had to speak sitting down — but Cecil encouraged him to speak again in his other Commission on the subject of minorities, and Nansen, the Norwegian delegate and former explorer, asked him to speak in support of Russian relief. This second Commission, however, put him on to its sub-committee which dealt with the organisation of Intellectual Work, a subject which, Murray told his wife, 'bores me stiff but I am one of the few people who know anything about it'. When he attended his first sub-committee discussion on 'this beastly Intellectual Travail' he found it to be 'devastating and drivelling . . . a Serb spoke twenty times, each time worse than the last. A Greek was mad, and Hennessy the Frenchman spoke about fifteen times.' It was an unpromising beginning to what was to become Murray's chief work at the League and in 1921 it seemed a diversion from more serious topics. On 12 September he was speaking in the Assembly itself on the need for the Council of the League to set up a Permanent Commission with power of enquiry on the spot to deal with minorities, and moving that the question of a national home for the Armenians should be referred to this Commission. He was better pleased with his performance on this occasion, taking pride in his ability to say everything in ten minutes, a far shorter time than anyone else took. But he found himself exposed to attack, for one of the Indian delegation attacked both the League and the South African delegation over the treatment of Indians in South Africa.

He became aware of the politics which ran through the Assembly independently of the merits of any issue, for the Indian who had attacked him, Shastri, nevertheless supported him in his proposal that various states be invited to give information about the opium traffic, in the face of opposition from France supported by Poland, Greece and Rumania. This opposition was ostensibly, said Murray, on the grounds that such a request would encourage spying and delation, although it was really by way of counter-attack in the battle over the white slave traffic. The Italian delegate opposed Murray's motion for relief of the Russian famine on the grounds that it was not a humanitarian but a political question, and therefore beyond the terms of reference of their Commission. His main battles were nevertheless with the French, especially on the question of the white slave traffic or, as it was called, the Traffic in Women and Children. The prohibition of this seemed to Murray a self-evidently worthy cause, but French opposition to the proposal was strong, because, conjectured Murray, they were anxious about their *maisons tolerées*, and they obstructed the passage of a Draft Convention, with Murray, as rapporteur on the topic, having to fight 'the Frog' — his word for the French delegate — all the way through the Commission and into the Assembly. Hanotaux, the French delegate, was 'dreadfully cross and upset' and Murray decided that on the other controversial question of the opium trade he had 'better keep in the background, as I was becoming persona ingrata to the French'.

As a first experience of the organisation which was to secure peace, it was disillusioning. The French in particular seemed to him difficult and obstructive on issues which were, in Murray's view, clear-cut moral ones, and when they looked like being beaten on one issue took to deplorable tactics on other important questions.

On 14 September, for example, in the matter of electing judges to the International Court, the French and their Eastern European ally, the Rumanians, supported the South American bloc which put in 'five dagoes at the head of the poll'. That was just the sort of occasion which brought out the worst qualities of the Assembly, and it constituted, believed Murray, a serious danger for the future. It produced unfortunate reactions in other delegations, including the British, for when Murray suggested to Sir Cecil Hurst, the Legal Adviser to the Foreign Office, that over the white slave traffic some attempt might be made to satisfy reasonable French anxieties, he received the answer that no one in the Foreign Office could agree; an apparent success would only inspire the French to demand more. This Franco-British hostility, a reflection of the deterioration in the relations of the two countries which had come with the Treaty of Versailles, worried Gilbert. Personally he was able to reach an amicable relationship with Hanotaux after their early battles, but he was more than ever convinced that the most urgent need was to include Germany, and if possible America, in the League. The absence of these two Great Powers made Franco-British hostility particularly dangerous for the future. 'We need another big civilized respectable nation.' It was not, however, simply a matter of a political numbers game in the Assembly. It was also, believed Murray, a question of the permanent machinery of the League. For, if all the Great Powers were not members, then the Secretariat which had begun by being predominantly British under so devoted a civil servant as Sir Eric Drummond, the first Secretary General, would by the rotation and *roulement* which were to be applied in Secretariat personnel, presently reach the point at which it had a South American chief and Rumanian and Greek supporters and then 'it will have less value. This is one of the great dangers. We do need Germany and the USA . . . It sometimes freezes one's blood to think what wretched material one has to build the League out of.'

Despite his unfortunate impressions at his first Assembly session in Geneva, Murray did not doubt that the League must be built. He remained a member of the South African delegation to the Assembly for one more session, during which he became a member of the Commission on Disarmament in substitution of his membership of that on Amendments to the Covenant. The latter had been frustrating in 1921 because of the legal uncertainty over the requirements for an amendment actually to be made: did the Assembly have to be unanimous or would a bare majority suffice? But Disarmament was equally frustrating because, in Murray's view, the military and naval advisers had no interest in seeing it achieved. Indeed, during that Assembly the situation became still worse, for the French occupied the Ruhr in 1922 to enforce German reparation payments and were apparently supporting Italy's breach of the Covenant over Corfu in return for Italian support over the Ruhr. But Murray's direct connection with the disarmament question ended when he ceased to be a South African delegate after 1922. The South African government then felt obliged to appoint one of its own nationals, and the only British government which felt able to appoint Murray to any official League position was the minority Labour government of 1924. Whatever their political complexion, British governments in any case felt it necessary that its delegation should speak and act with one official voice.

The League, however, had non-political aspects. The Committee of Intellectual Co-operation which was nominated in 1922 was composed neither of official nor of national representatives; its members were there as distinguished figures in the intellectual world, nominated not by national governments but by the Council of the League. The first President of the Committee was Henri Bergson, with Gilbert Murray as Vice-President. Other members included Mde Curie, representing physics and Poland, Destrée, a Belgian man of letters and former statesman, De Reynold, a Swiss Catholic literary man, and Rocco, an Italian lawyer. Its first secretary was a Japanese samurai turned Christian, Nitobe. The Committee met for the first time in August 1922. In the previous year, Gilbert had reported to the Assembly on the organisation of Intellectual Work, as *rapporteur* of a sub-committee of the Commission on Humanitarianism. The subject, he then privately said, was almost a joke, but he had to do the best he could with it. He had made a longish speech on 22 September 1921 and found that he was 'getting interested in the wretched business from having to explain and defend it' to a tired and inattentive Assembly. With the formation of the full Committee in the following year and upon making the aquaintance of his colleagues, he began to be more enthusiastic. Destrée he found to be a clever, colourful character, and Mde Curie 'wonderful', but his contemporary enthusiasm was not so great as his later reflections suggest.

Even in a committee concerned with learning and intellectual life he encountered the same anti-German feeling which he had thought so dangerous in the League itself. In September 1923, an argument over the collection and distribution of funds for the relief of Austrian universities which were suffering from the effects of the war led him to tell some home truths to his foreign colleagues. The Committee, he asserted, must make a perfectly clear pledge to treat all nations without distinction and it would be much better for it to hand over any money for distribution by other bodies. He pressed the point that Germany, rather than any more small nations, must be included, but in the following year he was exclaiming about the opposition to this proposal: 'those Frogs are at it again.' He was very angry with Bergson over his attitude to Albert Einstein's membership of the Committee. The latter had as a pacifist been critical of the League because of its potential use of force, and his letter to this effect was used by Bergson to maintain that, while he would be happy to have Einstein back on the Committee, he must first apologise for his attack on the League. He was not prepared to accept any other German. Murray took the matter up with Drummond, but before receiving an answer had already expressed his own views in a letter to *The Times*. Murray's was not the view Drummond held, and Murray then found that he too had to explain that his letter was not an attack on the Committee of Intellectual Co-operation to which he belonged. In the event Einstein returned to the Committee, but the incident showed Murray that, even in this non-political work, there were troubles ahead because of the strength of national feeling.

Bergson retired as president for health reasons in 1925, to be succeeded by the distinguished Swiss scientist H.A. Lorentz until 1928. In those three years Murray still worried about the French influence upon the Committee, especially since, in July 1924, the French government had offered to found and to fund with a million francs an Institute of Intellectual Co-operation to be situated in Paris. The Institute was to be placed at the disposal of the Committee of Intellectual Co-operation in Geneva but the direction of the Institute must be French. The offer was plainly seductive for a Committee which had no funds of its own. In Gilbert's words, it 'went wild with enthusiasm' and accepted with acclamation. It fell to Murray to point out to his colleagues that acceptance was not a matter for their decision but a matter for the Council of the League. He himself believed that to make Intellectual Co-operation dependent upon an Institute sited in Paris would be a most mischievous mistake. Nevertheless the Institute was set up. Murray was pressed to join the Board of Direction, an invitation he at first resisted, but as Vice-President of the League Committee, and its President from 1928, he felt that he could not refuse, whatever his misgivings. At root he was convinced that the Institute could not be international while it was wholly dependent on French money, while he felt the personal embarrassment of having his own expenses paid from this source. The League Council should not in his opinion have accepted the French offer unless other member nations were prepared to make similar gifts and no other Great Power ever did so. In particular, Murray was embarrassed by the consistent refusal of British governments, of any political colour, to provide any funds, although he tried to persuade them at regular intervals. He had little better success with the Dominions' governments. In 1927 he offered his resignation from the Committee, ostensibly on the grounds of his bad attendance, although he was in fact despondent about a number of aspects of the League, particularly the lack of progress on disarmament, and was aware that his Norwegian friend Nansen believed that the League in its existing form was doomed.

The rumours of Murray's possible resignation produced some unexpected expressions of concern. A French and a Rumanian colleague both told him how unhappy and disquieted they would be if he left, while Philip Noel-Baker who had had a long-standing concern with the League described to Cecil the effect which the possibility of Murray's resignation had had upon the Assembly itself and upon distinguished individual delegates such as the Czech, Edouard Benes. Knowledge of this reaction confirmed Lady Mary's view that her husband had, despite the bother the League caused him, 'done so finely and won such a position'. When in 1927 he was re-elected Vice-President, it was clear that Murray was at last in a position to take the lead in doing something to shape the future of Intellectual Co-operation.

His main problem was the Paris Institute. Its first director was Luchaire. It had soon become clear that, whatever his qualities, administrative skill was not among them, and in 1925 Alfred Zimmern, an Oxford don, was appointed Deputy Director. By 1927 it had become equally clear that Zimmern too was unable to supply the practical skills that Luchaire lacked, and that the relations between the two men had become impossible. De Reynold, whom Murray had originally regarded with considerable reservation as a conservative Swiss Catholic, was so despondent by mid-1928 that he too thought of resignation. The 1927 session he found to be so discouraging, the Institute so '*mal dirigé*' that he despaired for '*les valeurs intellectuelles et spirituelles que je représente — comme un âne porteur de reliques*'. Murray, whom he called *mon dernier espoir*, had become President of the Committee of Intellectual Co-operation, and De Reynold promised to support him in the necessary reforms. Murray's first thought was to secure proper control over the Institute's accounts by the Secretariat in Geneva, but Drummond told him that this was impossible unless a request came from the French government which would not make one. Murray next thought, through the establishment of national committees of Intellectual Co-operation in member states of the League, to offset the claim made by Luchaire and supported by Rocco in the International Committee in Geneva, that the Paris Institute was the sole organ of the Committee's work. By mid-1929 Murray had brought his Committee to the point at which Rocco and Destrée, as well as De Reynold, were agreed that Luchaire must go and that the means of doing this should be a committee of enquiry into the working of the Paris Institute, where Luchaire had begun a campaign for its 'rights' against the Secretariat of the League. The national committees when constituted were unanimous in their support for a committee of enquiry, and Luchaire himself showed its necessity when, in September 1929 after the decision about the enquiry had been agreed in Geneva, he attempted to dismiss Zimmern on the grounds that he lacked rapport with him. Murray prevented this on the obvious ground that, as the establishment of the committee of enquiry showed, there existed no full confidence in the Director, whose power to dismiss was in any case far from clear; any action must await the report of the enquiry.

When reorganisation was undertaken, as a result of the enquiry, the work of Intellectual Co-operation followed Murray's suggestions of 1929. The main Committee in Geneva, meeting once a year, he had then argued, could scarcely effect very much, but it could lay down a general programme of activity. It could work through committees and sub-committees of experts in particular areas. For example, a Museums office in Brussels; a Permanent Committee of Arts and Letters; a sub-committee on Education. It could establish a liaison with the Council of Scientific Unions and with such a meeting as the International Studies Conference, to which it could supply secretarial services. The Institute in Paris, with a new Managing Committee, a Director and a small staff, under the control of the International Committee in Geneva, formed the executive organ of Intellectual Co-operation which would carry out preparatory studies for conferences, and provide co-ordination and secretarial services for *ad hoc* committees of experts. Through bibliographical publications, it could foster intellectual co-operation. The International Committee and the Institute could co-operate with other League organisations, most notably the International Labour Office. To avoid the difficulties of a largely French endowment and a location in Paris, Murray accepted that the president of the Managing Committee and the Director of the Institute must be French, but by including the former within the International Committee, and by including members of the advisory or expert committees in the Managing Committee of the Institute, the work of Intellectual Co-operation could go forward.

This was broadly what the reorganisation achieved and Murray succeeded in carrying the French with him; they agreed that Luchaire must go, but *il faut s'agir sans brutalité*. In fact in April 1930 Luchaire offered his resignation which Murray accepted with some complimentary remarks about its wisdom at a time of change, and an expression of appreciation of the value of former services. He had expected a great row in the Committee meeting in Geneva in July when it considered the report of the enquiry. The French were prepared to accept Luchaire's resignation, but tried to make their acceptance a condition of getting various other things that they wanted. 'Blackmail', Murray called it, 'but my business is as usual to conciliate'. He did this successfully in spite of his anger at the French attitude, for in the meeting itself, although not in private discussions which were more difficult, Painlevé was reasonable and 'good humour returned with a long, silly speech by a fat, black Peruvian'. Rocco supported Murray, although Einstein, whom Murray believed had been 'got at' by Mde Luchaire, while 'nice', was 'a little childish'. Painlevé became President of the Managing Committee of the Institute and was presently succeeded by Edouard Herriot. The new Director was also a man with whom Murray could work, Henri Bonnet: 'all the good Bonnets are called Henri, all the bad ones Georges.' After 1930 Murray could begin to take pride in the work of Intellectual Co-operation which had now, under his presidency of the International Committee in Geneva, acquired the organisation which would begin to allow it to fulfil its important role.

In piloting the reorganisation through the shoals of an international committee, Murray had in his mind a definition of Intellectual Co-operation. There existed, he said, a certain standard of culture at which all civilised nations aim. The task of the League organisation was to provide the means of co-operation through which the civilised nations might achieve this — and by implication the uncivilised nations might be helped to want to achieve it. Murray was always absolutely clear that the central problem of the League was political: the prevention of war. But part of that prevention was the powerful but unseen sphere of the intellect in which interest and delight in the highest works of man caused differences of nationality to fade into nothingness. In some subjects, such as music, art and pure science, co-operation could flow naturally because it was not dependent upon language nor to any vital degree upon national tradition. Plainly there was a need to make art, music and pure science accessible across political and national boundaries, but the more serious difficulty was in those areas of intellectual work where language was an obstacle. Every language was a national tradition. Every national tradition was full of unexpressed assumptions, attitudes of mind. The first essential was to discover these and get them understood. That could only be done by the methods of conference, by personal intercourse between men of letters and science, and by conversation. This must be the first priority of Intellectual Co-operation which, with his awareness of the central political problems of nationalism and conflicts between sovereign nations, he began to call in 1931 'Moral Disarmament' in conscious distinction from Moral Rearmament.

This experience of direct involvement with an international organisation for peace, in which he worked side by side with men of different backgrounds and different principles from his own, who were nevertheless men of goodwill, obviously helped to move Murray from Liberalism, in a narrow sense, to Liberality, in the sense of its being the soul of western civilisation. Liberalism, as Murray had understood it, was a national British matter, primarily one of domestic politics, but Liberality was international, the reverse of that narrow nationalism which was the direct threat he perceived to the League of Nations. At Geneva and in Paris, his direct work was the task of educating opinion, of breaking down national barriers by promoting intellectual co-operation across them, but he realised that this was not enough. What was also needed was the education of public opinion within the individual nations of the League, and this was a much wider question than that of intellectual attitudes. Moreover, like the League itself, this national effort in public education was also a matter of co-operation between men of goodwill, of real Liberality, no matter whether they were Liberals or not. Side by side, therefore, with his work for the League itself went Murray's work for the League of Nations Union in Britain, the body organised to educate and to mobilize British opinion in support of the League.

Murray's involvement with the League of Nations Union ante-dated the creation of the League. In mid-1918 he took part in the negotiations which led to the amalgamation of the older League of Nations Society and the newer League of Free Nations Association, and he served on the Management Committee of the resulting League of Nations Union until 1920. He went off the Committee early in the year, with the comment to his daughter that it was 'only public jabber' and that he was trying to wriggle out of the Union's work altogether. If his hopes of a progressive national government under Grey or Robert Cecil had been fulfilled, a pro-League British government would indeed have committed British opinion by official action. It would have enlisted a majority behind it. As that hope of a progressive government vanished and Lord Robert Cecil began both to take an active part in the Union affairs and to develop a close and sympathetic relationship with Murray from their association in Geneva, the latter began to take more active interest in the Union. In 1922, while he was in Geneva, its Executive put his name forward for the position of Vice-Chairman and when Lord Robert, on taking ministerial office in Baldwin's government of 1923, felt obliged to resign his position as Chairman and instead to take the honorary position of Joint-President with Grey, Gilbert Murray became Chairman of the Executive of the League of Nations Union, holding the position until 1938, when he then became Joint-President with Cecil in succession to Grey.

As Chairman of the Executive of the League of Nations Union, Murray was committed to work which involved his presence at its headquarters in London once or twice a week. As with the Committee of Intellectual Co-operation in Geneva, much of the work fell upon the secretariat or permanent staff, but, where in Geneva this staff was provided from the professional civil service of the member nations, in London the Union had to recruit as it could and within narrower financial resources. After a few years of change and uncertainty, the Union finally secured as General Secretary Maxwell Garnett, a former Fellow of Trinity College, Cambridge, and a former Principal of the Manchester Institute of Technology. As General Secretary he remained as executive head of the staff of the Union until just before the Second World War, bringing enthusiasm and drive to its formative years. From a membership of 3,217 in November 1918 which had risen to nearly 41,000 two years later, the number more than tripled in Garnett's first year in post and thereafter rose very steadily. When Murray became Chairman of the Executive, membership stood at over 300,000 in more than 1,500 recognised branches. The Union's appeal for a million pounds, launched in 1921, did not indeed reach its target, although it raised a considerable sum. The Murrays themselves gave £1,500 to be paid over three years. It was not, however, finances which were Murray's chief concern as Chairman, nor even the strained relations within the Union, especially between Garnett and Cecil who complained to Murray in 1928 that the General Secretary ignored Executive policy and created an atmosphere of distrust, and in 1932 threatened that 'either he or I will have to go'. The real problem that Murray faced with the League of Nations Union was that its founders and its early Executive had never clearly decided what the role of the Union should be.

When Murray became Chairman in 1923, the objects of the Union, soon to be incorporated by Royal Charter, seemed clear enough: to secure acceptance of the League of Nations, to foster international understanding, to advocate full development of the League. These were objectives concerned with educating public opinion, but from the beginning it was hard to separate the activity which this entailed from political activity. While British governments were prepared to support the League, while Cecil himself held government office in charge of League affairs, as he did for most of the period up to his final resignation in 1927, the Union's work supported the government, no matter what its political complexion. Even the refusal by Baldwin's government to sign the Geneva Protocol in 1924 did not commit the British government to an anti-League policy while Cecil still remained a member of it. Nevertheless, the initial problem for the Union was to recruit Conservatives as members so as to broaden its base which, as Cecil had pointed out in 1919, was originally largely

Liberal and Labour. It was necessary to make it clear that to support the League was not a party matter. David Davies was clear in 1924 that the Union was primarily a propagandist body, not a committee of experts; it should lay down general principles and leave the rest to the government. If the Union was lukewarm in support of the government it would in his view lose the support that it was gaining in the country. In the same year Cecil was expressing his concern that the number of Conservatives on the Executive Committee was too low in proportion to the composition of the House of Commons as a reflection of national feeling; the Union must get as many Conservatives as possible, especially those who carried weight with the party leaders. He reminded Murray that, when there had been a similar and earlier problem with Labour representation, the matter had been overcome by consulting the leaders of the Labour Party even though the leader, Ramsey MacDonald, had been hostile to the Union because of an insult he believed it had offered him just after the war. In fact, in April 1926, the leaders of the Conservative Party themselves approached Cecil about increasing their representation on the Executive of the Union, and suggested that Duff Cooper and Hudson, parliamentarians who had some knowledge of foreign affairs, would be suitable members. They were duly co-opted.

The cross-party character of the Union, achieved, although not without difficulty, by the date of Cecil's final resignation from the government in 1927, soon came under strain. In July 1928, after repeated attacks upon the Union in *The Times*, a demand by what Murray called 'a Tory phalanx' for still more Conservatives on the Executive was really, he believed, an attempt to turn him out as Chairman. For, with Cecil's resignation from the government on the issue of the British refusal to accept equality with the United States as the basis of a reduction in naval armaments, the disarmament issue itself began to put strains on Conservative support for the Union. In July 1928 the Conservative government's view about the Kellogg pact which was proposed as an Amendment to the Covenant of the League, and renounced war as an instrument of policy, was cool: it wished to exempt certain kinds of war. Although Cecil and Murray themselves took the view that the Covenant already contained the Kellogg obligations, on this issue the Union began to appear to the Conservative government to be neither an educational not a propagandist body for the League, but a body which supported policies opposed to those of the government. It did not help that Murray in his 1929 Election Address explained that he stood on this occasion as an Independent, not as a Liberal candidate, because in the Union he worked with Lord Cecil and other members of the Conservative Party and with members of the Labour Party; but he went on to say that he was convinced of the danger of the present unmixed Conservative government with its 'dogged maintenance' of the right of private war, its refusal to accept the International Court, its policy of increased tariff barriers, and its lack of any clear policy of disarmament. His views on foreign affairs, he added, had been put before the public by the League of Nations Union. Such a clear identification of the Union with a line of policy which was not that of the Conservative government obviously created a dilemma for any Conservative Party member within the Union, although Murray believed that his views were non-partisan. They were those, he asserted, of men of Liberality in any party.

The 1929 election returned a Labour government, but that Party too had its fair share of anti-League members, although Arthur Henderson, the new Foreign Secretary, was himself pro-League. He gave Cecil a room within the Foreign Office and made him Deputy Leader of the British delegation to the preparatory Disarmament Conference. Henderson also signed the 'Optional Clause' by which Britain accepted the jurisdiction of the Permanent Court of International Justice. The effect, in Conservative eyes, was to identify the Union not simply as anti-Conservative but as actually partisan. The Labour government itself saw the Union somewhat differently, but even Philip Noel-Baker, who had long been associated with Cecil and the Union, when his party was in government, liked some of the Union's actions no better than the Conservatives had. In October 1930 he was protesting to Murray that resolutions of some of the regional councils of the Union were sidetracking the disarmament issue just when Henderson was giving a lead, and in June 1932 he and Henderson were, he said, 'astonished' by Murray's observation in the *Manchester Guardian* that Simon's plan for reducing naval armaments was superior to Hoover's. 'Of course I am sure you realize that unless we accept the Naval part, the French will be obliged by their public opinion to reject the Land part, and, therefore, the whole plan will be destroyed.' Nevertheless, the Union's policy began increasingly to look closer to Labour policy than Conservative and, after the fall of the Labour government and the split within the Labour Party, the Union began indeed to look like the real Opposition party, rather than the body its Royal Charter had defined. One ominous straw in the wind was the resignation of the Conservative Major J. Hills as Vice-Chairman of the Executive in January 1931, for he, said Murray, had been unfailingly co-operative in the conduct of Union affairs, especially where differences of party politics were involved. By March 1931 there was a visible rift along party lines in the Executive itself. In the following month it was clear that there was increasing difficulty both in raising money and in retaining subscriptions.

Murray was anxious to heal the rift, especially because he had come to have a high regard for a Conservative like Hills who was anti-pacifist, as was Murray himself, and yet had a real grasp of the importance of the League. His solution was to put forward a careful statement of a common point of view, although Cecil regarded this as an ambiguous formula by which different people would mean different things. Between them, however, they tried to reassure the Conservative members of the Executive that they were not regarded as a minority to be outvoted. The real remedy in Murray's view was to go all out for a political object which would interest everybody. Disarmament, he said, was that object. Here he and Cecil could reassure the Tories that they were not pacifists who sought unilateral disarmament by Britain but rather a mutual reduction of armaments, and they both proclaimed the actual need for armaments which, at the disposal of the League, could be used against aggressors against members of the League: In fact, Cecil and Murray were agreed on the need for an International Air Force for this purpose. Their problem, however, was that the Union contained many people, often former members of the Union of Democratic Control, who were pacifists and did not share their leaders' views, and such members always provided grounds for Conservative suspicion, no matter what assurance Cecil and Murray personally could give about their own views. In June 1931 the Edinburgh, Carlisle and Blackpool regional councils of the Union all wanted to devote their meetings and all of the Union's manpower to the cause of disarmament. Murray then had to remonstrate with them, in pursuit of his attempt to keep the Union out of party politics.

Disarmament was no easier a problem in the early 1930s than it has been in the nuclear age, although Murray came to believe, on the strength of Sir John Simon's own statements, that every technical problem had been solved by the end of the Disarmament Conference; only the political will was lacking. As an educational or propagandist body, disarmament was a topic on which the Union could do useful work. The Covenant of the League did not require those who signed it completely to disarm but rather to accept limitations upon armaments. The implication of this, in Murray's view, was that an international police force was necessary. Nevertheless, disarmament became a party issue and the Union, in concentrating upon it, achieved no unanimity. In March 1934 Cecil proposed a National Ballot on the Issue to the Executive which decided that, to carry it out, outside support was needed. A conference of other bodies was held late in the month: church organisations, peace societies and political parties. Of the last, Labour and Liberal agreed to support it; the Conservatives left it to their local branches only some of which co-operated. Murray was not himself enthusiastic. He believed that the issues could not be dealt with in clear simple questions, the answers to which would depend on the success or failure of the Disarmament Conference. If the Conference failed and there was then a scurry to rearm, people would not scrap any possible source of strength. An alternative course was public criticism of the Harmsworth press anti-disarmament referendum, and that, he thought, was the real business of the Union's canvassers.

Nevertheless, the Executive decided upon a Ballot which was held from mid-1934 to mid-1935. There were five questions, the last subdivided into two. They asked if Britain should remain a member of the League, if there should be an all round reduction of armaments, if military and naval aircraft should be abolished, if arms should be made and sold for private profit, if an aggressor should be stopped by sanctions or by military measures. Eleven and a half million people returned the questionnaires. Well over ten million answered 'yes' to four questions, but to the abolition of military and naval aircraft the 'yeses' fell to nine and a half million, and to less than seven million in answer to the employment of military measures to stop an aggressor. The Union hailed the result as an enormous success. Cecil was convinced that it had changed the government's attitude. Murray himself later pointed to the half million voluntary workers who had distributed and collected the ballot papers, as evidence of the Union's strength as a pressure group and of the spirit which had enthused the rank and file membership, but his original doubts were justified by the after-effects of the Ballot. The Conservatives had never really liked it, and, when the Union also gave evidence to the Royal Commission on Private Armaments, it lost some prominent Conservatives, such as Sir Austen Chamberlain. Murray tried to prevent this and to smooth things over, but he recognised that the Peace Ballot had put the Union in an anomalous position. When Chamberlain was saying that he could not be committed to what he regarded as a bad policy for the League and that Cecil simply overbore any dissent from his views, Murray suggested that an answer was to draw a distinction between resolutions passed at Council meetings which became official policy of Union and recommendations which had no such fundamental status. Chamberlain would have none of such subtlety as a solution to the split in the Union, while his fellow Conservative, Eustace Percy, frankly said that he loathed the whole Peace Ballot business and was disinclined to do anything more within the party which was being alienated from the Union. The Ballot, as he pointed out, presented the sharp issue of national sovereignty which, having been raised, would lose Conservative support for the Union. Murray was able to prevent a disagreeable discussion in the Executive by his handling of it, and later to discourage a member of headquarters' staff from sending a letter to the *New Statesman* personally attacking Austen Chamberlain, but the split was never really healed inside the Union. For, divisive as the policy issue was, there was the further question of the Union's associations in the campaign for the National Declaration.

To carry out the Ballot, the Union had had to seek co-operation with other bodies. Amongst these the National Peace Council was important, and it was part of an international movement. The temptation for some influential members of the Union was to join forces in a broad and united peace movement. Cecil took that view. So did Dame Kathleen Courtney. Murray did not. In October 1936 he warned Cecil that the International Peace Council in Europe was becoming militant left and, if there was to be any association between it and the Union, the Union must have control in order to stop the excesses which were likely to occur. The proposal for some kind of association split the Union still further. The West of Scotland branch was particularly concerned about the proposal and seemed to Murray almost to be putting him on trial about it. The churches, especially the Catholic Church, recoiled from the Union. The headquarters staff itself was bitterly divided and when, at their Christmas party in 1937, the customary pantomine included not merely some satire on the International Peace Council but also a caricature of an old and doddery Lord Cecil (actually ruled by Noel-Baker) there was a major row. Cecil wished to purge the staff. Murray thought that Cecil was wrong to take seriously what was a joke, albeit in bad taste, especially since he believed that Cecil's policy for the Union in respect of the Peace Council was also wrong because it committed the Union to association with men avowedly not of Liberality. Finally there was a compromise; and Murray, to his relief, was able to 'get rid' of the Chairmanship which had increasingly become a difficult and thankless task. He accepted instead the 'immense honour' of becoming Joint President with Cecil in succession to Grey.

As Chairman of the Executive, Murray had assumed responsibility for overseeing the day-to-day work of the Union, but the two days a week on which he looked into the London office were really not enough to be effective. His wife in 1925 had said that he was 'adequate (but not so great) at organisation of offices and the like'. It was not something that really interested him, although he recognised it as a duty. The League of Nations Union was in any case difficult. The General Secretary, Garnett, not only had bad relations with Cecil who wanted to interfere, but was frequently criticised by other members of the Executive who were on the Finance Committee and still more by the Branches which regarded headquarters as remote and extravagant with the money the regions collected. Murray found it difficult to control the administration of the Union. His talent was not for such administrative work, but for the chairman's role of conciliating different opinions on matters of policy, for offering guidance and counsel rather than for exercising control or executive direction.

He displayed the same talent in the Committee of Intellectual Co-operation and its *Comité des Arts et des Lettres*. In 1931 the latter included Bartók, Capek, Masefield, Mann and Valéry and its discussions on general issues seemed, like those of the main Committee, to be 'interesting, almost thrilling'. 'I don't know what has happened — people seem to have got free, to have ceased to fear.' By 1935, Murray felt that these meetings had got the League spirit; there was a feeling of unity 'or at least a friendliness which was quite remarkable'. He was impressed by the brilliance of some of its discussions: 'sometimes one realizes one's colleagues are clever people.' They, in turn, told him that they admired his chairmanship. 'I think it is chiefly that I am always punctual and listen attentively and smile at jokes,' Murray told his wife, but the words one of his colleagues actually used to him were his *autorité* and his *courteoisie érudite*. As Chairman Murray had once explained that his duty was 'as usual, to conciliate', and he described his method in the Geneva Committee to Isobel Henderson. He soothed his Italian Fascist colleague, Rocco, by writing elegaics to his niece. With the French Painlevé he made slightly profane jokes. He admired the Belgian Destrée's speeches as models of eloquence. In short, he consciously exercised his talent to please, to make himself agreeable, just as he had with his examiners at Merchant Taylors and with Lady Carlisle. That did not preclude firmness or *autorité*, but that word was used of him in 1935, after the withdrawal of first Italy, then Germany from the Committee of Intellectual Co-operation had removed men who despised Liberality. In the face of a real division of opinion, Murray sometimes seemed to conciliate by words which achieved an appearance of agreement but left the differences unresolved. Both Cecil and Austen Chamberlain felt that within the Union. Sir Robert Garran, the shrewd and experienced Solicitor-General of Australia who saw him in action at Geneva, thought him too conciliatory to be a good chairman.

Murray himself would not have disagreed. He could not think why colleagues admired his chairmanship and he was conscious of his failure to achieve the real objectives for which both the League Committee and the League of Nations Union existed: public education which would break down national barriers to the international cause of peace. 'I am ashamed', he wrote, 'of my failure in Great Britain to convince either the people or the Government.' His own chairmanship in the two bodies with which he was involved was, he knew, not the cause of the League's failure. That failure came from political and economic events outside both. After the failure of disarmament and the rise of aggressive nationalist governments to power in Europe and the Far East, hope for the League steadily dwindled. By 1936, after the outbreak of the Spanish Civil War Murray in Geneva was 'very nearly losing hope', although he 'did not in the least feel inclined to cease struggling'; but in Britain he also believed the Union to be failing. At its Scarborough conference in 1936 the resolution calling for the indefinite continuation of sanctions against Italy for its Abyssinian aggression seemed futile and destructive of public support at a time when German policy was causing the government to think not about the League but about re-armament. By early 1939, when he undertook his regular speaking tour to Union branches, he found his audience to consist almost exclusively of old radicals, British Women's Temperance Association types and schoolteachers. The Union had plainly failed to reach the young and the mass of the population.

This failure, both of the League itself and of the Union, was a failure of the cause of Civilisation, 'the cause which of all others I have felt most bound to work for'. Murray took some of the blame for his failure to educate public opinion in that cause, but he was more inclined to blame the failure on the lack of political will in the governments of the western world; and especially in Great Britain which had never been willing to contribute to the work of Intellectual Co-operation. Above all, he blamed the failure upon men. If only, he wrote, there had been in the Foreign Office at the successive crises of the League — the Protocol, the Manchurian incident, disarmament, Spain, Abyssinia — such men as Cecil and Henderson, not Curzon and MacDonald, Eden and Lytton, not Hoare and Simon, even an Austen Chamberlain, then 'we might well have had a disarmed world'. Not one of these men was a Liberal, but they were men of Liberality.

9 ANCHOR OF CIVILISATION

'The League', Murray told a correspondent in the mid-1930s, 'has ruined my Greek.' Certainly since the war he had given a great deal of his time and energy to the work. Indeed, as early as 1923, the Vice-Chancellor of Oxford University had asked him if he thought it proper to retain his chair while being Chairman or President of the League of Nations. Obviously the Vice-Chancellor had confused the League itself with the Union, but his mistake did not obscure the point. How could Murray fulfil his duties as Professor of Greek while engaged in so much public work? Murray endowed a lectureship to make sure his duties were discharged, but in terms of his own writing and lecturing the League's demands directly and indirectly occupied him at the expense of his 'real' work.

Nevertheless it was a deliberate choice, although not so clear a one at the time as it seemed to him in retrospect. The unity of his feelings and the common threat to all of his 'causes' which Murray had described to Lady Carlisle in 1917 remained. The enemy was war, for unless the World Order 'abstains utterly from war and the causes of war, the next great war will destroy it'. The League was therefore very important; indeed it was a duty which Murray could not shirk. It was inseparably linked with the cause of peace because, to Murray, peace was essential for the preservation of Liberality, and both were covered by the single banner: Civilisation.

Civilisation to Murray was not a purely material thing, although it had a large material element. As he explained it in a whole series of lectures and addresses, side by side with his work for the League, the chief characteristic of Civilisation was that it set man free from the pressure of daily fear of hunger or thirst or danger, free to do what he really wanted to do instead of merely what he must do to stay alive, 'free to make poetry and music, to pursue art and science, to think and speak and create'. These had been Murray's own personal ambitions, and there was a further indentification of Civilisation with his own life when he went on to associate it with Liberality. 'We have lost liberality in Europe because we have so largely lost the main elements of civilisation, and conversely we have lost these because we have so failed in liberality.' He did not

209

now use Liberality as an antithesis of Conservatism. On the contrary, the latter, 'by preserving the social order which it is the object of liberality to bring a little nearer to what the judgement of a free man requires', was a necessary complement to liberality. Nevertheless, 'civilised thinking means liberal thinking'. Liberality was the 'inner content of civilisation'; and fear of war and memories of war, by making Liberality impossible, were poisoning that Civilisation from within.

Given this view of Murray's, it is easy to see that the practical outcome was his devotion to the cause of the League which attempted the extermination of war which threatened the destruction of Civilisation. Given his devotion to Hellenism, it followed that the Greek world could strengthen the cause. The fugitives from anarchy in ancient times, he said, built a *polis*, city wall within which they were safe and could form a society. Thus security, the basic necessity of Civilisation, was attained. Modern states, he recognised, were unwilling to abandon their independent sovereignty and, since the old Roman solution of a single dominant state was out of the question, and a federation authority with real international power was equally out of the question, at least for the present, a Society of Nations was the inescapable solution. Inside this society men could observe justice, renounce war between themselves and practise collective security against non-members. This was the objective Murray proclaimed throughout the inter-war years, at first with hope, then with growing disillusion, finally with something close to despair. The direct failure was that of the League itself and of its organs and the failure of the League of Nations Union as an educational body. The indirect failure was that the message of ancient Greece had reached too few people in the hands of its interpreter to his generation.

Murray never believed that there was a direct lesson to be learned from Greece. Even in his wartime lecture on 'Aristophanes and the War Party', in which he drew a picture through the comedies of Aristophanes of Athens towards the end of the great war against Sparta, he did not draw a direct moral for England. Indeed he prefaced his lecture with a warning against the danger of reading the events of the past too exclusively in the light of the present. What he suggested was that, because history inevitably was to a great extent a work of the imagination, to understand it, it was necessary to use personal experience and to envisage the present much in the same perspective as it will bear when it too is a chapter

in 'the great volume of the past'. He knew that the Peloponnesian
War between Athens and Sparta had ended wrongly; it had
wrecked Hellas. 'Our war has ended right: and, one may hope, not
too late for the recovery of civilisation . . . we have such an
opportunity as no generation of mankind has ever had of building
out of these ruins a better international life and comcomitantly a
better life within each nation.'

Murray's own reconstruction of the Greek past had a part to play
in the preservation of Civilisation, but it was not a direct one.
Rather was it the indirect one of raising people's perception of what
might happen. Not 'Aristophanes and the War Party' but 'Poesis
and Mimesis', the Henry Sidgwick Lecture delivered in Cambridge
in 1920, explained what his interpretation had in mind. Aristotle's
Poetics were quoted with approval by Murray for the definition of
poetry (which meant also drama) as 'imitation'; not what had
happened, but what might happen. Murray also quoted Matthew
Arnold with approval: poetry was criticism of life. The two
definitions were not, said Murray, incompatible. Poetry might give
delight, but it might also help us to live better. 'We have imitated
the things we admired . . . seeing things that were beautiful and
trying to make others like them . . . We have formed ideals and our
ideals have guided us.' What Murray tried to do, through his
writings on Greece and his translations from the Greek, was to
reach those readers or listeners who wished for illumination on
'some question of the moment or the great riddles of existence'. A
poet, he said, ought to save souls; but, as one who had himself been
swept away in youth by the beauty of Shelley, he also recalled the
claim that poets are the great social legislators; and Liberality, the
inner content of Civilisation, was the result of the work of members
of a privileged class working to have their privileges extended to
others. Civilisation, in short, depended upon leaders, but these
leaders included in their ranks those who led, not through formal
offices or public work, but through their works of imagination.
Murray attempted both forms of leadership.

His tenure of the Regius Chair of Greek at Oxford would
normally have ended at the age of 65 in 1931, but, despite the
burden of his work for the League in Geneva, Paris and London,
he accepted an extension of five years to 1936. In 1926, at Harvard,
he obviously tried to influence the young in the lecture and tutorial
room by unfolding to them the Greek origins of the traditions of
Civilisation in order to catch their imagination with a vision of

what Civilisation once had been, so that they might feel called to the defence of their inheritance. But, as usual, Murray aimed beyond his immediate audience, and what he taught he put into books to reach and influence as wide a public as he could. His message had a consistency in the 1920s and 1930s with his faith before the war. In fifth-century Athens the human ape had achieved the unique moment of civilisation. In the nineteenth and early twentieth centuries he had the chance to achieve something different but similar. After the war the chance was still there. But his emphasis changed. It was not now that the chance should be grasped but rather that the chance itself should be preserved in order to be grasped. Where, pre-war, it was Euripides — the rational and progressive humanist — who preoccupied Murray, after the war it was first Aeschylus, with his concern with the 'deep unsolved mysteries of life', and then Aristophanes, the 'laughing philosopher' of a world at war and of its aftermath, although Murray's books on each of them were actually published in reverse order. Both of them had a message which Murray felt that he had not conveyed earlier, although he had seen them as part of the classical tradition.

Murray had selected Euripides for his attention in what he took for granted to be a secure world in which progressive causes would triumph. Immediately after the war, he selected Aeschylus. In late March and early April 1919, as he worked on its translation, the *Agamemnon* filled his mind to the exclusion, he said, of all else, and he went on in 1922 to translate the next play of the *Oresteia*, *The Choephoroe*, for publication in the following year, and completed the translation of the third play, *The Eumenides*, in 1925. The plays form a trilogy in which Agamemnon, leader of the Greeks against Troy, is murdered by his wife Clytemnestra, sister of Helen of Troy, by way of punishment. Agamemnon's son, Orestes, comes duty-bound to take vengeance on the murderess. Whether he takes vengeance upon his mother or not, he commits a grave sin. He takes the vengeance, but then come the Furies. What is to be the fate of a man who, in fulfilling his filial duty, kills his mother? That tragic theme preoccupied Murray in the wake of a terrible war. He saw in the three plays of the *Oresteia* 'the attempt of a powerful mind to think out in terms that are not quite our terms one of the deep involved mysteries of life — the problem of Sin, Punishment and Forgiveness'. The stimulus to Murray came from a contemporary situation in which Aeschylus seemed, as Euripides had seemed before the war, to have affinities. But it was not a simple process of finding a kindred spirit from the past to illuminate the problems of the present, nor of going from the present to look for affinities in the past. Murray's was a subtler mind than that, although he would not have denied that there were elements of both in what he did. The stimulus for his interest in Aeschylus was more complex than a contemporary political situation and its affinities with the distant past.

Aeschylus interested Murray not only because of his great tragic themes but because, as the subtitle of the book he later published in 1940 shows, he was 'the creator of tragedy'. He stood closer to the origins of Greek tragic drama than did Euripides, and therefore revealed Greek theatre at a formative stage. Disagreeing with other scholars, Murray placed *The Suppliant Women* closer to the original dance out of which tragedy arose than any other Greek play. *Prometheus Unbound* was pre-classical. *The Persians* was the earliest historical play in existence. *Seven Against Thebes* was the play most often quoted in antiquity itself. Whatever affinities Aeschylus' great tragic theme had for post-war Europe, it had the same fascination for Murray that the origins of Greek tragedy and Greek religion had had in pre-war days: the germs out of which a message of evolution and hope could be drawn. 'Out of little myths and ridiculous language' Aeschylus created tragedy. Out of poor material a great institution, the League, might be fashioned.

Throughout the 1920s and into the 1930s Murray translated Aeschylus' seven extant plays, as with Euripides making a new Greek text as he did so for publication in the Oxford Classical Texts series in 1937. What had gripped him about the *Oresteia* was the idea that sin could be pardoned, as Orestes was pardoned by the will of Zeus. The law which could so pardon could itself be understood and loved; it could become 'an inward inspiration, a standard of right living which men consciously need and seek'. There was hope and forgiveness after the bloody sacrifices of war. From the *Oresteia* in the early 1920s, Murray moved on to *The Suppliant Women* and *Prometheus* at the end of the decade. In the former he saw in the choral dance of women pursued by man Aeschylus' treatment of myths and legends in which the playwright sees a conflict 'and in each conflict he deepens the issue till it becomes one of the eternal problems of life'. In the latter play, he saw the story of the will to endure pitted against the will to crush.

Aeschylus became for Murray the protagonist of the moral revolution implied in the Olympian gods, as opposed to pre-Hellenic
blind and monstrous forces, and the expositor of the 'Third
Saviour' who rescues the world from death. This conception of a
Saviour made Aeschylus, for Murray, one who had introduced a
dangerous leaven into orthodox thought, for he would have liked
to believe that the ways of Fortune are strictly in accordance with
morality. Aeschylus, concluded Murray, had reached the conception of a supreme Tyrant, the enemy of man, and of a champion of
man standing up against him, a conception comparable to that of
the Old Testament picture of Job. Aeschylus' conception thus
became nothing less than the perfectibility of God or, turned from
poetic metaphor to fact, the brutal, non-moral external world has
'the possibility of evolving towards something more spiritual and
more concordant with our higher ideals'.

In this interpretation of Aeschylus Murray used his own perception of the moral dilemma of his own world to bring a coherence to
the Greek dramatist's view of his world, and then used that
coherent view attributed to Aeschylus to illuminate the situation of
contemporary western European civilisation. Naturally, given the
circularity of the method, the process was mutually reinforcing,
and for those in need of hope, attractive. But it was not a sound
historical method to study Greece through Aeschylus' plays. Since
only seven plays survive from the more than 80 which Aeschylus is
known to have written, there is no sound assumption that they
represent the playwright's ideas on the great problems and
mysteries of life, even if it were reasonable to believe that what a
Greek tragedian put on stage actually represented his own attitude,
a problem of method which recurs with Murray's account of
Aristophanes.

Murray was too good a scholar to ignore the reputation
Aeschylus had in his own day as the writer, not of tragedies, but of
satyr plays and, in Aristophanes' words, 'our Bacchic king' who
wrote more from Dionysiac inspiration than conscious art. Nevertheless, he explained away this reputation: Aeschylus had needed to
write within a ritual tradition which the audience knew and
expected in a play, and had attempted to transmute these 'ugly'
features. Murray also recognised that the themes he found in
Aeschylus — justice and forgiveness, virginity and love, honour
and loyalty — might seem too modern and civilised for an early
Greek poet; but he answered that, although they were put in

modern terms, these were things present in all human society. Greek scholars might be deluding themselves when they claimed so to understand a Greek of two thousand years ago, but he believed that the communication of beauty was a subtle and mysterious process which enabled people now living to have 'a more intimate communion with the thoughts of Shakespeare or Dante or Virgil or, it may be, Aeschylus, than with those of their next-door neighbours'.

In translating Aeschylus Murray himself wanted to communicate the beauty he found to his readers. His book of 1940 was intended as a guide book to the plays themselves, but in translating the plays themselves from 1919 onwards he provided a preface to each play — indeed his book incorporated much of this material — and added notes which might serve as stage directions to actors when the plays were put on stage. He had, he believed, adapted his earlier style to Aeschylus. The play he particularly cited in support of that belief was *Seven Against Thebes*, in which he thought he had actually imitated the Greek. It is hard to detect. Eteocles' opening speech is rendered:

Children of Cadmus, he must ponder well
His words, who watcheth in the citadel,
An ever-sleepless pilot, hand on oar.
For, if good issue, all the same evil thing —
May such not be — befall us, 'the king,
Great and alone', 'tis Eteocles must meet
The clamorous wrath of Thebes in every street
And curses: from all which may Zeus, whose own
Dear name is Saviour, safe preserve our town.

This is indeed a change from the Morris couplet he had used in earlier translations of Euripides, and the translation does not fall under T.S. Eliot's condemnation that Murray habitually used two words where the Greek uses one; he used half as many words again in this version. But the style still bears the marks of the Pre-Raphaelite, differing from his earlier work chiefly in the reduced number of gorgeous adjectives. The vocabulary still includes the 'My liege', and the 'thou' and 'thine' of earlier poetic diction:

Dost thou quake
At death and war, thou coward heart? he fumes
While o'er his helm three great o'ershadowing plumes

Toss in the wind, and 'neath his buckler bright
Wild brazen bells make music of affright;

If Murray thought that this style imitated Aeschylus, then his imitation is blurred by the English poetic associations of the diction he used. He also thought that one of Aeschylus' distinctions was his diction, his liking for 'gorgeous and thrilling' poetry, for language 'far more majestic than that of common life'. As an example he quoted a speech from *The Suppliant Women* in which a woman, wishing to throw herself over a precipice, uses six continuous adjectives to describe the place: 'A smooth goat-deserted, undeciphered, lonely-brooding, pendant-vulture's crag.' When he rendered this translation into verse, it became:

Some unbestridden, undescried
Smooth vulture-crag, in lonely pride
Hanging.

Given that Murray believed that Aeschylus reached for majestic diction, then it is easy to understand why he thought his own imitated Aeschylus. Nevertheless, in drawing the contrast with Euripides whose diction was 'clear, correct, simple and rejected bombast', Murray seems implicitly to be accepting that his Euripidean translations did not convey that poet's distinctive qualities to a modern audience. Ironically enough, however, it was the Euripides plays which actually reached an audience from the stage. The Aeschylus translations were seldom performed — Murray refused to allow the *Oresteia* to be done except as a trilogy — although *The Persian Women* was broadcast by the BBC in 1939 and *Seven Against Thebes* during the Second World War when the heroism of a besieged city had another contemporary message for its British audience. Murray was not happy with radio productions of tragedy: the actors were unused to Greek tragedy and the handling of the chorus presented even more difficulties on the air than it did on the stage. The 'new' comedy of Menander did better.

If Euripides was for Murray the playwright of rational, radical causes before war came to ruin progress, and Aeschylus the playwright who explored the great tragic themes in the face of hostile fate, after the First World War Murray began to see in a third Greek dramatist, Aristophanes, another poet who had a message for the modern world. When he wrote his *History of Greek Literature* in the 1890s, he had had little sympathy for Aristophanes, the man who made fun of Euripides and of the higher things of life. He had indeed translated one play, *The Frogs*, early in the century, but his real interest was in Greek tragedy, not comedy. In his post-war teaching at Oxford, he had prepared and delivered a course on Aeschylus in the 1920s, but by 1931 he had also become interested in Aristophanes: 'In times like these one often longs for the return to earth of one of the great laughing philosophers of the past.' In August he was laying the foundation of a course on Aristophanes: 'I treated him so wrongly in my old Greek literature.'

He set out, in the book he published on Aristophanes in 1933, to redeem this earlier picture. Aristophanes was no longer one who disliked Athenian democracy; he hated militarism and cruelty as much as he did the mob. He was not simply coarse and boisterous, a user of indecent language; so to regard him was 'a failure of historical or perhaps anthropological imagination'. Aristophanes, in the new picture which Murray now painted, found existing comedy indecent, coarse and common, and built it up into something artistic, intellectual and public-spirited. He removed its more glaring indecencies. But he too was working within a ritual pattern — the phallic ritual and saturnalian language which was the origin of comedy — so he could not remove the elements his audience would expect to find in a play. He was also working in an Athens at war, dominated by Cleon, the most violent of the citizens. Nevertheless he did not hesitate to attack policy towards Athenian allies and dependencies, nor (in *The Babylonians*) boldly to plead for peace and (in *The Acharnians*) against war, nor to attack Cleon (in *The Knights*). Aristophanes, on Murray's interpretation of these plays, stood against the will to win at any cost, by any use of force, and for the maintenance of ideals rather than this or that temporary gain. In *The Peace* he stood up not for his own city but for the whole of Hellas, and in *The Wasps* he championed the cause of the allied cities against Athens through an attack on the jury courts. The attack on Socrates in *The Clouds*, Murray explains, was not really an attack on something the poet hated, although Plato blamed the comedian's influence in bringing about Socrates' judicial murder, but rather a 'clash of humours'. Just as Aristophanes mocked at what interested him in the case of Socrates, so he mocked both Euripides and Aeschylus in *The Frogs*, not because he disliked their work, but because he was fascinated by it; although free with personal abuse of people he hated or disliked, there was no abuse of Euripides. Aristophanes, in short, mocked the things he loved, the higher things in his society.

On Murray's reading of Aristophanes, the thing the playwright most hated was war, because it meant misery for all Greece and degradation and brutalisation for Athens itself. After the hopeful peace of Nicias in 421 BC, there came rapid and growing disappointment. War came again and with it the ruin of Hellas and of civilisation. In the face of this disillusionment Aristophanes created *The Birds*, a great kingdom in the clouds, better than the reality of Athens. He no longer hoped that real peace would come, nor that politics would once again be in the hands of decent people. But in the realm of the Muses he could forget the world. It is tempting to read Murray's description of Aristophanes as self-description, a man's imaginative projection of himself. There is no doubt that the picture of a man who hated war because of what it had done and might still do to a civilised society, and who became disillusioned with the failure of the hopes raised by the peace made at the end of a terrible war, bears a marked resemblance to Murray himself.

But Murray, although he portrayed in his book on *Aristophanes* an analogous situation of which similar views were held, did not identify himself with Aristophanes. For he himself was never a man who mocked what he loved, and he certainly did not employ for any reason the obscenity for which Aristophanes was noted. Indeed, not only in the early translations which Murray made but still more systematically in the later ones, he omitted the obscenity completely. He recognised the difficulty; but Aristophanes' crudities were explained away, as other features of Greek society were explained away, as primitive survivals from the origins of comedy. That Murray found obscenity intensely distasteful is beyond question. When he read *All Quiet on the Western Front* which, with its horrifying picture of war, was by general consent a powerful anti-war book, he nevertheless found it too coarse; its author was skilful, although not so skilful that he could depict the brutalization without 'mentioning the unmentionable'. He had always found certain of Shakespeare's plays, above all *Measure for Measure*, 'disgusting'. Aristophanes might be excused by Murray's anthropological explanations, but in translation he had to be cleaned up. Even Murray's friends protested. Mackail told him that it was a masterly portrait, although he remained in doubt as to whether Murray had got the relationship between the playwright and Euripides right. 'But is it necessary to apologise for, or to explain away, his magnificent indecency by charging it all to the account of prehistoric ritual?' Murray admitted in reply that, as to Euripides, 'it is a question of proportion — I may not have got it right but I think in the main the matter has been stated too crudely'; but the matter of the indecencies he ignored altogether.

Aristophanes is probably Murray's worst book. He did not claim it to be scholarly, but, as many reviewers pointed out, it actually offended canons of scholarship by Murray's uncritical attitude towards and use of the sources. The more fundamental criticism was that Murray accepted a picture of Athens derived from Aristophanes' satires in his plays because of his anxiety to see Aristophanes as a founding father of the League of Nations. Nevertheless, whatever its considerable scholarly defects, Murray was doing what any preacher does: shaping a story to point a moral. And Murray *was* preaching. He was preaching the cause of Civilisation, after his experiences with the Italian Fascists and the Japanese militarists in his work at and for the League and in the very year in which the Nazis came to power in Germany. He had no doubt of the dangers threatening Civilisation and his message was hung upon appropriate classical pegs. With Aristophanes in 1933 he was preaching the cause of the League. With Aeschylus in 1940 the cause was not so directly politically pointed; it was the theme of tragedy, through experience of which comes a standard by which men might live: a purgation which also seemed to fit the times.

Contemporary analogies from these two Greek dramatists were obviously perceived both by Murray and by his readers, but to Murray Greek poetry had a deeper significance because it stood in a tradition which he identified with Civilisation. Before any illuminating analogies with the present were drawn, the Greek poets already represented a classical tradition which was an essential inheritance. Murray spelled this out in 1927 when he published the Charles Eliot Norton Lectures which he had delivered at Harvard in 1926 under the title *The Classical Tradition in Poetry*. In that book Murray restated his earlier beliefs on the origins of Greek drama. Comedy came from the mumming of rustics whose leers were a catharsis. Tragedy came from the Year-Daimon, the vegetation cycle: the provision of a scapegoat by which life was preserved. Both, of course, were poetic forms; and classical poetry, its metre originating in ritual dance steps, was central to it. So was poetic diction which was deliberately different from common speech. From tragedy in particular, poetry derived its essential quality of ecstasy and, through ecstasy, Beauty. Beauty was one thing by love of which mankind was united. The classical tradition kept alive the old Beauty which could be used to discover new. Such discovery was a need of the human soul. The classical tradition implied that some things were greater, more beautiful than others, and these would stand for ever. This tradition was Greek, transmitted through Rome with a confluent from Hebrew through Christianity, and with 'some bright torrents' from the pagan North. The river of tradition had, in modern times, broken into many streams, but Murray did not believe that Civilisation would, in spite of temporary and present appearances, throw aside Beauty simply because it needed time and effort to grasp and to understand. Civilisation, in short, entailed conscious and continuous effort to understand the classical past and to use it, not to imitate but to create new Beauty and to acquire a taste for it. If you were to ask who were the poets of the 'higher style' who had accepted this classical tradition and thus preserved the Beauty whose pursuit was the mark of Civilisation, Murray named Milton, Pope, Shelley, Keats, Tennyson, Browning and Swinburne. Even Shakespeare indirectly represented it. Murray recognised that there were other great poets. 'I must think about the great poets who can be so bad. Certainly Shelley can and Wordsworth and Shakespeare. Bridges and Binyon, yes, Masefield, yes. (Am I sometimes? I do hope so.)' But these additions do not really alter the descent of the classical tradition in poetry by which Murray tested the inner content of Civilisation: it allowed the search for Beauty which 'satisfied the need of the soul'.

Murray found Beauty no easier to define than others whom he admired: Keats, Shelley or William Archer. Indeed, he never attempted a concise definition; he left its meaning to become clear from his usage. He did not have a philosophical caste of mind, and had no interest in a theory of Beauty, but he plainly had an image of what he meant by the word. In his lecture upon Andrew Lang in 1947, for example, he recurs to the ideas which run through *The Classical Tradition in Poetry*. A poet appeals from emotion to emotion by his art. 'He creates a thing of beauty and you and I feel the beauty.' That Beauty is not simply a thing of the intellect, nor simply a thing of the senses. It is a thing to be apprehended by both although it is not fully expressible but rather belongs to 'the unfathomed mystery by which the mind of man is surrounded'. Beauty cannot be created except by 'loving effort after artistic perfection', perfection which can be measured by beauty of form in rhythm, metre and language. It is a striving not after literal Truth but after imaginative Truth, after 'things which are higher than ourselves'. That striving after perfection is to enable other minds to 'see a higher beauty, to have glimpses to greater nobility and joy'. Murray's use of the word Beauty, in the preceding quotations (which come from his sympathetic lecture on Andrew Lang), range him beside other Victorian romantics. The mysterious element in Beauty is stressed. But Murray used the word of poetry, of literature. He deliberately did not speak of Beauty in music for, being tone-deaf, he shared W.S. Gilbert's view that there were two tunes he could recognise: one was God Save the King; the other wasn't. Nor did he speak of painting. Beauty, for Murray, was a matter of language, of words, which had a formal or a sensual beauty but above all had meaning; they conveyed the Beauty of imaginative thought. Beauty lay in the message conveyed by words, in its imaginative Truth. Beauty, in short, was a construct of Civilisation which in turn provided the conditions of leisure which allowed the pursuit of Beauty.

In Murray's idea of Beauty, hard work and disciplined effort were essential. Beauty did not just happen; it had to be consciously created by painstaking effort and craftsmanship which, in poetry, he found to be singularly lacking in the younger generation which had discarded rhythm, rhyme and poetic diction. Of course poetic subjects were not limited to apple blossom, or swans, lakes, flowers and maidens in white dresses; it could be made out of blood, sweat and tears, out of 'mean streets and ordinary lives', but it was the spirit in which these subjects were treated that mattered. He doubted if good poetry had often been made out of 'disgust, boredom, dislike, dirtiness, envy and the denigration — or, as they now say, "debunking" — of things which are higher than our-selves'. The spirit must be the search for Beauty which satisfied the need of the soul.

The soul, as Murray was well aware, had other needs besides Beauty, but they were primarily linked in his mind with the pursuit of Beauty, of imaginative Truth. The message of Greek poetry was not only that of a central tradition of disciplined imaginative effort

— to be contrasted with modern failures which used common, non-poetic language and discarded the rules of the craft which made things of beauty — but also that of a search for God, or, rather, a sense of God. That had been the theme of his *Four Stages of Greek Religion* before the war. Freedom to pursue that search for what he had called to Bertrand Russell in 1902 'a thing like Heaven or God of which one can get glimpses in many different ways' was part of the inner core of civilisation. But just as the pursuit of Beauty through poetry involved rules and intellectual and imaginative effort, so the pursuit of Heaven or God involved rules. Supernatural religion was ruled out. When he published *Stoic, Christian and Humanist* in the same year as *Aeschylus: Creator of Tragedy*, Murray apologised in his preface for any hurt he might cause to those whom, on other grounds, he regarded as companions in the fight for Civilisation. He nevertheless repeated in 1940 his attack on revealed religion by recalling the revulsion he felt at the cruelty implicit in it, whether this was the parable of the Gadarene swine in which unoffending animals suffered, or the history of persecution and intolerance by the Christian church. Starting with the rational search of the Stoics for the Good, tracing the dimmed and distorted reflection of this search in the Christian religion of St Paul, he ended by justifying humanism: ethical and upright behaviour without supernatural sanctions. The atheist could be as ethical, indeed more ethical, than the man of faith, hope and charity. In doing so, he restated his early Utilitarian philosophy as he had put it to Russell in 1902. Utilitarianism was nearly the truth, 'but the end of life is in the processes of life'. By life, Murray meant the life of a civilised man who, inheritor of the classical tradition, had a duty to preserve that inheritance against its enemies and to enrich it by his or her own work in the pursuit of what, in Greece before its 'failure of nerve' he called in 1897 'Truth, Beauty and Political Freedom and Justice'. Forty years on, Murray had not changed his mind on the great issues of life, and during the 20 years up to the outbreak of the Second World War he frequently restated them, perhaps with the greater lucidity of experience and certainly with more public authority.

Murray's authority in those inter-war years was in part personal: his own character. With his establishment at Yatscombe he seemed to his many visitors to be totally secure in his convictions and serene in his belief. In discussion he could, as Arnold Toynbee said, be formidable behind the outward appearance of courtesy. Toynbee had good reason to know. He and Gilbert both felt that he filled the role of the son the latter never had. In the spring of 1928, Toynbee, having finished the annual Institute of International Affairs Survey for 1927, was pleasing his fancy by considering the philosophy of history. By October, three years later, he sent his father-in-law the first part of what he called his 'book of nonsense', *A Study of History*, although he did not really know whether it was nonsense or not. Murray read the manuscript and returned his comments within a few weeks. He did not think it was 'all my eye', but he thought Toynbee had an animus against western civilisation which he advised him to correct, and he had even graver doubts about his son-in-law's idea of a universal church which succeeded a collapsed civilisation. Toynbee agreed that churches and civilisations were 'inverse to each other', but explained that his ideas, like Plato's, were really metaphors: ideas conveyed in myth. Murray continued to read the manuscript of subsequent volumes and signed his comments on them 'The Old Rationalist' which reflected his doubts about Toynbee's thesis that civilisations had a cyclical life, and that in decline they were subsumed into what the author called a 'universal church' before a new civilisation in turn was born. Nevertheless he gave Toynbee's first volume of *A Study of History* a splendid send-off in a review in the *Observer* in June 1934. He believed the work would probably remain a classic, but in private he had thought that 'he lets his prejudices rather run away with him'.

Murray had a much stronger reaction to the volumes published after the Second World War in which Toynbee was then more overtly religious. Murray objected vigorously to the suggestion that the Greeks were secularist while nearly all philosophy is full of the idea of God. It was true that the Greeks had no God like the Jews' oriental king. What mattered, however, was that 'Man is king of all things' and that his use of his power should be just and equal. Murray had suspected Toynbee of some infection from his daughter's Catholicism in the early 1930s; the later volumes disappointed him very much because, he said: 'I can't help feeling that religion is a very primitive thing which is constantly being purged as [one] gets more civilised.' His disagreement with Toynbee, however, went deeper than religion for Murray still believed in Progress. He did not share Toynbee's brand of despair before the Second World War. Western civilisation was not inescapably doomed, whatever the dangers which seemed to threaten it. Man could — indeed must — defend it; he must not take refuge in religion which was a survival from the uncivilised past.

The difference between Murray and Toynbee was in part a matter of character and temperament. Murray was an optimist; Toynbee a pessimist. Nevertheless, Murray admired Toynbee's kind of scholarship because it was not narrowly professional but broad-ranging, in search, as he saw it, of imaginative Truth. Murray's own scholarship stayed within the bounds of the Hellenistic tradition, although it was equally speculative in character when he tried to recreate the Greek past through its literature. Murray's intention was to strengthen the inner core of Civilisation by revealing the beauty of Greek poetic tragedy to those who knew no Greek, but he still sought to underpin that faith by his work in Greek itself. Aeschylus' great themes, as Murray interpreted them, took their origin from his reading of the Greek text; and his critical edition of the plays, in the same Oxford series as his Euripides, went side by side with his translations. As he worked at Geneva and in London, as he translated from the Greek during his train journeys and in his hotel room, so he was 'raging to get at Aeschylus', he said in 1930. By 1935, as retirement from the Regius Chair drew near, he was able to devote more time to the text, work he found 'a great relief to the temper, though worrying'. By 1936 he had the proofs from the Press. Just as he believed that the search for Beauty required the leisure that Civilisation provided, so his editorial work required time which he never had in a life which had become filled with public work. At the age of 70, in any case, he believed 'I am certainly growing stupid'. The edition was not good. When it actually appeared in 1937 he was 'haunted by the number of misprints', but the defects went deeper than that. Fränkel, a German refugee scholar whom Murray had helped to bring to Oxford, had been, he said while constituting the texts in 1936, 'severe with me' over the problems of the Aeschylus manuscripts, into which he recognised that Fränkel put far more work than he did himself. But Murray had never belonged to the professional scholarly tradition which Fränkel represented. Notwithstanding his remarkable facility in Greek, Murray as an editor remained an amateur. More than that, at the end of his tenure of the Oxford chair he was as averse as he had been 30 years earlier, to 'mere' scholarship.

The result, in the later judgement of Paul Maas, another refugee scholar whom Murray helped to come to England, was a barrier in communication which led to a bad text. Murray felt that with Fränkel he came up against a brick wall because of the German's lack of imagination, while Maas thought that Murray's way was 'arbitrary'. No conscientious metrician, he declared in 1957, could accept Murray's arrangement of the Aeschylus texts, which because of his prejudice against Fränkel led to the production of an impossible text simply to avoid agreeing with him. Murray had done some work on the Aeschylus manuscripts. In the winter of 1937/8 he examined those in Paris during the meetings of the Institute of Intellectual Co-operation, but this was only after his edition had already appeared, in order to improve the reprinting. This did not occur until 1953, and although Murray, with the help of Maas and Hugh Lloyd-Jones, was working on a new edition just before his death, his edition was finally replaced with a new one because the cost of the corrections would have run into three figures and there had been many refusals by teachers of Greek to buy the original one without such corrections. Murray's reputation as a scholar has suffered because of this poor edition, for by contemporary professional standards it was amateur, a relic from another generation. In part, it was the result of pressure of other work in old age, but it was of course more than that. Murray had described his earlier textual work as a 'disgusting task'. Greece, not Greek, was his object. He edited the Aeschylus texts as an offshoot of his translations, not as his primary interest and duty, and because he believed he had a special insight into a fellow poet and playwright's meaning which no one else had seen. What he sought and what he saw was 'something eternal in human life'. That was what poetry was, even if what it said was not 'true in fact'. It was an unfashionable view of scholarship, the antithesis of what Fränkel stood for, a point well made by Edgar Lobel who held the lectureship endowed from Murray's income and who had also struggled with Murray's Aeschylus' re-editing in the 1950s: Gilbert Murray was a man magnificently endowed for the pursuit of truth, but he did not choose to pursue her; with Fränkel it is exactly the other way round.

Gilbert Murray's approach to scholarship created no 'school'. When he retired in 1936 he had the public reputation of the foremost Hellenist, but in the two volumes of commemorative pieces presented to him at a ceremony in Christ Church Hall, the one by academics, the other by established figures in public, literary and theatrical life, the evidence was of the width of his interests and activities, not of a group of pupils and disciples. The commemoration was not so much of the professor of Greek but of one of the last of the Victorian polymaths, a man who had moved easily across different fields in classical studies, in letters and in public life. Nevertheless, if he left no tradition in Greek studies, his influence continued in Oxford through his successor, E.R. Dodds.

Before Christmas 1935, with retirement due in the following summer, Murray had given some thought to his successor. Dodds, an Irishman and a conscientious objector during the First World War, had been a pupil, although not one who was close to Murray in the way that some of his other pupils were. But Dodds, appointed with Murray's support to the Chair of Greek at Birmingham, had an imaginative interest in the study of Greek religion. In late 1935 Murray suggested to Dodds that he might be a candidate. Dodds agreed to let his name be considered early in 1936. Stanley Baldwin, the Prime Minister, got on well with Murray, and characteristically asked his advice. Murray talked to Baldwin in April and then thought that the choice lay between Bowra and Denniston, unless further evidence became available about Dodds. The evidence did become available. A.D. Nock spoke with real enthusiasm about Dodds's book on Proclus, a neo-Platonic writer. Dodds, in Murray's own words, 'reduced Fränkel to speechless admiration'. Gilbert told Lady Mary that his own evidence, his memory of Dodds's 'extremely fine scholarship as an undergraduate', was a minor factor, but in putting the three men's names to the Prime Minister in 1936 he expressed doubts about Bowra whom he did not really think good enough, and he did not feel stimulated by Denniston, whereas Dodds was not only an extremely fine scholar but one whose breadth of interest was closest to Murray's own. It was Dodds whom he recommended to Baldwin, although Lady Mary herself had written strongly in Bowra's support, a letter which her husband passed to the Prime Minister. Mackail too was in favour of Bowra. Baldwin naturally took other advice; he 'properly and constitutionally' invited the Vice-Chancellor of Oxford to Chequers to seek his views, but the tone of enthusiasm about Dodds tipped the balance, especially since all the evidence about Bowra showed 'some hesitation about his scholarship'. Murray thought it the right decision, although he knew that it would cause widespread disappointment and ill-feeling in Oxford, and he felt unhappy for Bowra to whom he wrote praising his 'real brilliance of writing and teaching'. Nevertheless, he believed that Dodds was 'a good man' and Fränkel, in the face of hostile press publicity about the appointment, assured him that it was the right appointment. From Murray's point of view it undoubtedly was, for it combined fine scholarship with a breadth of interest that he believed vital for the future of Hellenism and therefore of Civilisation.

Murray's own contribution to both was recognised by the university, which conferred on him the honorary degree of Doctor of Common Law, a distinction given for public service, rather than the Doctor of Letters which would have been more appropriate for scholarship. He had a stature and a public reputation independent of any academic position, a place in public life. G.M., as he had come usually to sign himself, was a readily identifiable signature. Vacating the chair freed some of his time, although he continued on the Somerville College Council and served as Chairman of the College Library Committee. He had never, he admitted, devoted much time to college duties at Christ Church — hence some opposition to his election to an Honorary Studentship — for his personal tastes made college life uncongenial to him; he had in 1925 declined Julian Huxley's invitation, on behalf of a group of younger dons, to stand for the Wardenship of New College where he enjoyed lunching. He gave up undergraduate teaching with little regret, for the work had begun to tire him and the young he found increasingly unresponsive to his type of learning. Some of them, indeed, found his lectures, which included the singing of some of his own translated versions of Greek drama, distinctly embarrassing. Murray reacted nervously to lecturing to the young whom he found difficult to understand. In any case, by the time he retired the defence of civilisation had come to seem to him the overriding issue.

From his position in Geneva, as the 1930s went by, he had had a good vantage point to observe the gathering dangers to Civilisation. He had distrusted the French since his first attendance at the League Assembly and he never really revised his opinion. One of his respected colleagues in Geneva in July 1936 told him that France no longer counted in European power politics, and when Herriot told him in 1938 that all would still be well if Britain and France stood together, his reaction was doubt; is France really a strong nation? For, by mid-1936 some of his Geneva colleagues already believed that Hitler had got control of south-eastern Europe where the small nations were imitating the dictatorships of Italy or Germany. Murray had been disturbed by the early persecution of German intellectuals after the Nazis came to power — he had indeed helped many of them with hospitality at Yatscombe — and in 1934 the murder of the Austrian chancellor, Dollfuss, had thrown an even more awful light for him on the Hitler regime. He had long disliked Italian Fascism, since he first met Rocco at Geneva in the 1920s, and the combination of Germany and Italy was an obvious danger. His Swiss Catholic colleague, De Reynold, related to him in 1938 a conversation he had had with Mussolini who had told him how much he disliked the Berlin Axis, and how much he would like to be free of it *'mais ces stupides français'* would not give him the chance. The burden of this conversation was that Germany and Russia were revolutionary countries *'contre L'Église, contre la noblesse, contre l'histoire'* whereas he, Mussolini, was the opposite. The Duce's solution was a Four Power Pact, of France, Germany, Italy and England, otherwise the alternative was German or, worse still, Russo-German domination of Europe. With this kind of conversation as the background to his work in Geneva and Paris, Murray became increasingly 'utterly opposed to Fascism and Communism alike', the latter not merely from what he saw and heard in Geneva. He had been shocked by what he had heard Litvinov say about the Russian refugees: 'we have finished with them. Let them die.' He was even more shocked by what he saw of Communism in those close to him. In 1937 Philip, Arnold Toynbee's son, caused him considerable concern at a time when he was already worried about left-wing influence in the League of Nations Union. Communists, he came to believe, were like obscene creatures under stones, or men whose brains had been through an operation cutting out conscience, self-restraint and sense of shame. The danger of admitting Communists to such an organisation as the Union was, in the first place, that they were morally degraded, and in the second that they deceitfully used other organisations. In short, in defence of Civilisation there were allies you should not, could not have because of the nature of Civilisation itself. He quoted Commeret, a radical lawyer whom he met at the Quai d'Orsay, who deplored the tone of the British government which

talked only of 'interests'. 'Only on principles can you get any vision
of civilised nations.' Yet Civilisation itself could not include certain
traditions of European culture. Murray ruled out an inheritance
from Spain, for example. He had seen the Prado paintings when
they left Madrid during the Civil War; they were 'very nice, but
what a *horrible* civilization it was'. Murray saw the danger offered
by both Communism and Fascism, but the enemy was also within
Civilisation: supernatural, organised religion of which the Prado
pictures vividly reminded him.

By Civilisation Murray no longer meant the western European
heirs of the Graeco-Judeo civilisation, the civilisation of those who
lived within the security of the *polis*, with leisure to pursue their
own higher needs. He had never believed in a straight line of
progress from that Hellenistic past to the present; along the way
there had been a failure of nerve and then a re-emerging from the
primitive and the barbaric which had overwhelmed civilised man.
Authoritative or revealed religion was a mark of that primitive
regression, the appeal to blind faith or fanaticism which marked
Fascism and Communism as well as the Christian religion. The
leisure to pursue Beauty and Truth was the inner core of Civilisation, but what surrounded the inner core was the pursuit of
Freedom and Justice. With this meaning of Civilisation clear in his
mind, a paradox followed in his position. As a League of Nations
man, however much he might feel John Bullish when face-to-face
with foreigners, he was committed to the international cause of
Civilisation while at the same time believing that really it was only
Britain, and by extension the United States, which was the true heir
of Civilisation. For, looking at Europe which had also been heir to
Hellenism, before the Second World War it was clear to Murray
that the 'big' nations — Germany, Italy, Russia and Spain — had
all rejected the inheritance, and France was doubtfully strong
enough to bear it.

> I think Mussolini is right for once when he says that England,
> France and America represent conservative forces, that is, we
> want to conserve civilisation which is in danger of being
> destroyed partly by a general rejection of ethics and the worship
> of mere force, partly by poverty and Bolshevisation.

In the end, Civilisation for Murray came to be the inheritance
passed on by Liberal Victorian England. This was what he

defended in his Deneke Lecture in 1942. The nineteenth century in
Britain had seen the difficult struggle against the terrible by-
products of the Industrial Revolution: the abolition of slavery, the
reform of the penal laws, the purification of public life, the prevention of cruelty to children and animals, the regulation of labour
conditions and provision of social services, the emancipation of
Catholics, Jews, nonconformists and women, the spread of
education. Scientific, medical and material inventions were
unparalleled in history, and they had been accompanied by 'a most
wonderful flowering of British poetry and imaginative literature as
well as considerable achievements both in art and philosophy'. This
was a 'very splendid civilisation', which had come about because
members of a privileged class had worked to have their own
privileges abolished or extended to others; it was a Civilisation with
a most sensitive conscience about its own failures and hence with
the capacity to amend them. It naturally followed that the 'heirs
and continuators' of this civilisation must defend it, when the
threat materialised in September 1939.

War, by turning people into fanatics whose sole standard was to
win, was the single great enemy of Civilisation as Murray understood it. The ideology of War was the only thing worth fighting,
because it was that ideology, both within a nation and between
nations, which was the ruin of civilisation. In 1937, when Murray
wrote to Bertrand Russell saying that the dictators, the ideologues
of war, 'ought to be stopped', Russell had objected that 'in
stopping them we become like them'. Murray recognised that to
fight a war against the ideology of war involved some 'deviations'
from the normal standards of Civilisation, but his answer was
clear: 'I'd do anything for peace, but I can't accept the victory of
evil systems.' By April 1940, even Russell was finding it impossible
to maintain the pacifist position. The outbreak of war Murray
recognised as a failure of his generation, but he did not despair. In
December 1939, when he went for the last time to the League
Assembly in Geneva, he found the atmosphere 'encouraging . . .
the worm turning at last against these repeated violations of the
Covenant', violations which by that time included not only the
German attack upon Poland but the Russian attack upon Finland.
He drew encouragement too from the French Prime Minister,
Daladier, whose speech to the Assembly advocated the co-opera-
tion in war of France and Britain as a nucleus of a European
federation open to all like-minded nations, a view which in

Murray's opinion left the door open for the inclusion of an anti-Hitler Germany. Murray told Cecil that they must urge a step-by-step approach to closer European union, not a complete constitution for a federation, but he also made it clear that he did not regard such a federation as a substitute for the League of Nations. A Society of Nations was still the only answer to the problem of war. The idea might so far have failed 'but I think we have shown how it can be done'. But how much, after this war, would remain of 'the higher civilization of Europe'?

Meanwhile, the first objective must be victory. Although Murray still felt fairly sure that there were 'a good many things which decent nations will not do', he also believed that no belligerent would abstain from anything which would be really decisive. The war must be won or Civilisation would perish, but once it was won, notwithstanding the damage it had caused, it was only the one point of rejecting war that was essential: 'For the rest of our civilization and culture, I believe we should be far more concerned to preserve than to overthrow.' Throughout the war itself, now in his mid- to late seventies, Murray continued his educational work for Civilisation. 'I carry on a good deal of questionably useful work', he wrote to Jack Mackail, 'for the LNU, the London International Assembly, the Council for Education in World Citizenship, the British Council and other August bodies.' He also, to the distaste of his wife and some of his old friends, appeared from time to time on the BBC Brains Trust to deliver his message to a wide listening public, although face-to-face on the programme with its resident representative of the common man, Commander Campbell, he shared his friends' distaste for what he regarded as vulgarity. Nevertheless, he believed that through the programme he might do some good, in the sense that he could persuade his listeners of the values of Civilisation against the inescapable threats to them during the war. In doing so, he gladly accepted public recognition of his achievements. In December 1940, a dark period of the war, he was offered the Order of Merit for services to literature, and on this occasion he accepted the rare honour without hesitation, for there were again Liberals in Churchill's coalition government and the Prime Minister himself was the sole survivor in politics of Asquith's own Liberal government. Murray enjoyed the honour, and carefully recorded his private reception by King George VI at Buckingham Palace to confer the medal, but he also valued it for the public recognition the award gave to the cause for which he stood.

That cause was then conservative, the preservation of what he valued: 'I get rather impatient when people talk of the new world we are going to build.' Not a new world, but an old one: Liberal Victorian Civilisation; that was what Gilbert Murray thought even war was justified for. As the conflict went on, he began to worry that the League would be dropped and replaced with an Anglo-American understanding which would be too informal a system to preserve the peace. There might have to be something called by a name other than the League of Nations but the principle was clear. Indeed, it was fundamental, for the war was not to establish democracy nor to achieve family allowances nor to abolish the English public schools — all part of a 'new world' — but to put a stop to aggression and so to 'save our lives as a nation'.

The loose, general talk of a new world after the war was reflected in the League of Nations Union. Many of its members seemed to believe, in Murray's view, that it should advocate policies of domestic, social and economic reconstruction. This, Murray asserted, was not the Union's business. 'I often feel greatly out of sympathy with . . . [the] flock. I believe in the League of Nations (or, if you will, World Citizenship); they believe in Left politics with all appropriate prejudices.' He was 'rather inclined to resign the presidency', because he had become convinced that members clammered about Communism and domestic reform and were much less interested in League of Nations problems. It was, however, the left wing, he concluded, 'where we get most of our support'. There was the old risk of involvement with other societies — for example the New Commonwealth (David Davies' foundation) and Federal Union — which accepted parts of the Union programme but not all, and in any case were tempted to try to take over the Union. There was the old risk that conservatives and moderates were being repelled, especially by association with such a person as Konni Zilliacus who, said Murray, believed that peace could only come by communist revolution. He accepted the criticism that the LNU was saying the same old thing, but 'I firmly believe they are the right things to say'. It was dangerous to tell people that after the war they would be free from want; 'when people find they are not rich and happy they will turn against someone'. What disturbed him most of all were the 'masses of talented young idiots going pro-Russian'.

The dangers which Murray increasingly felt as the war went on were related to the Russian ally. Domestically there was the 'fundamental humbug' about Russia as the symbol of a new world after the war. Internationally, there was the doubt about Russian intentions and behaviour, for Russian principles were just like those of the Nazis. By mid-1944, three weeks after the Allied invasion of Nazi-occupied Europe, when the end of the war was in sight, Murray was convinced how awful the consequences would be: 'has there ever been a country with a good chance of conquering Europe who did not yield to the temptation?' The draft agreement at Dumbarton Oaks in late 1944, which looked like the Covenant with the kind of amendments the League of Nations Union had suggested, although the form and the language were different, pleased Murray. He much preferred that Russia should promise to behave, even if she did not mean to, but nevertheless she had 'a totally different standard from ours — a barbaric Asiatic one'. Civilisation, at the end of the second great war in his lifetime fought in that cause, was still in danger from international conflict, from a new barbarian threat, but that barbarism was also a domestic symbol, palely reflected in the Labour government elected in 1945. 'The Labour Party had told the working classes', said Murray to Toynbee in 1947,

that they were to do less work, have higher wages and that the country could plunge into all kinds of extravagant schemes of social improvement . . . it found that drastic economies had to be made, that hard work was needed, but it could not reverse its own policies . . . For the first time I am getting rather alarmed.

The anchor of Civilisation might not hold.

After Christmas 1931, Margaret Cole who was one of the few younger women on Christian-name terms with Gilbert Murray, wrote him a letter in which she addressed him as 'My Dear Monument'. She was given to teasing him, and herself, as a well-to-do radical. Facing servant problems in March 1932, for example, when her staff retreated to look after an aged mother, she mocked both of them with her 'really, the lower orders shouldn't have relations, should they?' She touched on two points about Murray. Even in the 1930s he was coming to seem like a monument to the Victorian era which she, in a younger generation, could respect but not wholly understand. He was one of the privileged people who had struggled to abolish their privileges or to extend them to others, while being also a figure of the Establishment. When a public figure above partisan politics was needed, it was Gilbert Murray who delivered the radio broadcast to mark the end of the General Strike and appeal for reconciliation after what, in the Murrays' view, was an act of domestic warfare. It was Gilbert Murray who, as his friends knew, was called upon for drafts of royal speeches on national occasions. It was Lady Mary, an integral part of the monument which was the Murray image, who, preserving a radicalism in domestic politics which came from her passionate attachment to the cause of the underprivileged, took in the Communist *Daily Worker* for her family but took great care that the servants should not see it. This aristocratic, high-minded, disinterested radical virtue was common enough in the nineteenth century when it had supported Greek and Italian revolutionaries against oppressive rulers. What puzzled contemporary radicals and socialists like Margaret Cole in the 1930s was the monument to Victorian England which Gilbert Murray consciously became.

It was the Second World War and its aftermath which saw Murray clearly stand out as the Victorian monument, an identification which was explicit in a well-known broadcast of 1947: 'A Victorian Looks Back'. Murray was not then quite 'the last of the Victorians', but he was one of the few left who had had a prominent career during the Queen's reign. In the post-war years, the Victorian civilisation which he had called 'very splendid' in his Deneke Lecture of 1942, came by 1954 to be a Golden Age. With the nostalgia and regret which are natural enough to old age, he had even come to regret what he had once so strongly defended: British entry into the First World War. 'If we had stayed out,' he wrote to Bertrand Russell in August 1955, 'the effects would have been less disastrous for civilisation if the Germans had been allowed to become complete masters of Western Europe, on more or less equal terms with the United States and Russia.' As it was, in the years after the Second World War, his overriding concern was, he told Arnold Toynbee, to make Hellenism 'a strong fortified island against barbarism', although he feared that we were in the Hellenistic age, where the real Hellenic nation was too small to stand alone, and the semi-barbarous masses had the strength. Would the United States play the part of Rome?

I begin to feel that we should aim not at a peaceful law-abiding world but at some form of unity of Christian or Hellenic civilisation, based of course on the Commonwealth, the United States and Western Europe but embracing India and Ceylon and whoever else may be willing to co-operate. I get the horrors when I think of enormous numbers of Russians, Chinese and possibly Arabs and of coloured people — a vast sea of barbarism round an island of Hellenism. I try to allow for prejudice, but somehow feel that our Hellenic or Christian standards and moral values are enormously precious approximations to truth.

This might be treated as an old man's dream, more especially since the inclusion of Indian and Ceylon was at variance with his views about the likely fate of those countries when their British educated elite faded away; but the theme so pre-occupied Murray and he repeated it in different ways so often in correspondence, broadcasts and public statements that there can be no doubt that it was a reasoned conclusion he had reached. It rested on the Victorian belief that its civilisation and culture were superior to any other and were worth defending by whatever means could be found. In 1948 he had already told his regular correspondent, Rose Macaulay, 'of course we ought to come to terms with Franco' in resistance to the menace of Russian barbarism, although he had not changed his mind about superstitious religion or authoritative revelation. He held a Victorian's belief that some cultures and civilisations really were superior to others; and they could be ranked in order of superiority. Modern, humane, liberal civilisation was Christian in the sense that Hellenism included a search for God in an undogmatic or agnostic sense. It was superior to a civilisation in which religion was intense, or closer to the vegetation rituals from which it sprang. But both were superior to the barbarism which menaced them both, for what the Communists had was a professed dogma, not a religion at all. The Victorian assumption about evolution and progress is clear. What concerned Murray, in the post-war years, with his Hellenistic analogy in his mind, was the danger of a failure of nerve in the face of the barbarian danger.

In its conviction of the superiority of its own civilisation the Victorian age has often been supposed to have been one of self-confidence, even arrogance, but in its eminent figures the private doubts, even the neuroses, have often been exposed. Where Bertrand Russell had roared with laughter at Lytton Strachey's exposure of some eminent Victorians, Gilbert Murray had not been amused; but he was ready enough to commission Strachey to write the Home University Library volume, *Landmarks in French Literature*, which described a serene, neoclassical world. Murray had denounced Max Beerbohm's caricature of the Victorian age as selfish and materialist: what age, he asked, was not? But, given the obvious threats to the heirs and continuators of 'a very splendid civilization', did his own nerve fail? Publicly it did not. In his 90th Birthday broadcast, which received wide publicity, he could assert: 'Our cause is not lost. Our standards are not lowered, but almost all that we love is in danger and must be saved . . . Perhaps those who have endured to the end will come into their own.' 'That', said Arnold Toynbee, the prophet of a declining civilisation, 'is magnificent.' Murray displayed confidence. As he told Lewis Casson in 1942, 'in this horrible age of violence and disorder, one wants to hold up a standard of order, beauty and dignity in the midst of tragic doings', but when an old friend and frequent holiday companion, Professor J.A.K. Thomson heard his broadcast, 'A Victorian Looks Back', in 1947 he told Gilbert that it was 'absolutely right to make it rather more optimistic than in private conversation: the country needs heartening'. Murray saw that as his duty, although he wondered from time to time if Toynbee was not right that our civilisation was in decline. Nevertheless, he more usually felt, as he told his wife in May 1947, in the face of tragedy: 'in the meantime we must go on with our normal duties and even pleasures, like good children.'

His remark was made in the face of a family death, but it represents Murray's general attitude to life in old age. The Murrays had been uncomfortable during the war, for Yatscombe was difficult to maintain with petrol and fuel shortages. In 1942 they had tried to lease it and thought of moving to a smaller house in Oxford or a flat in London, for Lady Mary had to carry the shopping out to Boar's Hill. They found no one to take Yatscombe and Lady Mary, also in her mid-seventies, struggled on, with Rudolf Olden living in the cottage, the house full of grandchildren and refugees, with neither maids nor cooks who would stay for long. She rose at six o'clock in the morning to do the housemaid's work before break-fast, and then often bicycled down into Oxford to give whatever help she could to the unfortunate. Gilbert himself was often away from home, in London, at the Executive of the League of Nations Union or to take part in the BBC Brains Trust which his wife despised. He at least managed an annual holiday: in the summer of 1941 and 1942 in south-west England, in 1943 at Lettice Fisher's cottage at Godalming, in 1944 with the Cecils at Hayward's Heath. Lady Mary attended to her duties in Cumberland, where she dealt with the business of the Murray farms and tenants, inherited from Lady Carlisle. By the end of the war both were suffering from the infirmities of old age. Gilbert had a tiresome neuritis in his left arm, and in 1945 suffered from loss of appetite, while Lady Mary was in the Acland Nursing Home in Oxford being treated with M and B for a pneumonia. Yatscombe was still proving difficult to run and, while Gilbert agreed that it would be easier for her if he stayed away from home, he thought the solution was for them to live more simply: cold lunches, not cooked ones, an egg and cocoa supper, and more household work for himself, such as looking after his own bedroom and the study. In early 1946, however, he too was in the Acland for a blood count and later in the year was having injections to keep it normal, while in mid-1946 his wife suffered from a burst blood vessel in the head. When Cecilia, Lady Mary's sister, died in May 1947, Gilbert told Mary that they knew it was bound to happen: 'we shall soon follow her.' In fact, both lived for ten more years, but in 1949 Lady Mary began to lose her hearing, and became very nervous and depressed, although she seemed to Gilbert still 'to be doing the farms rather strenuously'. In the following year she began to lose her memory and her understanding; she seemed, her husband told Arnold Toynbee, to be unable to finish sentences she had begun. Gilbert was tired and distressed by her condition, and he did not like to leave her alone more than he was obliged to, for his company seemed to be one of the few things she still cared for. She could still clear the table and even wash up, but she could not read nor do the accounts, although she was, he told Janet Spens, gentler and she did not seem unhappy. She liked to see new faces at meals and was quite good at recognising old friends whom Murray encouraged to call.

Nevertheless, the marriage became a one-sided relationship. By the summer of 1952, Lady Mary was unable even to send a postcard in reply to her husband's frequent letters when he was away from home, and the household itself became more and more dependent upon servants who were increasingly hard to find and to retain. Murray himself became more and more dependent upon secretaries, and these too were hard to find and to keep. In 1952 he was complaining that where, before the war, he had been able to get girls who had Firsts in Greats, these days an applicant had a Fourth in Mods, no secretarial training and was unable to drive a car. When he did find a capable girl, such as Lorna Chubb, they were usually soon lost by marriage. No one was really able to fill the gap left by his wife's decline, for he had become accustomed to having her manage the household and financial affairs, and to arrange the practical details of his life, even choosing his companions for afternoon walks on Boar's Hill. With the effective loss of his lifelong companion, Gilbert Murray privately became 'lonely and pining and worried about death duties', he told Rosalind in August 1953. He could not think it likely that his wife would live much longer, and he was bewildered by what he should do if she should die. He would need someone to run the household, but he knew that Rosalind could not, while Barbara Hammond, Lawrence's widow, and Janet Spens, his old Glasgow pupil and Oxford colleague, were themselves too old and frail. In a shadowed present, private and personal as well as public and political, his thoughts naturally turned to a Golden Age in the past, and to his own childhood, although he found himself shy of completing his autobiography.

To the loneliness he felt because of family circumstances, there was the simultaneous sense of isolation by the death of friends and companions in the causes for which he stood. Charles Archer, William's brother, a frequent pre-war holiday companion and regular correspondent, died early in the war; he severed a valued link with that period of his life when Murray was involved with the theatre and the world of letters in London. The death of George Bernard Shaw he felt very much, not because Shaw was an ally in public causes — indeed Murray thought him simply mischievous — but because he too reminded Murray of the same period of his life as Archer. With the deaths of Jack Mackail and Lawrence Hammond his links with his classical, literary and radical past seemed to snap. He acquired during the war one new friend, Rose Macaulay, a Liberal descendant of the historian, on the occasion of the loss of her library by German bombing, but there was not the same shared store of common memories. The relationship, in Victorian fashion, was chiefly conducted by correspondence, but in 1953, finding the late eighties to be neither so nice nor so cheerful as the age of eighty (which was much the same as seventy), Murray told Rose Macaulay that he always paid the fares of his grand-children, nieces and nephews who came to see him, and he would gladly place her on the list if she would come.

With Rose Macaulay, Gilbert Murray discussed politics, books, family, as he had with his older friends. Of those, only one with whom he felt a communion of interests survived: J.A.K. Thomson, Professor of Greek at King's College in London University. Their acquaintance went back to the pre-First World War period, when Thomson, then at St Andrews, wrote to him about Homer after *The Rise of the Greek Epic* was published. In 1923 Murray had helped to secure the London chair for Thomson who thereafter was a regular holiday companion in Switzerland during the summers when Murray attended his meetings in Geneva, for J.A.K. was in whole-hearted and admiring agreement with Murray's kind of scholarship. When he read *The Classical Tradition in Poetry* in 1927 he wrote that he did so with complete agreement and extreme pleasure: 'why, after you, should I write about literature?' He shared, too, Murray's political development. In February 1950, they both voted Conservative for the first time in their lives, in part because he, like Murray, had come to believe that Socialism sapped the Victorian work ethic: 'where would you and I be if we had been afraid of overwork?' This identity of interest and concern led Murray to share the belief that there were 'few scholars of our type left . . . The present scholars at universities do "research" and the non professional scholar, like Gladstone and Asquith . . . is almost extinct.' The sense of isolation is clear. When Murray read Karl Popper's book *The Open Society and Its Enemies* in 1947, and saw

the great denunciation of Plato, Aristotle and Hegel, his reaction
was to wonder who Popper was. When Ventris deciphered the
linear B script as Greek, Murray, accepting the fact, reasserted that
it was absurd to pin Homer to a definite date, but recognised in
1953 that 'we shall have to think again about all early Greek
history'. When, three years later, in August 1956, the
Encyclopaedia Britannica asked him to revise his article in the last
edition on the origins of Greek tragedy and comedy, he confessed
to Eric Dodds that he might have been carried away by his enthusiasm for the A.B. Cook/Frazer/Jane Harrison discoveries and the
Year-Daimon/Vegetation Ritual thesis. He appealed to Dodds for
help, because he did not then feel equal to revising his views, and he
wanted him to point out 'some new books which I ought to consider'. His mind was not closed on scholarly matters, but again the
sense of isolation from modern scholarship was there; and the sense
of old verities being swept away.

Murray never, however, felt completely isolated in his Victorianism
in the modern world. During the war, Sybil Thorndike and Lewis
Casson told him of the success of Greek tragedy in his translations
in the Welsh mining valleys, where *Medea* was as popular as
Macbeth, one coal-miner crying out: 'This is the play for us; it
kindles a fire;' while a performance of *The Trojan Women* in
London was seen by an old cockney barrow woman and her
friends, who told Dame Sybil that 'it was lovely; and we all 'ad a
good cry . . . them Trojans was just like us, we've lost our boys in
this — war'. After the war John Gielgud revived *The Trojan
Women* in 1946, with Murray attending, as of old, the rehearsals.
In the same year Casson directed *Electra* at the King's Theatre in
Hammersmith, and Murray agreed to revise some of the more
distinctly Victorian idioms such as 'Woe is me' and 'Ah, me',
although those idioms were still carefully retained in the D'Oyle
Carte productions of the Gilbert and Sullivan operas. In those
works, however, such expressions were intended for comic effect,
and Gilbert Murray accepted the difference of context, for he had
himself turned to the production of Greek comedy as well as
tragedy. In November 1941 he told Lewis Casson that fragments of
Menander had been found in Egypt and that he was 'filling in one.
No one could call it a great play but it is a specimen of a style of
drama hitherto unknown and practically the origin of modern
comedy of an artificial type — Molière, Congreve, Sheridan.' He

was at a loss for a name for his play by 'Menander and Co', thinking of The Shorn or Shaven Head, until G.B.S. suggested 'The Rape of the Locks'. The translation was finished in 1943, but Tyrone Guthrie, who read it with great pleasure, could not see any opportunity to produce it in the near future. Nevertheless it was comedy which now attracted Murray, the New Comedy, which he believed expurgated the grossness of the Old Comedy which came from the old Dionysiac fertility ritual. When in 1948 he translated another tragedy, *Oedipus at Coloneus*, he was disappointed because it was not as good as his Euripides translations and he doubted whether he would publish it, although in fact he did. He found it more congenial to assist Menander with a translation of *The Arbitration*, and, suitably expurgated, to translate Aristophanes' *Birds* as a 'rather lovely' Gilbert and Sullivan piece.

The Arbitration was staged at the Maddermarket theatre in September 1945 and again at the New Theatre in May and June 1946 but, although it was sufficiently like modern comedy of an artificial kind, there was a problem with staging. As the producer pointed out to Murray, the cast did well but the audience 'allowed themselves to be overawed by the "translation from the Greek" and "Gilbert Murray" on the programme, and so took it too seriously'. In the post-war years, however, Murray was less interested in productions upon the stage, although he readily gave permission for dramatic societies, colleges and schools to put on his versions. He had become interested in the medium of radio or, as he called it, the wireless. In February 1947, the BBC broadcast *The Frogs* which disappointed him. In September 1949 he was, he told Rose Macaulay, enjoying immensely the BBC rehearsals for the broadcasting of *Medea*, although disappointed that the actors emphasised the drama, not the poetry. In August 1952, when the BBC produced *The Arbitration*, Murray attended the rehearsal and liked the producer and the actors but the medium turned the play from something meant to be seen into unseen talk. The actual technique, however, was rather well done, using a narrator. Murray tried to improve the performance by correcting one actor who had a tendency to talk comic cockney, and feared that the play might be vulgarised by such attempts to 'brighten' it. When he heard the broadcast, he said to Mary Stocks, widow of an old Oxford colleague and a BBC radio personality on 'Any Questions', that he thought on the whole it had been very well done, given the difficulty of trying to make a play into a broadcast. His main criticism was that the play was taken too fast, so that it was hard to follow even if you knew it well, as he did; anyone who did not would be bewildered. The technical problem interested him, linked as it was with the old difficulty of the chorus in Greek tragedy, to which a new solution had to be found when it was dramatised for radio. His interest gave him pleasure, for his mind was still open to a new challenge, but as much because it took him back in memory to the days with his friends at the Royal Court Theatre.

'The present is burdensome. The future dark. Only the past bears contemplation.' Those words were not Gilbert Murray's, but they are true of 'the last of the Victorians'. With the death of Lady Mary in September 1956, a great sadness fell on Murray. The loss of a lifelong companion, even though Lady Mary had in a sense left him several years earlier, was 'surprisingly heavy' to bear. He confessed to Mary Stocks in October 1956 that he was 'old and senile'. But as a Victorian, his personal burdens and the private pleasures of work which interested him were no excuse for shirking public duty, however much he wished to be rid of it. Since the war he had had the gravest misgivings about the direction of British society. Socialism had been destroying the value of hard work. The Welfare State had failed to distinguish between the deserving and the undeserving needy; and it was leading to the tyranny of the common man. He had argued this with Margaret Cole in 1953 and she, like a good socialist, had answered: of course the common man should have more humility; so should his betters; and asked G.M. to answer two questions. At what point in history do you think we went wrong? What do you wish to see done now? She suggested to him two alternatives, one of which was patently absurd. Put the genie back in the bottle or give guidance. Murray was not dissuaded from his belief that democracy was proving a failure. Perhaps the choice lay between despotism and Fascism (as defined by Rocco, not as in reality), and socialism in its full form was on the side of tyranny. He repeated the point to Arnold Toynbee. A clear-sighted intelligent group must lead the mass, as it did in nineteenth-century England: good *fascismo*. 'I don't see how the country can be properly governed by people who want more wages for less work and whose political knowledge comes from the *News of the World* and the *Sunday Pictorial*.' What was necessary was an educated oligarchy, although education was being diluted by soft options like Modern Greats and History which did not have the rigour of the hard subjects like Greats and Mathematics. The evidence of this dilution of the educated oligarchy he found in the taste which preferred T.S. Eliot or, still worse, Ezra Pound to the great tradition in poetry: it was 'amazing' that a poetry prize could be given to the latter. He had commented on it, he told J.A.K. Thomson, to Jan Masefield who replied that he should remember that there were mad people in all periods, not only the present. Murray did remember it. He reflected that it was 'rum what effect Ezra Pound and fifty years of war had had on public taste', and still carried the burden of trying to preserve a peace which might preserve Victorian Liberal civilisation.

Increasingly disenchanted as he was with the United Nations and the United Nations Association, he did his best to pass on the torch of the League. In August 1947, at the age of 81, he travelled to Paris to consummate the not altogether easy union of the Committee of Intellectual Co-operation with UNESCO. His bust, by Epstein, still stands in its Paris headquarters. He brought, said the incoming chairman Dame Kathleen Courtney, peaceable good sense to the Executives of the United Nations Association, but by 1950 he was disquieted by Communist influence in the UNA, by 1952 depressed by the organisation's tendency to become involved with the domestic affairs of member nations and the passing of unrealistic resolutions, by its tendency to produce schemes of world government rather than practical policies, and by the lack of weightier people on the Executive. He continued to lend his name to the Association, but the faith which he had had was not there. As early as June 1948 he told his wife that 'we old stagers are always in danger of being undermined or swept away by people whose aim is not international peace but extreme party feeling'. The United Nations Association Executive, in short, was not an educated elite giving guidance, but an undistinguished lot which was, in Murray's view, increasingly unrealistic. He continued to offer advice to Dame Kathleen but his views were increasingly minority ones within the UNA, because he found it increasingly difficult to support the United Nations itself, unless its Charter was revised, and for this he found no support, after Cecil's withdrawal, in the United Nations Association.

His attitude to the United Nations itself was consistent with his view that Civilisation and Peace were the most important things in the post-war world. As the civilised European nations withdrew from the rule of their empires and colonies, 'the real trouble', he said to Mary Stocks after an 'Any Questions' broadcast in 1953, 'is that we have told these miserable Indians and South Americans that they are everybody's equal and must have all their rights, and culminated the foolishness by giving them universal suffrage which hardly any nation in the world is capable of using properly.' The consequence for the United Nations was the dominance in the Assembly of a 'horde of little semi-civilized states'. 'The world', he told J.A.K. Thomson, two months before his own death, 'was no longer ruled by civilized powers; it was at the mercy of a mass of little barbarous nations in the United Nations;' and it was hard to see how the machine could be mended.

Murray wrote these words a few weeks after he had made an open break with many of his United Nations Association colleagues and his friends and allies in the cause of international organisation for peace. When President Nasser of Egypt nationalised the Suez Canal, and the British and French took military action in November 1956, Gilbert Murray took a public stand in support of the British government of Anthony Eden. The case, he thought, was crystal clear. A small barbarous nation had clearly broken an international agreement. The United Nations, because of the veto in the Security Council and the horde of little semi-civilised nations in the Assembly, had no power to act to enforce an international agreement. Beyond that, he wrote to Arnold Toynbee who was far away from England at the time, lay the wider threat to civilisation from barbarism. Nasser was a successful dictator, with all the anti-West nations — Arabs, North Africa and most of Asia behind him, and behind that the Russian conspiracy against the West and its civilisation. Not surprisingly some of his old friends and colleagues were outraged. Asquith's daughter, Violet Bonham-Carter, said: 'How could you?' Philip Noel-Baker neither saw him nor wrote to him again. Dame Kathleen Courtney told him that she did not differ as much as he supposed she would, but that it was difficult to get away from the fact that Britain and France did use force without reference to the United Nations and did not carry out the obligations of the Charter. Still, Murray received some support. Naturally the Prime Minister, Eden, was grateful, and sent his private secretary to discuss the situation. More surprisingly Norman Angell, a well-known dissenter from traditional foreign policy in the First World War era, wrote to congratulate Murray on his letter to *The Times*, taking the view that it was a disservice to the United Nations Organisation to pretend that 'it can do what at present it obviously cannot'. Sir Robert Menzies, the Prime Minister of Australia, would certainly have agreed, for he, after attempting to resolve the situation with Nasser, fully supported the British action. Ironically enough, in January 1956, he had proposed Gilbert Murray for the Nobel Peace Prize for 1956, with the support of Angell, Harold Nicolson, Salvador de Madariaga, Lord Samuel, Earl Attlee, Lord Thurso, Alexander Cadogan, Robert Cecil, Henri Bonnet and other prominent men, and with the support of the governments of New Zealand, Ceylon, Rhodesia and Nyasaland, and with the expression of the Indian government which, as a matter of policy, neither nominated nor supported candidates for the prize, that it would be happy if this year it was awarded to Gilbert Murray for his long and devoted work for peace. Both Norman Angell and Robert Cecil had gained the Nobel Prize for Peace in earlier years; but this was one honour that was not conferred on Gilbert Murray. He himself had come to value peace only for the sake of Civilisation. And for Civilisation, like a good Victorian, even peace might be sacrificed. He had never wavered from that view since 1914.

There is a different kind of irony at the end of Gilbert Murray's life. Another of his consistently maintained views was that opposed to dogmatic, institutional, authoritative religion. He had always carefully distinguished this from a sense of God. In 1944 he was telling Rose Macaulay that people did not understand when he talked of a mystery, 'something beyond our grasp we simply do not know and must not dogmatize'. He made the same point to Bertrand Russell ten years later.

> Then about faith. What I wrote about beauty, physical and moral, was I think based on a sort of faith, that is, on a strong consciousness that beyond the realm of our knowledge there was a wide region in which we have imperfect intimations or guesses or hopes. Most of the so-called faiths are these, intimations worked up into the form of definite myths or dogmas, almost all of them anthropomorphic. The myth is mostly invented, but the faith at the back of it has at least a good deal of probability about it . . . It is in some ways the most interesting part of life, the great region in which you must be agnostic but nevertheless you have something like conviction.

What could be more in the tradition of Liberal Victorian thought, and that within three years of his death? Yet, after Murray died at Yatscombe on 20 May 1957 the rumour began to spread that on his deathbed he had been received into the Roman Catholic Church. If that is true, then at the end of his long life he reached a conclusion which, by contrast with other facets of his personality and conviction, was neither a development of long-held interests and views but a repudiation of them. Certainly most of his family and friends saw it in that light at the time, and the end of a life which had seemed so much of a unity was marked by public and bitter division.

Gilbert Murray became ill on 16 April 1957. On 10 April he had written to Thomson that one of the troubles of old age was that your tastes were out of fashion; you loved the poetry and painting of your youth and were repelled by those who found them a bore. Six days later he lapsed into unconsciousness and a telegram was sent to his daughter saying that her father was not expected to live more than 24 hours. She arrived at 7 p.m. in the evening of the same day. Her father did not recognise her and seemed to be in a coma. Rosalind as a Catholic thereupon telephoned the parish priest, Father Crozier, to tell him that her father was dying and to ask him to pray for him. Shortly after this telephone call, recorded his daughter some weeks later when controversy had arisen over her actions, Gilbert Murray regained consciousness and 'seemed to want something'. She asked him if he would like the priest to come. Her father, she said, opened his eyes, nodded and quite clearly answered 'yes'. Father Crozier came on 17 April. According to Rosalind, he asked the sick man: 'do you know who I am?' The clear and firm answer which she heard was: 'yes'. The priest then asked: 'do you want the blessing of the Church into which you were baptised?' Answer, firm and clear: 'yes'. The priest bent down and talked to him in a low voice, Rosalind going to the other end of the room, not wishing to hear what was said. At the end of the low-voiced conversation, Father Crozier administered Extreme Unction, and then left. But Murray lived on for four and a half weeks, although never again, in his daughter's opinion, fully conscious.

Rosalind Murray recorded these events on 26 June 1957. Father Crozier gave a later version to Alexander Murray, Gilbert's grandson, on 21 June 1982 which differs in some details. In this account, Rosalind telephoned not on the night of 16 April, but about 2 p.m. on 17 April and asked the priest what he could do for her father. He replied: 'I could perhaps give him a blessing', but said, since he was told he was 'asleep': 'no hurry about the whole matter . . . don't wake him up . . . if he'd like me to come and see him, I will do so.' At 5 p.m. Rosalind rang him again to say her father was 'perfectly wakened', and Father Crozier went to Yatscombe where he chatted to Gilbert Murray and asked: 'would you like to see [me]. Reply: 'yes'. The priest then said to Rosalind that there were two things. Had he left instruction to be cremated? Rosalind replied that the Will had not been opened. Was he a member of the masonic order? Rosalind replied that her father abhorred all secret societies. Either point, before the Second Vatican Council, would have inhibited the priest, but he was, as he put it, 'clear'. He then took Murray's hands and said: 'You're very ill. Would you like the sacraments of the church in which you were baptized?' Gilbert said: 'yes' and clutched the priest's hand. Rosalind then moved away, and the priest administered the sacrament. He then heard nothing more for three to four weeks, when early one morning Rosalind rang to say her father was dying, and the priest went to Yatscombe where he and Rosalind said the Prayers for the Dying, and then he left.

Murray's will instructed that his body be cremated, as it was, and the ashes then lay in the Anglican church at Lanercost, close to Naworth Castle and Carlisle, until the Dean and Chapter of Westminster consented to their burial in the Abbey. When the two thousand invitations to the Abbey ceremony on 5 July were sent out, in the third week in June, the *Sunday Dispatch* newspaper rang Father Crozier and asked if it was true that he had received Murray into the Catholic Church. The priest asked what their source was. The reporter refused to divulge it. Rosalind gave an interview to the *Sunday Dispatch*, but on 19 June 1957 her solicitor wrote to the Editor stating that she did not wish it to be published until she had seen the proofs; while on 21 June her Catholic son, Lawrence, was also in touch with the newspaper about the interview. The paper 'splashed' the story on 22 June, and it was then taken up by other papers, which raised with the Dean of Westminster the question of an Abbey burial if Murray had become a Catholic. Family, friends and Father Crozier publicly put their views in the interval before 5 July; and privately there were some bitter exchanges, centred upon the propriety of Rosalind's actions.

There is no doubt that on 17 April Gilbert Murray was given the

Last Sacrament by Father Crozier in the honest belief that that was what he wished. There is no doubt that the priest and Rosalind genuinely believed that Gilbert Murray's attitude to religion had changed in the last months of his life. Father Crozier, for example, has recorded that, when Lady Mary was very ill, Rosalind came to stay at Yatscombe and naturally went to Mass. She asked the priest to pray for her mother and he agreed, also asking her to give Gilbert, whom he had met, his kind regards and to tell him that he was praying for his wife. Just after Lady Mary's funeral, Rosalind and her father went for a walk past his church, and Rosalind told Father Crozier that she then told Gilbert that prayers were being said for Lady Mary. She said that her father stopped, looked at her and said: 'why didn't you tell me this before?' That evening, after his daughter had left Yatscombe for the North, Murray telephoned the priest and asked him to come and see him. Father Crozier did so and Gilbert thanked him for the prayers. He then talked about Glasgow. There were further 'chats' between the two of them, usually about an hour in length, and during the first of them the priest had asked what Murray's philosophy of life was. Murray, said Father Crozier, replied that he felt 'there is some great power behind the universe . . . of course, it's beyond the mind of man'. The priest said: 'well, to a certain extent that's the teaching of the church.' 'O no', answered Murray, 'the teaching of the church says . . . it's black or white.' 'Do you mean St Thomas' articles?' asked Father Crozier. Murray invited him to come again and on 31 January they discussed religion. In this second chat, the priest said that Murray had asked him for the First Vatican Council definition of the church, and during a third visit for afternoon tea on 22 March, when Rosalind was again there, Father Crozier read it out. Murray asked for a copy, which the priest delivered to him the following morning. Murray asked him to call again, but the priest explained that he was busy during Lent and would call again after Easter. It was on Tuesday in Holy Week that Gilbert Murray was taken ill; on Wednesday that Father Crozier came to administer Unction. His belief, shared by Rosalind from what the priest told her and what she had seen and heard while she was at Yatscombe, was that her father's attitude to religion had changed from his lifelong conviction.

This opinion was supported by Janet Spens who, on 7 July, told Rosalind of her last conversation with Gilbert Murray on 12 April. She believed that he knew it was their last meeting. He asked her:

'who are the great poets of our time?' and answered himself: Tagore and Tennyson, because they wrote on the great subjects of life and death. They went on to discuss Tennyson, and Murray replied to her question that *In Memoriam* and *Idylls of the King* were the great poems. He added that Andrew Bradley had once 'blamed me for not realizing how completely Tennyson covered the ground', the whole question. In reply to a question whether he agreed, Murray answered emphatically: 'yes, I do.' Janet Spens understood this to mean that Gilbert Murray accepted Christian doctrine as expounded in Tennyson and had got her there to tell her so, because she thought he believed it his duty to put it on record that he had reached that conclusion; a conclusion reached, Janet Spens added, over months, not suddenly, and reached before his last illness. Tennyson's poems and a request for the copy of the definition of the church: are these firm evidence for the belief that Gilbert Murray had changed his views on religion? *In Memoriam* is not a specific statement of Christian doctrine; it implies no more than grief in a person who had a totally undogmatic sense of God. Since Murray linked it with Tagore who was neither Christian nor dogmatic, his agreement with the poets does not necessarily bear the interpretation Janet Spens places upon it. Nor does the request for the Vatican definition imply more than an interest Murray had had in religion for much of his professional life and still revealed by his discussion with Bertrand Russell in 1954. The Vatican Council definition of the church, in any case, states that:

> The divine mysteries by their own nature so far transcend the created intelligence that even when delivered by revelation and received by faith they remain covered with the veil of faith itself and shrouded in a certain degree of darkness so long as we are pilgrims in this mortal life, not yet with God.

With much of that statement, Murray would have agreed in 1954; it is not inconsistent with what he then said to Russell or Rose Macaulay or Arnold Toynbee when he was still explicitly an agnostic and sceptical of organised religion. Yet, there can be no doubt that Rosalind and Father Crozier believed Murray to be veering to the Catholic Church. Certainly both hoped for it, and Father Crozier, on his visit of 17 April, plainly came prepared with Holy Oil to administer the Last Sacrament. To both of them, after all, the salvation of a soul was in question.

Both Rosalind and Father Crozier were bitterly criticised within the family for what they did, especially after Isobel Henderson's testimony became known. She paid Murray a visit on 19 April, two days after the priest's visit. She did so by his invitation and she found him 'quite lucid'. His attitude to religion she described as 'not hostile, but detached'. Having heard Oxford rumours of Father Crozier's visit, she casually asked if the priest had been to see him. Gilbert Murray replied: 'No, my dear. No one has been to see me except you.' That statement went to the heart of the question those who were angered by what had happened were asking: was Gilbert Murray lucid, in possession of his faculties, on the evening of 17 April when he was given Extreme Unction and thereby re-admitted to the Catholic Church? Rosalind was clear that her father was, but she had also repeatedly told her son Philip that during the last five weeks of his life her father would not recognise his grandson if he came to see him. Philip also pointed out that, even if his grandfather was not in a coma, he was still very ill and that what had happened was the result of questions to a very sick man, not requests by him of his own volition. Moreover, there was a significant discrepancy in his mother's and the priest's account: she stated that her father had been asked if he wanted the blessing, not the sacrament, of the church. The former did not mean re-admission, as did the latter.

Amid such acrimony, Gilbert Murray's ashes were laid in the Abbey in Poet's Corner, not far from those of another great humanist, Casaubon. Some of the antagonists regretted the quarrel; for some it was a matter of principle and they could not fail to stand up for what they believed. In one sense the angry argument seems an irony after a life so often assumed to be harmonious and serene, but hostility to organised religion was the one issue on which Gilbert Murray himself became militant, even late in life. In another sense, agnosticism about the significance of what happened on his deathbed is symbolical: the sense of mystery with which many a Victorian replaced dogmatic faith. Perhaps the last word should be left with Douglas Woodruff. 'Unless a man makes a formal and deliberate act while in full possession of his senses, he should be credited by his contemporaries as having maintained the convictions of a life time.'

Verae Humanitatis Exemplar
Quo Vivente Graecorum Veterum Litterae
Revixerunt
Nec De Concordia Gentium
Fas Erat Desperare

1866   1957

The real irony is that his epitaph in Westminster Abbey should be in Latin, not Greek.

BIBLIOGRAPHY

Unpublished Sources

The nature of the materials for a life of Gilbert Murray enabled me to dispense with footnotes. The bulk of the sources for the book is contained in the collection of his papers in the Bodleian Library at Oxford, access to which is by permission of his Literary Executor. Those papers were — and I wish gratefully to acknowledge my debt — carefully sorted by his original joint Literary Executor, Isobel Henderson, and his former secretary, Jean Smith. The Bodleian Library holds the list of their contents, arranged by individual correspondents and subjects. The quotations or references in my text can therefore easily be tracked down. The two ladies, however, did something more. They wrote to each of Murray's main correspondents asking that his letters should be returned, either to be placed with the collection or to be copied for deposit in the archive. Most correspondents did so. In any case, especially from the First World War onwards, Murray often typed his letters and kept copies. So both sides of a correspondence are often preserved in Murray papers. Other relevant collections, which for the most part replicate the Murray archive contents, are listed below. The arrangement and listing of the Bodleian collection has enabled me, by quoting in the text the name of the correspondent and the date of any letter, to dispense with footnotes to the source. In the same way, where a reference is to informants I have consulted, the name has been mentioned in the text.

The main parallel collections of papers are:
Asquith Papers (Bodleian Library)
Cecil of Chelwood Papers (British Library)
H.A.L. Fisher Papers (Bodleian Library)
George Bernard Shaw Papers (British Library)
Other papers are still held privately by the Murray and Toynbee families.
The Public Records Office holds material relating to Murray's time at the Board of Education. St John's College, Oxford, holds material relating to his undergraduate days.

Published Sources

Gilbert Murray's Publications

The following is a select bibliography, containing works quoted or referred to in the text. Lectures are not listed where they were later included in published collections of essays. A complete bibliography is held by the Bodleian Library.

Gobi or Shamo: A Story of Three Songs (Longmans, Green and Co., London, 1889)
The Place of Greek in Education, Inaugural Lecture (James Maclehose and Sons, Glasgow, 1889)
A History of Ancient Greek Literature (Heinemann, London, 1897)
Carlyon Sahib (Heinemann, London, 1900)
Euripides Fabulae, vol. i (Oxford Classical Texts, 1901)
Euripides Translated into English Rhyming Verse (George Allen, London, 1902)
Euripides Fabulae, vol. ii (Oxford Classical Texts, 1904)
The Trojan Women of Euripides, transl. (George Allen, London, 1905)
The Electra of Euripides, transl. (George Allen, London, 1905)
The Rise of the Greek Epic (Oxford, 1907)
The Interpretation of Ancient Greek Literature, Inaugural Lecture (Oxford, 1909)
Euripides Fabulae, vol. iii (Oxford Classical Texts, 1910)
Iphigeneia in Tauris, transl. (George Allen and Unwin, London, 1910)
Medea, transl. (George Allen, London, 1910)
Oedipus, King of Thebes, transl. (George Allen and Unwin, London, 1911)
Four Stages of Greek Religion (Columbia University Press, 1912)
Euripides and His Age (Williams and Norgate, London, 1913)
Rhesus, transl. (George Allen and Unwin, London, 1913)
Alcestis, transl. (George Allen and Unwin, London, 1915)
The Stoic Philosophy, Conway Lecture (George Allen and Unwin, London, 1915)
The Foreign Policy of Sir Edward Grey (Oxford, 1915)
Agamemnon, transl. (George Allen and Unwin, London, 1920)
Essays and Addresses (George Allen and Unwin, London, 1921)
The Problem of Foreign Policy (George Allen and Unwin, London, 1921)
The Choephoroe, transl. (George Allen and Unwin, London, 1923)
Five Stages of Greek Religion (Oxford, 1925)
The Eumenides, transl. (George Allen and Unwin, London, 1925)
The Classical Tradition in Poetry (Oxford, 1927)
Ordeal of This Generation (London, 1930)
The Suppliant Women, transl. (George Allen and Unwin, London, 1930)
Prometheus Bound, trans. (George Allen and Unwin, London, 1931)
Aristophanes: A Study (Oxford, 1933)
Seven Against Thebes, transl. (George Allen and Unwin, London, 1935)
Then and Now (Oxford, 1935)
Aeschyli Tragoediae (Oxford Classical Texts, 1937)
Liberality and Civilisation (London, 1938)
The Persians, transl. (George Allen and Unwin, London, 1939)
Aeschylus: Creator of Tragedy (Oxford, 1940)
Stoic, Christian and Humanist (George Allen and Unwin, London, 1940)
Antigone, transl. (George Allen and Unwin, London, 1941)
The Rape of the Locks, transl. (George Allen and Unwin, London, 1942)
Anchor of Civilisation (Oxford, 1942)
The Arbitration, transl. (George Allen and Unwin, London, 1945)

Victory and After (University of Leeds, 1945)
The Wife of Heracles, transl. (George Allen and Unwin, London, 1947)
From the League to the U.N. (George Allen and Unwin, London, 1948)
Andrew Lang: The Poet (Oxford, 1948)
Oedipus Coloneus, transl. (George Allen and Unwin, London, 1948)
The Birds, transl. (George Allen and Unwin, London, 1950)
Hellenism and the Modern World, (BBC publications, London, 1953)
Ion, transl. (George Allen and Unwin, London, 1954)
The Knights, transl. (George Allen and Unwin, London, 1956)
An Unfinished Autobiography (ed. J. Smith and A. J. Toynbee), (George Allen and
  Unwin, London, 1960)

Select Bibliography of Quoted, Relevant or Background Published Works

Asquith, Lady C., *Diaries 1915–19* (London, 1968)
Asquith, M., *Autobiography* (ed. M. Bonham-Carter) (London, 1952)
Barratt, W. S. (ed.), *Euripides Hippolytus* (Oxford, 1964)
Beaverbrook, Lord, *Men of Power 1917–1918* (London, 1956)
Beerbohm, M., *Around Theatres* (London, 1953)
Beerbohm, M., *More Theatres 1898–1903* (London, 1969)
Birn, D., *The League of Nations Union* (Oxford, 1981)
Blake, R., *The Unknown Prime Minister* (London, 1955)
Bowra, C. M., *Memories* (London, 1966)
Bowra, C. M., *On Greek Margins* (Oxford, 1970)
Brailsford, H. N., *The War of Steel and Gold* (London, 1914)
Britain, V., *The Women at Oxford* (New York, 1960)
Buchan, J., *Memory Hold the Door* (London, 1940)
Burrow, J. W., *Evolution and Society* (Cambridge, 1966)
Burrow, J. W., *A Liberal Descent* (Cambridge, 1982)
Cecil, Viscount, *A Great Experiment* (London, 1941)
Chamberlain, A., *Politics from the Inside* (London, 1936)
Conacher, D. J., *Euripidean Drama* (Toronto, 1967)
Courtney, K., *Extracts from a Diary during the War* (London, 1927)
Crewe, Marquess of, *Lord Rosebery* (London, 1931)
Dodds, E. R., *The Greeks and the Irrational* (London, 1950)
Dodds, E. R., *Euripides Bacchae* (Oxford, 1960)
Dodds, E. R., *Missing Persons* (Oxford, 1976)
Egremont, M., *Balfour* (London, 1980)
Eliot, T. S., *Critical Essays* (London, 1961)
Finley, M. I., *The Use and Abuse of History* (Cambridge, 1977)
Fisher, H. A. L., *An Unfinished Autobiography* (Oxford, 1940)
Gilbert, M. and Gott, R., *The Appeasers* (London, 1963)
Gooch, G. P., *Under Six Reigns* (London, 1958)
Goody, J. (ed.), *Literacy in Traditional Societies* (Cambridge, 1968)
Grey, Viscount, *Twenty Five Years*, 2 vols. (London, 1925)
Guthrie, W. K. C., *The Greeks and Their Gods* (London, 1950)
Haldane, Viscount, *An Autobiography* (London, 1929)
Hamer, D. A., *John Morley* (Oxford, 1968)
Hammond, J. L., *C.P. Scott of the Manchester Guardian* (London, 1934)
Harrison, J. E., *Prolegomena to the Study of Greek Religion* (Cambridge, 1903)
Harrison, J. E., *Themis* (Cambridge, 1912)
Hazlehurst, C., *Politicians at War* (London, 1971)
Henley, D., *Rosalind Howard, Countess of Carlisle* (London, 1958)
Hinsley, F. H., *British Foreign Policy under Sir Edward Grey* (Cambridge, 1977)

Howe, M. (ed.), *Holmes–Laski Letters*, 2 vols. (Oxford, 1952)
Jenkins, R., *Asquith* (rev. ed.) (London, 1978)
Judd, D., *Balfour and the British Empire* (London, 1968)
Koss, S., *Lord Haldane: Scapegoat for Liberalism* (New York, 1969)
Kelly, M. (ed.), *For Service to Classical Studies* (Melbourne, 1966)
Lang, A., *Custom and Myth* (London, 1885)
Lang, A., *Myth, Ritual and Religion*, 2 vols. (London, 1887)
Lloyd-Jones, P. H. J., *The Justice of Zeus* (Berkeley, 1973)
McCallum, R. B., *Asquith* (London, 1936)
Mallet, S. C., *Herbert Gladstone* (London, 1932)
Ogg, D., *Herbert Fisher* (London, 1947)
Percy, Lord E., *Some Memories* (London, 1958)
Platenauer, M. (ed.), *Fifty Years (and Twenty) of Classical Scholarship* (Oxford, 1968)
Pycior, S., *The Most Ineffectual Enterprise* (Ann Arbor, 1978)
Rae, J., *Conscience and Politics* (London, 1970)
Robbins, K., *Sir Edward Grey* (London, 1971)
Roberts, C. H., *The Radical Countess* (London, 1962)
Russell, B., *The Amberley Papers*, 2 vols. (London, 1927)
Russell, B., *Justice in Wartime* (London, 1966)
Russell, B., *Autobiography*, 3 vols. (New York, 1967–9)
Samuel, Viscount, *Memoirs* (London, 1945)
Shaw, G. B. S., *Florence Farr, Bernard Shaw and W.B. Yeats* (Dublin, 1941)
Shaw, G. B. S., *Commonsense About The War* (London, 1915)
Shaw, G. B. S., *Bernard Shaw's Letters to Granville-Barker* (ed. C.B. Purdon) (London, 1956)
Shaw, G. B. S., *Collected Letters* (ed. D.H. Lawrence) (London, 1965)
Sykes, C., *Evelyn Waugh* (London, 1975)
Taylor, A. J. P. *The Trouble Makers* (London, 1957)
Toynbee, A. J., *Acquaintances* (Oxford, 1968)
Toynbee, A. J., *Experiences* (Oxford, 1969)
Trevelyan, G. M., *Grey of Fallodon* (London, 1937)
Turyn, A., *The Byzantine Manuscript Tradition of the Tragedies of Euripides* (Urbana, 1957)
Tylor, E. B., *Researches into the Early History of Mankind* (London, 1878)
Vickers, B., *Towards Greek Tragedy* (London, 1973)
Vickery, J. B. (ed.), *Myth and Literature* (Nebraska, 1966)
Walters, F. P., *A History of the League of Nations*, 2 vols. (Oxford, 1952)
Waugh, E., *The Diaries of Evelyn Waugh* (ed. M. Davie) (London, 1976)
Webster, C. K., *The League of Nations in Theory and Practice* (London, 1933)
Webster, T. B. L., *The Tragedies of Euripides* (London, 1967)
West, F. J., *Hubert Murray: The Australian Pro-Consul* (Oxford, 1968)
West, F. J. (ed.), *Selected Letters of Hubert Murray* (Oxford, 1970)
West, F. J., *Biography as History* (Sydney, 1973)
West, F. J., 'The Australian Expatriates: Gilbert and Hubert Murray', in A.F. Madden and W.H. Morris (eds.), *Australia and Britain* (Sydney, 1980)
Wilamowitz-Moellendorf, U.v., *Greek Historical Writing and Apollo* (Oxford, 1908)
Wilson, G., *Murray of Yarralumla* (Oxford, 1968)
Zimmern, A., *The League of Nations and the Rule of Law* (London, 1936)

INDEX